796.4
FIX   Fixx, James F.

E 80-061

            Jim Fixx's Second
            book of running

BOOKS BY JAMES F. FIXX

Games for the Superintelligent (1972)
More Games for the Superintelligent (1976)
The Complete Book of Running (1977)
Solve It! (1978)
Jim Fixx's Second Book of Running (1980)

JIM FIXX'S
SECOND BOOK of
RUNNING

The all-new companion volume to **The Complete Book of Running**

James F. Fixx

Random House
New York

JIM FIXX'S SECOND BOOK of RUNNING

796.4
FIX

E80-061

All rights reserved under International and Pan-American Copyright Conventions.
Published in the United States by Random House, Inc., New York and
simultaneously in Canada by Random House of Canada Limited, Toronto.

Parts of Chapter 2 first appeared in *Scene*. Portions of Chapter 13, in
modified form, were first published in *Signature* and *The Complete
Runner's Day-by-Day Log and Calendar*. Chapter 15 was
written on assignment for *Sports Illustrated*.

*Grateful acknowledgment is made to the following for permission
to reprint previously published material:*

American Journal of Epidemiology: Graph, "How Exercise Prevents
Heart Attacks," by Ralph S. Paffenbarger, Jr., M.D., is reprinted from the
American Journal of Epidemiology, Volume 108, 1978. Reprinted by per-
mission of the *American Journal of Epidemiology* and Ralph S.
Paffenbarger, Jr., M.D.

Litton Educational Publishing, Inc.: Chart from *Nutrition and the Athlete*
by Joseph J. Morella and Richard J. Turchetti. Copyright © 1976
by Litton Educational Publishing, Inc. Reprinted by permission of Van
Nostrand Reinhold Company.

W. W. Norton and Company, Inc.: Chart adapted from *The American Way
of Life Need Not Be Hazardous to Your Health* by John W. Farquhar, M.D.,
by permission of W. W. Norton & Company, Inc. Copyright © 1978 by
John W. Farquhar. Originally published as part of *The Portable Stanford*,
Stanford Alumni Association, Stanford, California.

Library of Congress Cataloging in Publication Data

Fixx, James F
Jim Fixx's Second book of running.

Includes index.
1. Running. 2. Jogging. I. Title. II. Title:
Second book of running.
GV1061.F56   796.4'26   79-5533
ISBN 0-394-50898-X

Manufactured in the United States of America

23456789

Illustrations by David Noyes
Designed by Carole Lowenstein

For Kitty,
who has brightened more miles
than she knows

How much happiness is gained,
and how much misery escaped,
by frequent and violent agitation of the body.

—Dr. Johnson

Foreword:
Out of a Corner

If you use the word *complete* in a title, as I did in *The Complete Book of Running*, you pretty much paint yourself into a corner. It becomes difficult, unless you're willing to subject logic to uncomfortable stresses, to write a second book on the same subject. Nonetheless, not long after publication I found myself brooding about a sociological paradox and wondering whether logic was, after all, sacred.

When I started writing *The Complete Book of Running* there was no more than a ripple of the tide that was soon to engulf the United States. Except for a handful of publicly athletic celebrities such as Jacqueline Onassis, Dick Gregory and Joseph Heller, practically everyone who ran did so obscurely and, because running was still more an eccentricity than a sport, diffidently. Running wasn't a subject that came up at cocktail parties or in executive offices, and certainly not in the White House. Suddenly, within a matter of months, all that changed. When I sat down to write, there had been perhaps 6,000,000 runners in the United States. Now there were easily 25,000,000. Magazines carried articles about running and its wonders, both real and imagined. The *New Yorker* printed cartoons about it. Housewives put on warmup suits to go to the A&P in. Even the most obscure races and places became clogged with participants.

One day, while running in the desert outside Phoenix, I saw a conical mountain in the hazy distance. When I got closer I saw that it was so steep and craggy that it would be difficult to walk to the top, let alone run. My spirit of adventure aroused, I searched out a trail and started plodding toward the peak. Soon I was sweating hard. My heart pounded. My legs turned to useless weights. Finally I came to the brow of the summit. There, to my astonishment, was a gray-haired woman in running shoes. She told me she ran up and down the mountain every day except Sunday, when for variety she ran fifteen miles across the desert. She said that at one time she had run the mountain twice a day. She found, however, that ever since she had turned sixty-five she tired more easily. Once a day now seemed enough.

In writing *The Complete Book of Running*, in short, I'd had in mind a running society that no longer existed. Undaunted by my lack of prescience, the book quickly hit a brisk stride. Before its first two years were over, to my astonishment, it had gone into thirty printings and fourteen foreign editions. It had climbed to the top of most of the best-seller lists, including two in Australia and one in Argentina, and simply perched there for months on end, as tireless as any long-distance runner. Soon it had sold a million copies from Rome to Tokyo and almost everywhere in between, and my shelves slowly filled with such titles as *Guia Completo de Corrida, Alles over hardlopen* and *Das komplette Buch von Laufen,* books I had written but could not read. To a writer long accustomed to being mostly unnoticed, it was wonderful fun. Still, whenever people asked me about my writing plans, I replied, truthfully, that I didn't intend to write any more books on running. Although it was repeatedly pointed out to me by those with a more commercial literary bent than my own that just about anything I decided to write on running would undoubtedly sell in at least modest quantities, I didn't want to write a book for that reason alone. Anyhow, I had plenty of other things to do.

I would not, I suspect, have broken my vow of silence had it not been for several overseas trips. During the months after publication I found myself spending time in Athens, London, Birmingham, Newcastle, Paris, Florence, Venice, Melbourne, Sydney, Brisbane and Auckland, not to mention dozens of cities in the United States. As I did so I became aware that my view of the running phenomenon was turning into something considerably different from what it had once been. Like the Apollo astronauts who, strolling on moon dust, became the first human beings to see our earth whole, I now began to see the running experience whole. It was apparent, first, that running was not the localized American phenomenon I had imagined it to be. Second, I came to feel that if only because of its sheer magnitude, running possessed an importance that transcended its well-publicized physical and psychological benefits. Finally, I became convinced that even though much of the press was still treating running as if it were another of society's passing fancies, the sport was in fact here to stay.

I began to notice, too, that other aspects of running were changing in significant ways. An inventive epidemiologist in California was conducting important studies that were going largely unreported. Psychologists and other investigators were developing fresh insights into human motivation; their work bore directly on why some people, knowing running could do them some good, never begin or, once having begun, give it up. Other psychological investigators were exploring the baffling frontier where muscle and mind interact. New information was available about nutrition, about training, about avoiding and treating injuries, and about the effects of running on such subgroups as women, children and older people. Although the standard 26.2-mile marathon was increasingly popular, races longer than that distance were attracting unprecedented numbers of participants and in the process were revealing much about the physical capacities of human beings. All sorts of new running equipment, some of it inspired by opportunism but much of it thoroughly useful, was available. Not least, the journalism of running, previously so tidy and monochromatic, had become a fascinatingly unruly thicket. Where once we had had only one nationally circulated running magazine, now there were several, each with its distinctive fare and followers. I began, in spite of myself, to see that the makings of a second book lay quite legitimately at hand. This, with apologies to any logicians in the audience, is it.

JAMES F. FIXX

Contents

JIM FIXX'S
SECOND BOOK of
RUNNING

1 ////
What We're Running Toward

Notes on the Significance of Putting One Foot in Front of the Other

A decade or so ago a hospitable but, as it was to turn out, incautious Michigan woman named Jeanne Bocci decided it might be fun to invite a few friends over for a four-mile New Year's Eve run followed by dinner. A dozen or so people showed up. The next year, word of the party having spread, twenty people were there. "It was strictly for fun," a woman who recalls the gathering told me. "The race was completely low key. Afterward Jeanne served spaghetti and that was it." Low key or not, the event continued to grow until no fewer than 250 people turned up for dinner one New Year's Eve. Even though the Boccis had by then moved to a bigger house, the place nearly split at the seams. In 1978 the dinner, now having acquired an official sponsor, Detroit's Hughes & Hatcher department store, had to be held at an armory. De-

spite an ugly midwinter downpour, 3,200 turned up to run
and 3,500 came to dinner. "It's nice that it's grown," said Mrs.
Bocci with disbelief, "but I can tell you I don't want to be the
one to do the cooking next year."

When Jeanne Bocci invited her dozen pioneers over for that
first New Year's Eve party, and for a long time afterward, neither she nor the most farsighted prophet of popular enthusiasms could have foreseen what was going to happen to running or why. At the time, it was among the most obscure of all
sports. Pursued by a handful of lean and gristly true be-
lievers who gathered in out-of-the-way parks on occasional
Sundays to race, it remained far from the general consciousness. From time to time, it is true, a Roger Bannister or a
Gunder Hägg would surface on the sports pages of newspapers, but most runners ran without public notice and certainly without any hint of public approval. I remember standing as a child on a curb near my parents' home in a New York
City suburb, watching a haggard, sweating string of runners
pass, and hearing an oversize woman murmur with fervent
disbelief, "They must be crazy." It was a succinct summary of
the prevailing attitude toward the sport.

In time, however, several events occurred. Together they
were to turn running into a phenomenon the likes of which the
world had never witnessed.

First, in 1968, an evangelical Texas physician, Dr. Kenneth H. Cooper, wrote a book, *Aerobics*, that took much of the
mystery out of the exercise question by telling Americans, for
the first time in a widely read nonscientific book, exactly how
much of various activities they needed in order to achieve a
reasonable degree of cardiovascular fitness. Running was
among his recommended exercises.

Second, an appealingly boyish American marathon runner
named Frank Shorter put running squarely into the public
consciousness by bringing a gold medal home from the 1972
Olympics.

Third, American involvement in the Vietnamese war ended,
and much of the country, weary of its troubled preoccupation
with external matters, turned with relief to thoughts of itself

and means of self-betterment. That there was an unabashedly narcissistic strain behind the shift in no way diminishes its relevance to the running movement.

Fourth, word began to spread beyond the core of the running community that the sport was one of the most effective ways to become thin, look young, and regain waning vigor.

Finally, in mid-1977, the press discovered running. Suddenly runners were turning up everywhere. Advertisers, ever alert for trends, began using runners in newspaper and magazine ads. Runners, including at least one running author, appeared in dozens of television commercials.

Prodded by these developments, the number of runners in the United States increased from 6,000,000 to 20,000,000 or more in an explosive three-year span. As I write these words the likelihood is that there are as many as 40,000,000 runners in the nation. More than ever, we runners are emphatically not alone. At whatever hour we go forth for our daily run, perhaps a million other Americans are doing exactly the same thing. In the process they are, incidentally, proving Thorstein Veblen mistaken. In his *Theory of the Leisure Class*, published in 1899, Veblen argued that recreation is exclusively reserved to the moneyed class and is, in fact, one of the characteristics that distinguishes it from the working class. This is patently no longer the case. Geoffrey Godbey, a Penn State professor, recently wrote in an essay entitled "Theory of the Leisure Mass" that by the 1970s outdoor recreation, including running, was becoming thoroughly democratized.

The United States has experienced scores of mass enthusiasms, including a few involving sport. Perhaps the closest parallel to the running movement was the sudden growth of tennis that, beginning in the 1960s, created a nationwide surge in sales of equipment, construction of tennis facilities, and laments about tennis elbow. The comparison, however, goes only so far. Unlike tennis, running requires little skill or aptitude and practically no equipment. Almost anyone, no matter how unathletic or even downright clumsy, can benefit from it and, with modest application, be assured of measurable improvement. While many new tennis players, discouraged after a year or so to discover that their abilities have struck a plateau, give up in discouragement, almost no one who starts running stops. Even if many of today's participants were to cut down on their mileage, give up racing, and generally make less to-do about their running, the sport would almost surely continue to grow.

Although its long-term significance remains to be assessed, it is already apparent that the running movement has brought changes that would have been unimaginable a few years ago. When I started running in the late 1960s a race that attracted 100 participants was a major event. Today there are dozens that routinely draw 1,000 or more starters. In a recent five-month period the Road Runners Club of America, the nation's chief organizer of races, added 44 local chapters to its roster, bringing its total to nearly 250.

Sermons have been inspired by running. ("There is not so great a gap between the physical and the metaphysical as we are wont to imagine," Rabbi Sheldon Wayne Moss told a congregation in San Diego in early 1979), and more than one observer has specifically identified running with religion (Bob Anderson, publisher of *Runner's World*, wrote not long ago, "Someone once said, 'For humanity to survive, it will have to invent a new religion.' The religion has been invented. It is the religion of the runner"). The identification may not be as bizarre, and it certainly is not as unusual, as it seems at first glance. Not long ago, at Holy Innocents Episcopal Church in Atlanta, the Reverend Robin Myers inaugurated "joggers' masses" at which participants first attend a service, then warm up, run 2.2 miles, and gather for breakfast afterward.

The traditionally less athletic half of the population, its women, have turned in vast numbers to running. At one point an investment company that was thinking of financing a running magazine calculated that women were taking up running at a rate as much as 30 percent greater than the rate for men.

Insurance companies, convinced of the benefits of vigorous exercise, have taken to offering reduced rates for runners.

Newspapers, among them the *Boston Globe* and the *New Orleans States-Item*, have begun to carry regular columns on running.

In broadcasting its weather reports, a New York City radio station, WNEW-FM, has been known to tell listeners how good or bad a day it is for running.

Finally, the running explosion has set off reverberations far from the nation's borders, creating what amounts to a global running community. Even in England, where until recently running was confined largely to serious competitors, the boom is starting. The general secretary of Britain's Road Runners Club, Peter Goodsell, told me recently that applications for membership have been increasing at a sharply growing rate for the past seven or eight years. Comparable patterns are reported in other parts of the world, not least in New Zealand, where, as we shall see in Chapter 13, some 32,000 people recently participated in what was at the time the world's largest race, and in Italy, where no fewer than 50,000 official entrants and uncountable unofficial runners participated in the 1979 Stramilano.

When any enterprise becomes as popular as running has become, a suspicion inevitably arises that there must be something wrong with it. Thus, from the beginning, a backlash was predictable, and that of course is exactly what eventually occurred. Its beginnings were equable enough. In August 1977, at almost precisely the time the rush toward running was starting in earnest, a newsletter published by the President's Council on Physical Fitness and Sports wondered mildly whether the strength and scope of the fitness boom weren't being exaggerated. "There is a reasonably large and growing core of practicing physical fitness converts, and there are many millions more who have bought the gear and have the inclination," the respected government body observed. "If they can be persuaded to join the ranks of the physically active on a permanent basis, reality will more closely resemble the picture painted by the current wave of publicity." At about the same time, *Runner's World* asked where the boom would ultimately lead. "What effect will this mercurial growth have on the sport?" asked one of its writers. "The answer is unclear as yet, but it is clear some sharp growing pains lie ahead."

The inception of the backlash's more rancorous stage can be dated with equal precision. The hostilities began with the publication in 1978 of Vic Ziegel and Lewis Grossberger's *Non-Runner's Book*, a cleverly conceived if unevenly executed parody that offered, according to a jacket blurb, "advice and reassurance for the millions of Americans who want to know 'Is it all right if I don't run?'" Ziegel and Grossberger's spoof was both lighthearted and good-natured. Still, its brisk sales suggested a darker dimension: that plenty of Americans sympathized with its implicit theme that running had become a monumental nuisance and runners themselves relentless bores.

From that time on, there were skirmishes aplenty.

An increasing number of municipalities started passing legislation decreeing where, how and in what sort of dress runners could do their running.

An increasing number of runners were struck by beer bottles, verbally abused and frightened half to death by resentful and vindictive automobile drivers.

New York magazine jumped on the backlash wagon with an article by John Van Doorn that it billboarded "The Physical Elite. They Run. They Work Out. They Think They're Better Than You Are."

Reacting to publicity following the death by heart attack of Congressman Goodloe Byron, who was a thoroughly trained marathon runner, a sizable segment of the population, including some of the press, decided that maybe running wasn't good for people after all. Nor did President Carter's subsequent collapse during a hilly 10,000-meter race help the running cause.

Dr. Christiaan Barnard, the heart transplant innovator, called running "a dangerous mania." Lest anyone suppose his comment was a slip of the tongue, a few months later he specifically identified running with masochism, saying, "I see no difference between this form of recreation and that bought for a simple fee from the ladies who specialize in chain mail bras, leather panties and a brace of whips."

When the syndicated "Dear Abby" newspaper column asked for reactions to the jogger-versus-motorist squabble, mail reportedly ran fifty to one in favor of motorists. One reader expressed a common attitude: "If it's exercise they want, why don't they go to a gym or exercise at home?"

Soon after Dr. George Sheehan, a New Jersey cardiologist who was among the earliest to articulate the rewards of running, published a collection of metaphysical essays entitled *Running and Being,* he was called an "old fool" and a "consummate windbag."

Finally, even the running community itself began to scrutinize the increasing influence of big business, and in some cases just plain bigness. *Running Review*'s headline "The Hidden Rot of Commercialism" summarized a prevailing view.

However dismayed some runners may have been by the virulence of the backlash, in moments of self-analytical candor many admitted that they themselves were partly to blame. They had made claims for their sport that were flatly untrue, and they had greatly exaggerated its benefits and pleasures. Thoughtful observers like Joe Henderson, the former editor of *Runner's World,* could try to restore sanity with comments like the following:

> We need to praise running for what it is. There are safer ways to exercise than this, better ways to meditate, quicker ways to get high, truer ways to find religion, easier ways to have fun. I don't deny that running gives some of these things. But praising them too highly hides what we really have here—a sport which like all sports has both pain and joy, risk and reward.

And so could the *Washington Post*'s Colman McCarthy, himself a marathon runner and one of the most consistently persuasive writers on the subject:

> As we let ourselves get light in the head from the aroma of flowery praise that the media initially blow toward every fad, we were also inhaling the sweet-scented guff that runners themselves were emitting.

And Ed Ayres, the perceptive editor of *Running Times:*

> Like precocious children who have received too many pats on
> the head from doting relatives, more than a few of us have be-
> come spoiled and insufferable. Some of us have become just a
> little too aggressive in our criticism of people who smoke, eat
> junk food, and get fat. We flaunt our fitness a little too much not
> to make others feel uncomfortable.

Whatever the excesses of action and reaction, the continued
noisy fuss over running has largely obscured the fact that in a
profound sense the sport is changing the world. Not the whole
world, of course, but significant corners of it. As a paradigm of
the change, consider the case of George Mize, a 340-pound Illinois steelworker. One day in early 1979, Mize, sick of always
having been, as he put it, "that fat guy," started running.
When I was in touch with him less than a year later he was
down to 208 pounds and was still on the decline. As
indisputable proof of his accomplishment he proudly mailed
me a pair of his abandoned blue jeans. I measured them. They
were fifty-four inches at the waist.

Just as significant as the shrinkage of Mize's dimensions,
however, were the alterations in the way he viewed himself.
"You might not imagine," he told me, "the mental influence
my weight loss is having on me. I've been complimented so
much lately I almost feel guilty about the whole affair. It's not
natural." The change in Mize, like the change in thousands of
other runners, amounts to nothing less than a new view of
human possibilities. Men and women who once thought of
themselves as irretrievably middle-aged have come to see
themselves as young again. People who rarely ran a step
cover five miles a day without breathing hard. By the hundreds of thousands, runners all over the world are realizing
that it is not necessary, as Dylan Thomas put it, to go gentle
into that good night, that they can rage against it and, through
running, perhaps postpone the going for a while. They are
realizing, in short, that their day-to-day health is their re-
sponsibility and not a doctor's. Should they break a leg or become seriously ill, they are entirely willing to see a doctor, but

they know it is primarily their own business to keep themselves well.

It would be a mistake to ascribe this change in perception to a sudden access of good sense peculiar to our own era, for it is in fact not a discovery at all but a rediscovery. John Dryden observed that "the wise, for cure, on exercise depend." Later, Samuel Johnson remarked, "How much happiness is gained, and how much misery escaped, by frequent and violent agitation of the body." More recently the historian George M. Trevelyan said, "I have two doctors, my left leg and my right."

It would be a mistake, too, to suppose that, through running, the world is on the verge of being freed from the scourge of sickness. For one thing, despite everything running does to benefit the cardiovascular system, it seems to have no influence whatsoever on the incidence of many diseases, including cancer. For another, its scope notwithstanding, the running movement is clearly limited. As recently as 1979 a full 41 percent of the American population, by its own testimony, got no exercise at all, and another 28 percent exercised for only two and a half hours or so every week. Moreover, the running movement is largely concentrated in the upper middle class. In studying the sport's dimensions not long ago, the public opinion analyst Louis Harris found that 53 percent of highly active Americans had annual incomes of at least $15,000, while 22 percent had incomes of at least $25,000. As revealing as any single fact is this one: in a major marathon held in the late 1970s, one out of every two participants held a graduate degree.

It is nonetheless apparent that the growth of running and the general increase in concern about physical fitness, whatever their limitations, reflect a significant shift in attitude. A study by Yankelovich, Skelly and White showed recently that 46 percent of Americans have taken steps to improve their health and that 70 percent believe most Americans are more concerned with taking care of themselves than they were a few years earlier. It may not be everything a physical fitness visionary could ask for, but it's a beginning.

A significant question, of course, is whether it will last. The

Harris study called running, like calisthenics, a "fast-rising" activity, in contrast with walking, bowling and softball, which are "level" and with bicycling, hiking and swimming, which are "losing." Neil Amdur, the *New York Times*'s track and field authority, has written, "The foundation for long-term growth has been laid.... Running will endure—perhaps not as a boom or rage but, more importantly, as the vehicle for a fulfilling life." Similarly, when Hank Herman, the managing editor of *Family Health* magazine, looked into the question by talking, as he put it, with "just about everyone who could be expected to have something meaningful to say about how the running scene would look ten years from now," he concluded: "The verdict was resoundingly clear: In 1989, the roads and running tracks won't be any less jammed with bipeds than they are today. If anything, there'll be *more* runners out there." Running's biggest growth period is no doubt leveling off, but it is almost certain that the sport will continue to grow well into the 1980s and perhaps beyond.

Running, as every runner discovers, is not just drudgery but sport, amusement and a telephoneless, bossless escape into freedom from everyday pressures. It is, I suspect, something more significant, too: the leading edge of a major and perhaps lasting change not just in how we take care of our bodies but in what, ultimately, we think of ourselves.

2

Is Running Really Good for Us?

At Last, a Patient Scientist Provides an Irrefutable Answer

From a distance the San Leandro Hills, rising in serpen-
tine brown creases from the eastern edge of San Francisco Bay, look much like a pile of old baseball gloves badly in
need of neat's-foot oil. One recent dawn, just as the first splash
of sunlight was exploding through the eucalyptus trees and
onto the shadowed flanks of a crease known as Wildcat Can-
yon, a compact human figure with thinning hair and an incon-
gruously cheerful expression could be seen running hard
along a blacktop road. It was in fact a Stanford University
professor in his late fifties named Ralph S. Paffenbarger, Jr.,
and he was engaged in an arduous and repetitive ritual. Every
so often, as he reached a forbiddingly steep portion of the
pavement, he would break into a sprint and, his heart banging
against his rib cage, ascend until his breath came in famished

increase in physical activity to a level of about 2,500 calories a week.

Heart attacks per 10,000 man-years of observation

TOTAL HEART ATTACKS

NONFATAL

FATAL

Less than 500 / 500-999 / 1000-1999 / 2000-2999 / 3000-3999 / 4000 or more

Calories expended each week in physical exercise

Source: American Journal of Epidemiology, 108, pp. 161-175, 1978

306

gasps and his legs threatened to carry him no farther. Then, having rested by covering a few hundred yards at a relaxed lope, he would repeat the self-torturing procedure. Paffenbarger had been doing this for an hour and his shirtless body glistened with sweat. He was feeling good. He was also feeling optimistic. At home, in a desk drawer, was a red, white and blue envelope containing a British Airways round-trip ticket; within a few days his efforts would be put to the test when he tried to run the 53.5 miles from London to Brighton. Paffenbarger was not greatly worried. In recent years he had competed in eleven Boston Marathons, six or seven 50-mile races, four races of 100 miles, and a 72.6-mile race around Lake Tahoe. And why not? His physique, 145 muscled pounds sculptured economically onto a five-foot, eight-inch frame, is ideally suited for attempting unthinkable distances. Once, in fact, he ran for nearly twenty-nine hours, stopping only to drink fluids, and on another occasion was one of only three runners to complete the 100-mile-long Western States Endurance Run. Five times that many people had been at the starting line.

Paffenbarger's most celebrated achievements have not, however, been in running at all but in an activity only intermittently related to it. It is a medical subspecialty known as epidemiology, a world of computers, probabilities, graphs, charts, tables and the arcane convolutions of inductive logic, all of it employed to determine the causes of diseases, both contagious and noncontagious, and how they spread. In the entire United States there are at most 500 epidemiologists. Among them Paffenbarger has few peers, for over the years he has not only managed to solve some of the most stubbornly resistant medical mysteries but has also provided an unassailable answer to a seemingly simple but bafflingly complex question: Is running really good for people?

Unless you are knowledgeable enough about both logic and statistics to understand the difficulty of proving that one circumstance causes another, you might innocently suppose that the relationship between exercise and good health had long since been demonstrated, at least to the satisfaction of anyone but an irredeemable nit-picker. It was, after all, a full quarter-century ago that J. N. Morris and two other investigators, comparing the heart attack rates of drivers and conductors on London's double-decker buses and of clerks and mail carriers in the city's postal system, discovered that the conductors, who spent much of their time walking up and down collecting fares, suffered only half as many heart attacks as the more sedentary drivers, and that the mail carriers had significantly fewer heart attacks than the clerks. The same pattern was, moreover, found in later studies of workers, clerks, business managers and professional men in Philadelphia; section men, switchmen and clerks in the U.S. railroad industry; farmers and professional men in North Dakota; full-time farmers, part-time farmers and nonfarming residents of Evans County, Georgia; exercising and nonexercising cigarette smokers; Canadian farmers, miners, laborers and business executives; and sedentary and nonsedentary residents of Britain, New York City, Israel, Scotland and Westchester County, New York.

Even though all the studies corroborated Morris's findings, a troublesome ambiguity remained. The reason for the link between exercise and good health was not at all clear. Two explanations were, in fact, possible: 1) exercise might, as most investigators intuitively suspected, lower the incidence of heart attacks; or 2) those who are healthier and thus less subject to heart attack in the first place might be more likely to exercise. If the second possibility was the correct one, then it might turn out that no amount of exertion, no matter how diligently pursued, could lower heart attack risk. If you were going to have an attack, you'd simply have one. This possibility seemed quite likely when Morris published a second report in the prestigious British medical journal *The Lancet* subtitled "The Epidemiology of Uniforms." Comparing jobs held with uniform size, he found that when they started work the drivers weighed more for their height than the conductors. Since overweight in itself increases heart attack risk, maybe people who were more disease-prone to start with had naturally drifted toward the more sedentary assignments. In that case, job duties would have had no influence on subsequent health.

It was within this atmosphere of scientific puzzlement that Ralph Paffenbarger, as a fledgling epidemiologist, first went to work back in the 1940s. For a long time he had known he wanted to be a doctor. When he was in the fifth grade in Columbus, Ohio, he developed mastoiditis, had an operation and spent eleven days in a hospital. "It was something new in my life," he says. "The place fascinated me. Right then I started thinking about being a doctor."

Paffenbarger took premed courses at Ohio State, went on to the Northwestern University medical school, interned at Evanston Hospital, and in 1947 joined the Public Health Service. As an intern he had witnessed two polio epidemics. The disease fascinated him. Now, in the Public Health Service, he had a chance to study it in detail. Assigned to the Center for Disease Control in Atlanta, he looked into such questions as whether having had a tonsillectomy increased the risk of polio (it did), whether being pregnant increased the risk (it did), and whether the common housefly, *Musca domestica*, was responsible for spreading the disease (it wasn't). It was his first exposure to epidemiology, and he loved its haunting combination of logic and mystery. In his late twenties, he seemed to be well on his way to a career in the epidemiology of polio. Then, in the mid-1950s, Jonas Salk and Albert Sabin came along. Suddenly there was no longer any polio for Paffenbarger or anyone else to study. "It was time," Paffenbarger says with a wry shrug, "to stop being interested in polio."

Although his plans were momentarily awry, Paffenbarger was not discouraged. He is, as more than one acquaintance has discovered, a hard man to discourage. A few years ago, mostly as a joke, friends invited him on a two-week, 223-mile backpacking trip along California's John Muir Trail. Paffenbarger, who had never before been backpacking and knew nothing about the sport, went out and bought a $12 pair of hiking boots. Eight days into the trip the soles peeled away from the uppers. Rick Buxton, one of his fellow backpackers, taped, tied and wired them together. As they hiked Buxton told Paffenbarger there was no way he could last another week with his shoes in that condition; he would have to head home at the next turnoff.

"If they come apart again," Paffenbarger asked, "can't you put them together again?"

"I suppose I could," said Buxton, "but I wouldn't recommend it."

Paffenbarger finished the hike. He still keeps the tattered boots as a souvenir.

Paffenbarger moved to the Robert A. Taft Sanitary Engineering Center in Cincinnati. There, while other scientists studied such garden-variety problems as air pollution, food and water sanitation and radiological hazards, he turned to the epidemiology of a bafflingly unpredictable mental illness known as postpartum psychosis that sometimes afflicts women after childbirth. (It was, and still is, Paffenbarger's suspicion that many if not most mental disorders are not of psychological origin at all but are caused by hormonal imbalances.) Meanwhile, old friends had found their way to the National Heart Institute—now the National Heart, Lung and Blood Institute—in Bethesda, Maryland. In 1958, when an opening occurred, they asked Paffenbarger, who by this time had a Ph.D. in epidemiology from Johns Hopkins, whether he would like to look into the epidemiology of heart disease. Paffenbarger said he would. It was a decision that was ultimately to produce answers to some of medicine's most elusive mysteries.

When epidemiologists investigate a disease, they follow a well-established procedure. First, they read whatever has been written about its clinical nature, what causes it and how current concepts suggest it is most effectively prevented and cured. In the case of heart attack, this wasn't much of a project. In the 1950s not much was known about it. The literature was accordingly sparse.

Second, they study the disease's behavior. Does it spread quickly or slowly? Does it move from one person to another? Are insects involved? Viruses? Or do physiological abnormalities lead to its occurrence?

Finally, they talk to anyone who might be able to suggest

promising avenues of inquiry. Here Paffenbarger was lucky. His boss, James Watt, simply said, "Paffenbarger, do it the way you want to do it." Paffenbarger started visiting knowledgeable doctors. One day he paid a call on the late Paul Dudley White, President Eisenhower's personal physician and one of the leading heart specialists of his time. White told him that with only a few exceptions, such as that of a perspicacious investigator named Ogelsby Paul who had recently begun studying the heart attack rates of Western Electric workers, no one, in his opinion, had thus far paid sufficient attention to the relationship between exercise habits and cardiovascular health.

For an epidemiologist the vacuum was made to order. First, it involved a major disease, one that had been identified as early as 1912 but about which little had been learned. As late as World War II, for example, the distinguished cardiologist Sir Thomas Lewis was still insisting that heart attack patients should stay in bed for six weeks or more. "During the whole of this period," he wrote in his book *Diseases of the Heart*, "the patient is to be guarded by day and night nursing and helped in every way to avoid voluntary movement or effort." Today some patients are out of bed within two or three days.

Second, enough anecdotal evidence existed to make it likely that some sort of relationship, no matter how tenuous, existed between exercise and heart attacks. Nor was the likelihood of success in any way diminished by the well-considered view of Paul Dudley White, an avid bicycle rider and exercise enthusiast.

A layman can easily understand the principal research technique of epidemiology. The investigator searches out a sufficiently large number of healthy subjects, takes whatever history seems relevant, and waits to see what happens. As soon as enough heart attacks, tumors or ulcers have occurred, he looks to see whether they have a pattern of antecedents or are merely random. Though simple in concept, epidemiology has a formidable built-in difficulty: you often have to wait for an extremely long time before cause, if any, produces effect, if any. A person first studied at age twenty may not come down with a disease for half a century. Even for a man with Paffenbarger's patience, half a century can seem a long time to wait.

Sometimes, fortunately, a way around the problem can be found, but only if someone, years earlier, obligingly recorded histories of the group you want to study, thereby in effect compressing time into a workable span. Paffenbarger wondered, therefore, whether somewhere there might not be such a group, perhaps associated with an organization that requires periodic physical examinations. Eventually he thought of colleges and universities. Searching for usable records, he visited the University of Minnesota, Ohio State, the Berkeley campus of the University of California, West Point, Annapolis, the Coast Guard Academy, M.I.T., the University of Massachusetts, the University of Wisconsin, Bryn Mawr, Mount Holyoke, Radcliffe, Smith, Vassar and Wellesley. At none of them did the records prove adequate, although the Coast Guard Academy's came close, falling short only because the academy had fewer graduates than Paffenbarger felt he needed in order to give his study proper statistical heft. Turning at last to Harvard, he found what he was looking for: meticulous medical histories going all the way back to 1916 as well as, from 1938 on, answers to a considerable array of psychosocial questions. There were 36,500 such records, and almost all the people they described, thanks to the university's fund-raising zeal, were currently traceable. For an epidemiologist the documents were a treasure trove. Almost simultaneously Paffenbarger found another cache of usable records. These were at the University of Pennsylvania and covered the years 1931 to 1940 for 13,500 men and 3,000 women. Among other questions, they asked whether the students were subject to nervousness, insomnia, worries, self-consciousness, secretiveness, oscillating moods and feelings of persecution. Paffenbarger finally had what he needed.

A continuing problem nonetheless nagged at him. No matter what his findings or how great their statistical validity, a critic would still be able to argue that that familiar bugaboo, self-selection, was a factor. Suppose, as Paffenbarger was almost certain would happen, people who exercised proved to have fewer heart attacks than those who didn't. There would be no way of showing that they were not healthier in the first place. That might, in fact, be the very reason they exercised more. Although he would, to be sure, have demonstrated a relationship, he would not have proved what he was looking for: causality. He set to work but kept looking for something more.

Finally, in 1968, he found it. Years earlier, some 6,000 San Francisco longshoremen, aged thirty-five to sixty-four, had had physical examinations. All, regardless of what kind of work they might have preferred, had worked for at least five years as cargo handlers. Thus Paffenbarger finally had a population in which initial self-selection was not a factor. When the longshoremen had had their physicals, furthermore, there was none of the mechanization and use of shipping containers that was later to lighten their work; cargo was moved by brute muscular force. Over the years, however, work conditions changed. Moreover, many of the men were promoted to supervisory posts or reassigned to less demanding jobs. Through records kept by their union Paffenbarger was able to discover which of them had had heart attacks. If, therefore, a relationship between exercise and health were found, it would almost unquestionably be one of cause and effect. More importantly, the same relationship could be presumed to hold with the Harvard and University of Pennsylvania graduates. The college graduates and the longshoremen, one of the groups wonderfully large, the other wonderfully free of Paffenbarger's most troublesome logical and statistical puzzlements, gave him a corroborative triangulation no previous researcher had enjoyed.

Nor was Paffenbarger daunted by the complexity of the record-keeping and analysis involved in the project. Not long ago, in order to take a closer look at his work, I spent parts of three days with him at his home in Berkeley and at his offices on the Stanford campus in Palo Alto and the University of California campus just down the road from his house. Each morning, before driving off in his five-speed diesel Rabbit, he entered in a spiral-bound notebook the date and odometer mileage. One morning I asked him why. "I like to keep track of things," he said.

Our longest day together was spent at Stanford, where Paffenbarger serves as professor of epidemiology in the medical school. His office, which is on the ground floor and overlooks a sunny courtyard, has only two decorations on its pale yellow walls. One is a calendar. The other is a photograph of himself and a friend, Peter Mattei, running together in a 100-mile race. In a walnut bookcase is an assortment of books on epidemiology, as well as *Dr. Sheehan on Running,* Bill Bradley's *Life on the Run, The Magic of Walking* and a paperback copy of Gertrude Stein's *How to Write.* Paffenbarger was wearing tan chinos, brown suede running shoes with triple parallel stripes, and a silver belt buckle as big as a man's hand that he was awarded for completing the Western States Endurance Run. On it was engraved "100 Miles—1 Day."

Paffenbarger talked about his studies. "By its nature," he said, "epidemiology is crude. The epidemiologist works with very rough data. Suppose some guy says he climbs five hundred stairs a day. There's just no way to verify what he's told you. You've got to take his word. Otherwise, we don't have many problems. We've lost track of only 0.62 percent of our Harvard men. They may disappear for a while but we almost always find them again, so we have practically a complete followup. With our first mailing we may get a two-thirds response. Our next mailing will bring it to 75 percent. With the third we get it up to 90 percent. It would be even higher except that a lot of secretaries think their bosses are too busy to answer us, so they never see the darned questionnaire. Some people, I suppose, really are too busy. One fellow wrote on his questionnaire, 'Drop dead.' When we sent a second request he said, 'Drop dead again.' We'll keep after him, but I'm not hopeful."

Because Paffenbarger is mining his study subjects for dozens of kinds of information, not all aspects of his analysis can be undertaken at once. I talked with a young computer programmer named Shelley Hurwitz, who sits at a desk in Paffenbarger's outer office when she is not at Sequoia Hall, where the computers are kept. Ms. Hurwitz has a pretty face, a deskful of green-and-white printouts, and a worried look. You can flog a computer only so hard, she explained. This is one reason the Harvard and University of Pennsylvania graduates have been yielding information for nearly a decade and a half now, and why Paffenbarger expects to be working the same vein for years to come.

His first report, in the *American Journal of Epidemiology*, appeared in 1966. Thereafter, as analyses were completed, he published slices of the total study in such publications as the *American Journal of Public Health*, the *Journal of the American College Health Association*, and the *Journal of the National Cancer Institute*. Among his incidental findings have been these:

It is possible, many decades in advance, to predict the incidence of fatal stroke by examining blood pressure, weight, cigarette smoking, family history and college participation in athletics. Furthermore, the likelihood of stroke is greatly increased if a student had a blood pressure greater than 130/90, was more than 20 percent overweight, smoked more than ten cigarettes a day, was not an athlete and had a parent who had died from any cause but particularly from cardiovascular or kidney disease.

It is similarly possible to predict the onset of hypertension. People subject to hypertension, a predisposing factor in heart attack and stroke, are likely to have a systolic blood pressure above 130, a pulse rate above 90 beats a minute, and a parent with hypertension. They are also likely to be overweight first-born children who spend fewer than five hours a week at sports.

Adults are more likely to develop diabetes if as students they had a family history of diabetes, complained of heart irregularities and a sense of exhaustion, had a low vital capacity, were overweight, had a systolic blood pressure above 130, drank coffee and tea, and consumed fewer than seven glasses of water a day.

Habitual coffee drinking is the best predictor of peptic ulcer, while milk consumption best identifies those likely to remain ulcer-free.

Whatever one's exercise practices, heart attacks are more likely among sons of blue-collar workers, and high blood pressure is less likely among those who at one time or another have moved from city to city—a sign, presumably, of adaptation to a mobile society.

Hodgkin's disease is more likely among people who as youths contract few contagious diseases, have a parent who died early, particularly from cancer, and are overweight, smoke cigarettes and drink coffee.

Accidental death is more likely among those who attended boarding school rather than lived at home, smoke cigarettes and drink alcohol, drop out of college and complain of nervousness, insomnia and the other psychological characteristics mentioned earlier. In the same alumni population suicide is more likely, except that potential suicides are more apt to have lost their fathers early in life either through death or parental separation.

It was, however, when Paffenbarger began to look at the cause-and-effect relationship between exercise and cardiovascular health that he made his most arresting discoveries as well as those with the greatest relevance to those of us who run.

In at least a general way, the conditions that create heart attack risk have long been known. Chief among them are cigarette smoking, overweight, high blood pressure and sedentary living. Paffenbarger set out to study them with enough mathematical precision to determine the relative importance of each. For the first time such precision was possible because of the magnitude of his two study populations and because they spanned much of the range of possible human activity, from the extremely active longshoremen to the more sedentary Harvard and University of Pennsylvania graduates. Using a technique known as multiple logistic risk analysis, Paffenbarger plotted various combinations of risk factors to see not only what their cumulative effect might be but also in what ways and to what degrees risk might be reduced. As the numbers piled up, the evidence grew that exercise could to some extent overcome every known risk factor, both separately and in all possible combinations. Cigarette smokers who exercised heavily had only two-thirds as many heart attacks as sedentary smokers. Overweight people who started exercising reduced their heart attack risk by as much as one-quarter. Those with high blood pressure could cut their risk by more than half. And so it went, risk factor by risk factor. Exercise could reduce, and in some cases nullify, the effects of everything from diabetes to family history.

When Paffenbarger looked into the effect of altering combinations of risk factors, he found that even larger gains were attainable. As the table below shows, a sedentary person who smokes cigarettes and has high blood pressure can reduce risk by a full 88 percent if he alters all three factors, while someone who neither smokes nor has high blood pressure can reduce his risk by 28 percent merely by becoming more active. The implications not just for individuals but for the health of the nation at large are considerable. Among Paffenbarger's college graduates, for example, only 8.2 percent suffered from hypertension. Thus even if they were all treated and their blood pressure became normal, the reduction in heart attacks for the total population would be slight. In the case of exercise, on the other hand, the potential gain is enormous. Since 60 percent lead sedentary lives and are thus in increased danger of heart attack, persuading them to exercise could produce an important reduction in heart attacks.

REDUCING YOUR HEART ATTACK RISK

Sedentary life style	Cigarette smoking	High blood pressure	Heart attack rate*	Potential risk reduction†
Yes	Yes	Yes	201	88%
Yes	Yes	No	66	60%
Yes	No	Yes	102	76%
No	Yes	Yes	80	68%
Yes	No	No	35	28%
No	Yes	No	50	48%
No	No	Yes	42	41%
No	No	No	26	—

* Per 10,000 person-years
† If yeses are changed to noes

Analyzing his statistics, Paffenbarger was able to determine with unprecedented precision the amount of exercise needed to achieve a protective effect. When he used a graph to plot heart attacks against energy expended, he found that the curve descended sharply until about 2,500 kilocalories a week. Because a mile of running consumes about 100 kilocalories, that works out to the equivalent of three or four miles a day. This, Paffenbarger points out, is the minimum amount of exercise, of whatever kind, that will produce a significant reduction in heart attack risk. A person that active is 64 percent less likely than a sedentary person to have a heart attack.

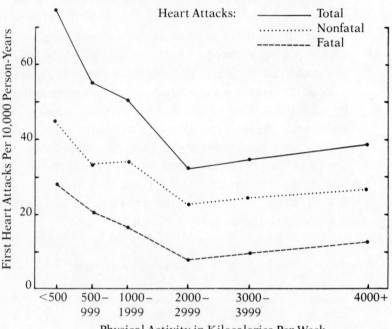

HOW EXERCISE PREVENTS HEART ATTACKS

Paffenbarger cited, incidentally, a methodological curiosity in the graph, which appears above. Beyond 2,999 kilocalories a week the protective effect appears to diminish. He suspects, however, that this is not what actually occurs at all. He told me, "Our questionnaires inquire about the number of flights of stairs climbed and ask that ten steps be considered one flight. I've got a hunch that some people count the steps they climb every day but forget to divide by ten. They tell us they climb fifty flights when they really climb five. I'm pretty sure that rise in the graph is nothing more than an artifact of our methods."

Should you decide to run right off the end of the graph and cover more than forty miles a week, you will probably continue to enjoy greater protection, but only to a point. The graph below, which translates Paffenbarger's longshoremen findings into running equivalents, suggests that if you in-crease distance from fifty miles to a hundred or so a week you will cut your heart attack risk in half. The gain is not, however, as great as it may at first appear, since at fifty miles your risk is already comfortably low, having been cut by nearly two-thirds in the first twenty-five miles alone. Paffen-barger himself runs seventy or seventy-five miles a week and frequently puts in hard quarter-mile bursts. "There is excel-lent evidence," he told me, "that periodic hard running does a lot more good than just coasting along all the time."

BEYOND FIFTY MILES A WEEK

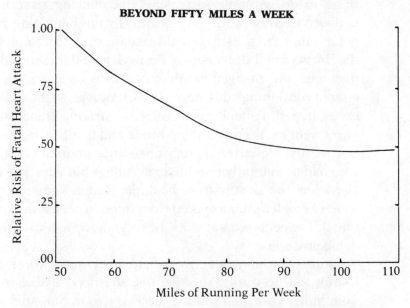

Given the current state of physiological knowledge, exactly why exercise so effectively reduces the number of heart at-tacks can only be guessed at. One problem is that so many changes take place in an active man or woman that no one has so far been able to determine which is most significant. A

Stanford colleague of Paffenbarger's, Dr. Peter D. Wood, has found that the blood of trained runners contains greater concentrations of high-density lipoproteins than that of nonrunners. It is high-density lipoproteins that patrol the bloodstream, removing the cholesterol that narrows arteries and thereby produces heart attacks. Similarly, Dr. Thomas G. Pickering of New York Hospital–Cornell University Medical Center recently reported that the blood of runners is less viscous than that of nonrunners and therefore flows more freely and forms clots less readily. Other researchers have documented running's favorable effects on cholesterol and triglyceride levels, blood pressure, obesity, cigarette smoking, the efficiency of the heart muscle and even, as will be seen in the next chapter, psychological stress.

Like Paffenbarger's longshoremen studies, his college studies eventually suggested that self-selection has little if anything to do with the increasingly convincing relationship between exercise and good health. In the beginning it appeared that the question might remain moot, for analysis of the Harvard and University of Pennsylvania data showed that men who had engaged in athletics during college seemed to enjoy a continuing advantage. Then, however, as the evidence accumulated, Paffenbarger noticed a striking trend. As the years went by, the advantage shrank and finally disappeared. Eventually, a quarter-century or so after graduation, a man who had been totally unathletic in college but who now exercised was almost sure to be healthier than a former campus sports hero. If a stubborn skeptic wanted to persist in arguing that self-selection was at work, he was now up against a formidable obstacle.

A dozen or so years ago Paffenbarger and two or three friends took to getting together one afternoon a week in Joaquin Miller Park, just south of Berkeley, for a run. Afterward, as the sun fell behind the redwoods and live oaks, they would sit in a quiet glade down a hill from the parking lot and open a few bottles of cold Hamm's. The group grew, and today on a good night as many as sixty or seventy men, women and children turn up. One recent day Paffenbarger invited me to join them. We ran ten hilly miles. As we were finishing, coasting down a dusty dirt path that curled along the edge of a hillside, we could see a big campfire and smell the hamburgers. "I think running is going to last," Paffenbarger was saying. "People who run find their lives so much more enjoyable. Everything works better. Their cardiovascular system. Their gastrointestinal system. Even their ability to think. I suspect most of the people who are running today are going to continue right on into old age. I hope I do." We cooled off, drank a bottle or two of beer, and ate two hamburgers and a big piece of cake. Then we went back to Paffenbarger's house in Berkeley and slept the sweet sleep of the innocent and the overfed. A few hours later, at dawn, Paffenbarger was banging on my door, summoning me to another run. Half asleep, I put on my shoes and, helpless in the face of all the charts, graphs and tables that had swarmed through my dreams, went.

3 ///
Frontiers

The Mind of the Runner Is Both Baffling and Tantalizing

*N*early two decades ago, long before the current army of researchers had begun to look with fascination into the relationship between physical conditioning and the workings of the human brain, Dr. Paul Dudley White addressed the graduating class of the University of California medical school. An outspoken champion of exercise, White argued that the time-honored Western dichotomy between mind and body rests on a fallacy. Contrary to what many of us suppose, he told the audience, the brain cannot function at anything close to maximum power unless the body is in excellent condition. Intellectual health, he insisted, depends on the proper circulation of blood to the brain. "Here," he said, "are located both our mental activities and our very souls and personalities, and we must keep it healthy and free from the disadvantages of poor physiological and psychological functions, and from defects of blood supply due to obstructions of the arteries."

In the years since White uttered those words, scores of scientists have verified their truth. The evidence is, in fact, beyond dispute that mental ability—such capacities as learning potential and academic achievement—almost invariably increases as physical fitness improves. It is plain, moreover, that running and other high-intensity activities bring a number of other far-reaching psychological changes. The precise mechanisms by which running affects us so deeply are still being investigated and debated. Some authorities think the changes result from nothing more than an elevated body temperature or an increase in the brain's blood supply. Others suspect that they are brought on by running's hypnotically repetitive rhythms. Still others argue that they result from the release of morphinelike chemicals called endorphins or from a natural stimulant called norepinephrine.

If, however, much remains to be discovered, much is already known. Since the mid-1970s, when I first began to look into the question in preparation for writing *The Complete Book of Running*, researchers of almost every imaginable variety have been exploring the psychological dimensions of our sport. By early 1980 an organization called the International Association of Running Therapists had even come into being, and at its first meeting had turned to such topics as—I am quoting from the official agenda—"Runners: Divorce and Marriage," "Runners and Ego Psychology," and "Women Runners and the Myth of Atalanta." At another conference, held a few months earlier under the auspices of the Cornell University Medical College, an endocrinologist reported on the incidence of emotional disorders in runners, a psychologist described personality change among runners, a cardiologist discussed the influence of a runner's body type on his or her personality, one psychiatrist described the effects of running on depression and two others discussed running as an adjunct to psychotherapy. Finally, a team of tirelessly athletic researchers reported on what they learned when, using bicy-

cles and portable tape recorders, they interviewed participants during a hundred-mile footrace on Long Island. (One of
the things they learned was that after ten or twelve hours of
running some people aren't particularly eager to be interviewed.)

These are only a handful of the topics currently under study.
Within the past few years it has become apparent that the
mental aspects of running are one of psychology's most promising frontiers, one beyond which lie not only uncharted physiological and psychological territories but fundamental philosophical issues as well. If, for example, we ultimately confirm
that human beings experience maximum psychological integ-
rity when they exercise strenuously rather than when they are
largely sedentary, this finding would clearly suggest the sort
of life humankind was in effect designed for. It would also suggest how far most of us have allowed ourselves to drift from
our intended path. For whatever the societal confusions of our
time, it is clear that we live in the twilight of the Industrial
Revolution's long first phase, the period in which our ma-
chines have been unable to function without physical effort on
our part. For two centuries you and I have been needed to
place raw material in position, to pull levers, and to remove
finished products. Now, in the second phase, computers and
their uncomplaining robots are beginning to perform all these
functions, leaving for us only one role at which we continue,
however tenuously, to excel: thought. If, despite history's current tide, humankind in its fundamental nature requires not
thought alone but strenuous movement too, it may be that
only our play—running or some physically demanding sub-
stitute—will preserve us. When we run we may be strengthening not just our cardiovascular systems and sanity but our
evolutionary grasp of life on this planet.

It has long been apparent that psychological alterations
occur to a more marked degree in running than in other activities, including even such arduous sports as swimming and bicycling. At a scientific conference a few years ago A. N. Rosen-
berg of Princeton University speculated on why running
confers more pronounced psychological effects than, for ex-

ample, swimming does. "Running," he said, "is qualitatively different from swimming in the sense that a swimmer will often go down the same lane repeatedly. A marathoner generally won't use the same road more than twice, once in each direction. I think the fact that one is traveling to different places has a lot to do with the mentality of the runner." At the same conference a psychiatrist suggested another possible reason for running's psychological power. "If it is true," he said, "that man is the greatest long-distance land animal on our planet—that is, that man can run down any other land animal—this indicates that there may be a biological or evolutionary pattern or archetype which resonates to very deep levels of our unconscious."

At a second, more recent conference a Yale psychiatrist, Dr. Victor A. Altshul, described how one of his patients had benefited from a combination of running and psychotherapy. At the end of Altshul's talk a member of the audience asked him: "Do you think running has anything special that other sports don't have?"

"Yes," replied Altshul, who is himself a runner. "Its contentless character. There are no split-second decisions as in other sports. While you're running you don't have to think about anything."

Whatever the precise cause, it is common knowledge, now abundantly verified by numerous studies, that runners are more likely than other athletes to experience striking psychological alterations. Thus far, the most comprehensive attempt to understand their nature is Valerie Andrews's 1978 study *The Psychic Power of Running*, a wide-ranging if misleadingly titled exploration of running's effects on our mental lives. What is noteworthy, of course, is not that such a book was written, but that it is thus far the only work of its kind. We simply do not yet know much about why running has such a profound effect on the human mind. Nor, for that matter, have we catalogued with any precision the variety of mental readjustments running causes. For the moment all we know is that their scope is considerably broader than even the most daring

researchers suspected in the early days of the current running
movement.

In *The Complete Book of Running* I cited several studies and
quoted innumerable fragments of personal testimony suggesting that in one way or another runners feel better psycho-
logically than nonrunners. At the University of Southern California, for example, Dr. Herbert A. deVries and Gene M.
Adams found that in some cases fifteen minutes of moderate
exercise reduces nervous tension more effectively than tranquilizers do. At Purdue University another study demonstrated that after a four-month running program volunteers
became more stable, self-sufficient, imaginative and confident. The kinds of change documented in such studies were, I
noted, succinctly summarized by a former Olympic marathoner named Ted Corbitt, who suggested that running is
"like having your own psychiatrist."

Much of the information I was able to gather about the subject at that time was, however, distinctly impressionistic and
therefore unsatisfyingly inconclusive. Except for a few pioneers like deVries, few researchers had looked closely at the
psychological effects of exercise. One underlying reason, no
doubt, was a deeply rooted Western conviction that except in
unimportant ways the mind and body are independent, in
contrast to the Eastern view that they are fundamentally indi-
visible. Another reason, perhaps the main one, was that practically nobody thought there was much of anything worth in-
vestigating.

Now we know differently. At the Cornell conference mentioned earlier, eight distinguished specialists and an audito-
rium full of psychiatrists, psychologists and laymen spent a
whole day exploring the psychological ramifications of running. Although learned arguments were frequent and occasionally vehement, on one aspect of the proceedings there was
never a moment's disagreement: the effects of running are
more numerous than even the most visionary dreamers of a
few years ago imagined. It would, in fact, be a formidable task
to attempt even a sketchy summary, for in addition to forty

or more full-scale studies of exercise and personality alone, the literature is filled with hundreds of reports on exercise and mental health, exercise and intelligence, and exercise and other aspects of human and even animal psychology, not to mention uncountable speculations, hypotheses and theoretical meditations. The range of these writings is extraordinary. All manner of excellent new evidence exists, for example, that running in itself, even in the absence of psychotherapy, contributes to mental health. Although no one understands exactly why, people who run seem to call into being an otherwise elusive internal direction finder that guides them away from psychological distress. Examples are easily cited:

Kenneth H. Sidney, a researcher at Victoria Hospital in London, Ontario, put thirty-four men and women, all of them aged sixty or older, on a fourteen-week conditioning program. Four out of five reported improvements in psychological well-being, and those who trained hardest felt the best.

S. N. Blair, a researcher from the University of South Carolina's Human Performance Laboratory, questioned employees of a Greenville, South Carolina, firm, the Liberty Corporation. He found that those who exercised during their leisure time were more satisfied with their jobs than sedentary employees. (A similar study in Canada, however, showed that while a fitness program decreased absenteeism at an insurance company, it didn't have any measurable effect on how workers liked their jobs.)

It has been well established, too, that exercise has a marked effect on anxiety. At the University of Wisconsin, two researchers recruited 177 men and 38 women for an exercise program. After their workouts most subjects felt less anxiety than before. A researcher named Wesley E. Sime has found, furthermore, that among university students exercise reduces the anxiety typically associated with examinations. It does so, in fact, more effectively than tranquilizers—and without the mind-dulling effects associated with such drugs.

Exercise has a similarly salutary effect on depression. Not long ago Gerald D. Tharp of the University of Nebraska studied sixty-five students and YMCA members who exercise regu-

larly and fifty-six who did not. He found that the more active
subjects manifested significantly less depression. Another researcher, Dr. John H. Greist, and three associates reported in
The Physician and Sportsmedicine: "The freedom and the
renewed capacity to think creatively on most runs greatly re-
lieves persons who have been mired in depressive rumina-
tions. A depression-free interlude on the run, even if short-
lived, renews hope that the illness itself will be time-limited."
Dr. Robert S. Brown, a psychiatrist, summarizes the phenomenon this way: "Depression seems to be uncommon among
athletes."

Interestingly, however, such a diminution of depression
takes place only during and after high-intensity exercise.
When Brown compared the effects of running with those of
less strenuous sports, he found that softball players, for example, experienced no discernible reduction in depression, and
that tennis players reported only a slight reduction.

Running is not, of course, a psychological panacea. In the
view of a Harvard Medical School psychiatrist, Dr. Earl G.
Solomon, it does, however, impart benefits that are attainable
in few other ways. As a case in point he recently described a
technique for altering one's state of consciousness and thereby
improving the efficacy of psychoanalysis:

1. Take a one-hour run, at a pace Solomon described
   as "a gentle lope."
2. During the run repeat the word *one* or the more
   mantralike syllable *om*.

Doing these two things simultaneously, he explained, "produces a runner's high, a healthful, pleasant experience." The
runner, he said, becomes relaxed and refreshed and enjoys a
feeling of renewed vitality. For reasons that are not clear, rap-
port with an analyst may increase and resistance to therapy
lessen. A California psychiatrist, Dr. Thaddeus Kostrubala,
who for a number of years has routinely used running as part
of psychotherapy, reported recently that he too has found it "a
powerful therapeutic tool." In many cases, he told a recent

gathering of his colleagues, "the need for medication de-
creases."

Other investigators have reported that people tend to
dream more, in greater variety and more vividly as a result of
running. Some psychiatrists, including Kostrubala, feel that
this is all to the good, since dreaming presumably enables the
dreamer to become aware of drives that might otherwise remain irretrievably buried in the unconscious.

Exactly why all these psychological improvements occur is,
as already noted, not yet known. A psychologist named James
C. Brown, however, offers a theory in his book *The Therapeutic
Mile:*

> One value of running, an important value among many and, in-
> deed, the value of playing any game, is that it can serve as a sim-
> ulation of life. Running can be used to serve as a micro-life expe-
> rience without the extreme consequences of failure. It serves as
> an ideal learning experience in that it allows you to experiment,
> to learn new skills, and to practice without suffering the real-
> life effects of less than goal achievement.... Running allows
> you to observe yourself under life-in-miniature conditions.

So much for psychological benefits. Earlier I mentioned an
innovative study that was conducted during a hundred-mile
race. The investigators, Drs. Paul Milvy, Michael H. Sacks and
two associates, hoped to find out how mental ability changes
as a result of extreme fatigue. Every three hours, therefore,
they questioned participants in the grueling race, including
Don Ritchie, the eventual winner, who covered the entire
course at an average pace of just over seven minutes a mile. In
addition to having Ritchie and his fellow runners describe
how they felt, they asked them to repeat four-, five- and six-
digit numbers, to reverse two-, three- and four-digit numbers,
to add numbers and, at the end of each interview, to recall
three common objects (such as *hat, book* and *lamp*) that they
had been asked at the beginning of the interview to keep in
mind. Surprisingly, even in the last of their series of interviews, when they had run roughly the equivalent of three consecutive marathons, mental ability held up well, and the ca-

pacity for reciting numbers backward actually improved. "The runners remained sharp and clear," said Sacks. Just as the high-mileage training regimens of recent years have shown that men and women are more durable physically than had previously been suspected, so we may now be discovering that even physical efforts of almost unendurable intensity do little, if anything, to undermine mental functioning. A few years ago, when I held an office job in Manhattan and did much of my training in Central Park during lunch hours, I often felt fatigued by midafternoon. It may be, however, that I wasn't shortchanging my employer as badly as my Puritan conscience suggested.

If many of the effects of running are undeniably beneficial or, like the foregoing, merely neutral, others may not be. Yale's Dr. Altshul recently told a gathering of his colleagues that the unquestioning enthusiasm for the sport that has prevailed during the past few years reminded him of attitudes toward marijuana in the 1960s. "If you were a right-thinking liberal type," he said, "you were convinced marijuana couldn't hurt you. In exactly the same way we were all convinced until recently that running couldn't possibly do you any harm. Three years ago at meetings like this one the speakers would all sound like evangelists for running. Now we're more cautious."

Several investigations show why.

Dr. Richard A. Dienstbier, chairman of the psychology department at the Lincoln campus of the University of Nebraska, recruited twenty-two male and eight female students in order to study the differing psychological effects of running various distances. At two-week intervals, as the thirty students trained for a marathon, Dienstbier evaluated them for such characteristics as anxiety, fatigue, cheerfulness and tolerance to stress. In one test the volunteers, wearing earphones, were subjected to almost painfully loud sounds of breaking glass, bursting balloons and high-speed automobile crashes. Evaluating their reactions, Dienstbier found that while, as expected, numerous psychological improvements take place after a short run, many of the benefits fall off sharply after a longer, more exhausting workout. After a run of marathon distance, for example, susceptibility to both anxiety and stress is typically greater than after a relaxed six-mile run. More running, in other words, is not necessarily better; it may, in fact, be distinctly worse.

In another study a New York City physician named Edward Colt, assuming runners would turn out to be mentally healthier than nonrunners, conducted psychiatric evaluations of thirty regular runners aged twenty-three to forty-nine. In a randomly chosen control population, he knew from previous studies, well over half would be free of any history of psychiatric disorders. Among his running population, he was surprised to learn, less than half were, in his words, "psychiatrically well." Because Colt studied relatively few runners, it would be a mistake to make too much of his findings. Nevertheless, they suggest that running may not be the all-purpose remedy some hopeful observers have argued it might be.

The same Dr. Kostrubala mentioned a few paragraphs ago has reported that running can even give rise to delusions. Two, he said, are particularly common: the delusion of cardiovascular immortality, and the delusion that running prevents cancer. Neither is true. The most that can be alleged is that running, as mentioned in the preceding chapter, markedly improves cardiovascular health. So far as even the most painstaking researchers have been able to determine, it has no effect whatever on the incidence of cancer.

Perhaps the most prominent exposition of the psychological dangers of running has come from a researcher named William P. Morgan, who serves as director of the Sport Psychology Laboratory at the University of Wisconsin in Madison. Running, Morgan insists, can turn into a dangerous addiction, especially for those who cover as much as ten miles a day. Addicted runners, he says, work out even when injured and are likely to neglect important aspects of their lives. He wrote recently: "Exercise addicts give their daily run(s) higher priority than job, family, or friends. They run first, and then if time permits, they work, love, and socialize." Furthermore, he has said, such addiction is progressive: "Just as the drug addict must keep upping the dosage in order to create the same quality of sensation, the addicted runner must increase the duration or intensity of his activity in order to maintain that all-consuming exercise high."

Morgan's argument is, needless to say, partly a question of definition. Practically no one, after all, uses the word *addiction* when referring to people who spend inordinate amounts of time making money, playing at politics or pursuing the opposite sex—activities perhaps even more hazardous than spending a quiet hour or two in a park or on a country road. Still, it is perfectly true that running's peculiar appeal has at one time or another tempted many of us to do more of it than we have felt we ought to.

Despite its growing comprehensiveness, the catalogue of running's benefits and dangers is far from complete. Not long ago I was in touch with a psychologist named Frederick N. Dyer, who is affiliated with the Army Research Institute for the Behavioral and Social Sciences. Citing the limited research that has been undertaken on the psychological effects of exercise, Dyer provided me with a provocative list of unanswered questions. Among them were these:

Do upsetting situations seem less upsetting after a person has increased his or her cardiovascular endurance?

Does cardiovascular conditioning improve the ability to control emotions?

Is the severity of phobias reduced by cardiovascular conditioning?

What effects do training sessions of varying intensities have on phobias, aggressiveness, emotionality and stress tolerance?

What are the effects of cardiovascular conditioning on sexual appetites and performance?

What are the physiological mechanisms by which cardiovascular endurance influences emotional stability, stress tolerance, phobias and so forth?

Not long ago Dr. George Sheehan wrote in *Runner's World:* "Whatever the emotion, whether it range from annoyance to rage, from disquiet to terror, from guilt to remorse, one of the best remedies is vigorous action. Sport is the therapy best suited for the instant treatment of emotional distress." Many runners and, increasingly, many researchers would agree. Because running holds such promise, it is likely that it will be studied with increasing diligence. In order to enjoy the benefits of the sport, however, you and I need hardly wait for the full array of scientific findings. It is enough to know that in running we may have discovered a reliable way to ease much that troubles our lives. As I write these words I have just come home after racing in a sleety downpour. When I left my house this morning I had much on my mind—deadlines, the press of chronic overcommitments, an assortment of other vexations. I would be exaggerating if I said they have disappeared. The race, however, put them in their proper place; they are no longer quite so troublesome. Someday, perhaps, scientists will explain why this change occurs. When they do, they will only be telling our minds what our bodies, in their mysterious wisdom, have never needed to be told.

4 ///
The War on Sloth

Strategies for Overcoming Inertia

*O*ne recent spring, just as the azaleas were starting to bloom in southeastern Missouri, a forty-three-year-old surgeon named Jean René Dupont decided to organize a class for new runners. With the encouragement of the administrator at the Missouri Delta Community Hospital in Sikeston, Dupont, who had been running for ten years, got word of the program to his colleagues and some friends. Four women and sixteen men joined up. Because of round-the-clock schedules the whole group was seldom able to run at the same time, but whenever possible members worked out together for mutual encouragement and camaraderie. Most were soon able to cover two to three miles without stopping. Dupont was delighted. "Those runners," he told me proudly, "were as highly motivated as any group could be."

No one, including Dupont, fully understands what happened next. One member dropped out because of the pressures of his medical practice. Several others, citing the same reason, soon dropped out, too. By late summer only a dozen of the original twenty remained. "Then the bad weather came," said Dupont, "and that was it. By that time I was the only one running. I'm still running—alone." Meditating ruefully on the experience, he told me, "People will do almost anything to get out of exercising. I have been most unsuccessful in encouraging people to run."

If we lived in a properly logical world the motivational problem would not be as troublesome as it is. Most of us, after all, want to be healthy, feel good, look young and live a long time. Since even modest amounts of exercise are likely to help achieve all those ends, simply realizing that fact should be enough. But since when has reasonableness had much influence on human affairs? The mind, as we all know, is ingeniously inventive at devising excuses, and equally inventive at concealing what it is so persuasively doing. "Some people," says Lee Spade, a Columbus, Ohio, psychologist, "are genuinely self-destructive. To better their emotional and physical well-being runs counter to a deep-seated need for self-harm." Similarly, Dr. Peter O. Knight, a Florida cardiologist, told me, "During my fifteen years of medical practice I have heard practically every reason one can offer to avoid exercising. In the final analysis the majority of people have a psychological barrier that allows them to rationalize their status as being unique: that is, the preventive medical benefits of exercise are for the other guy, while they themselves are in some way not vulnerable to disease. It is just not convenient to look too closely at reality." Even dedicated runners know the siren song that beckons them to run fewer miles than they should or to run less often. How much more beguiling, therefore, is that song to a person long accustomed to the pleasures and indisputable rewards of slothful living.

Nor, for that matter, does it take much effort to brush aside the advice of authorities who tell us we should exercise. Not long ago a distinguished physician told me that despite fatherly badgering and an occasional ill-tempered grumble one of his sons continues to smoke cigarettes, a clear health risk by any standard other than that of the Tobacco Institute's sleepless minions. Reflecting recently on such frustrating paradoxes, I found myself wondering whether there might not be at least a few motivational principles to help counteract, however feebly, the evident appeal of continuing to do nothing. I therefore started talking with people who might shed light on the question, among them doctors, coaches, YMCA and corporation fitness directors, preventive medicine specialists, and scores of ordinary runners who, in one way or another, have been successful, or in some cases revealingly unsuccessful, in persuading others to exercise. Out of nearly fifty such conversations emerged, first, a vivid sense of the difficulty of the task. At the same time I caught an occasional hopeful glimpse. There are tested motivational techniques that may make it easier to embark on a running program and, once embarked, to stick with it. Most of these techniques, moreover, are equally applicable to ourselves and to those we may be trying to encourage. Significantly, too, such psychological force-feeding is usually necessary only at the start of a running program. Once a participant discovers that running isn't just hard work but fun, too, motivation pretty much takes care of itself.

Part of the inertia problem is that too many of us were taught to look on exercise as punishment, or at the very least as an activity that isn't notably pleasurable. A Roselle, New Jersey, runner named Fred Schumacher told me, "I've found that many people resist exercising because of a previous bad experience—physical education in school or physical training in the service." Dr. Gail Shierman of the University of Oklahoma's Physical Education Department said, "Some of the negativism stems from poor physical education programs in the public schools, where the teacher uses jogging or pushups as a disciplinary measure." I myself vividly remember a high school football coach for whom, in cases of training-rule violations, pushups were the sovereign remedy. Particularly for women, overcoming society's anti-exercise preachments can be a stubborn problem. Barbara L. Wood, a staff member at the University of Maryland Counseling Center and the organizer of a women's running program, said, "Women have not, typically, spent their lives surrounded by voices urging them toward sports. Many times the voices have, in fact, said quite the opposite. To expect women to take a deviant stance and maintain it, solely on the strength of their own internal voice, may be asking a bit much."

The problem is compounded by the fact that exercise isn't all fun at the beginning. Muscles protest. Lungs burn. The next morning you feel creaky and sore. Nor, usually, do you improve as quickly as you'd like. "The beginning is the most difficult," says Schumacher. "The rewards are almost nonexistent and the sacrifice required is measurable."

For all these reasons, persuading yourself or anyone else to start running is seldom easy. I spoke, in fact, with only one person, a cardiologist, who claimed never to have experienced any difficulty. "I tell my patients," he said dryly, "that if they don't change their way of life they're going to need a coronary bypass operation. When they start thinking about having someone cut into their heart, they're anxious to take steps to avoid it." Most of us, however, are not jolted quite that arrestingly into a sense of the urgency of exercise. Truth to tell, we probably feel fairly good without it; it is only our puffing with exertion and the girth of our waistlines that suggest that all may not be entirely well within. We realize, therefore, that if we are going to be moved to start running, we are probably going to have to do most of the moving ourselves; no obliging cheerleader will come along to prod us into it. Dr. Art Mollen, a Phoenix preventive medicine specialist and a tirelessly articulate champion of running, writes in *Run for Your Life*, "Beyond a few tests and some prescriptive advice, there is really nothing I can do to you or for you. If anything happens, it will be because you will do it to and for yourself." Other observers, lamenting their inability to goad people into exercising, agree. A Montreal psychiatrist, Jacques Plamondon, wrote me a long, thoughtful letter on the futility of expecting doctors to motivate us. "Physicians have done little in understanding motivational aspects of staying in good health," he said, "and less so in practicing sports like running." Dr. Max L. Irick, a Missouri physician, told me, "I have found that encouraging people to exercise when they have not expressed the desire to is generally useless. It has been my experience that the average individual needs a source of inspiration more than a source of information." Robert Nixon, an Illinois college professor, author and marathon runner, said, "Before a person will act he must feel a fairly strong need." Finally, Betty H. Bones, the wife of a Richmond pediatrician and a regular runner, summed it all up in a terse hypothesis: "It may turn out that motivation is all from within."

Mrs. Bones's suspicions are convincingly supported by the work of a University of Rochester psychologist, Edward L. Deci. A specialist in motivation, Deci argues that too many people regard themselves as being buffeted by external forces when in fact they have considerable control over how they will behave. "Responses," he writes, "need not follow automatically from stimuli. People can decide how to respond to various stimuli." Should Deci's view be correct, then we ought to be able to overcome objections to exercise not by convoluted psychological machinations but simply by deciding that we need exercise and are therefore willing to bestir ourselves and get some.

If, however, the sources of motivation lie within, so, of course, does motivation's opposite, the mechanism that generates excuses. Excuses are, in fact, so indigenous a part of exercise that Mollen devotes a whole chapter to them. "I tell my patients right from the start," he writes, "that their excuses will not work on me, that I know them all anyway, having heard them a hundred times. So, I inform them, why waste your breath unless, maybe, you have a rare excuse specimen I have not heard and could add to my collection?" The beginning runner needs to be as unyielding with himself as Mollen is with his patients. My friend Walter Guzzardi has the right idea. When I asked him how he managed to struggle from his bed every morning to run his two and a half miles, he replied, "I don't make a decision every morning. I made a decision once, long ago, to run every day. When I wake up, the decision is already made." In Guzzardi's puritanical scheme of things there is simply no room for excuses.

Not everyone, of course, is able to be so stern with himself. Nonetheless, almost anyone, by searching diligently, can find motivational devices that work. As Philip K. Wilson, executive director of Wisconsin's renowned La Crosse Exercise Program, observed recently, "The motivation of an individual is truly a factor specific to that individual. What is meaningful and motivates one participant may be meaningless and not a motivator to another individual." Staff Sergeant Ronald C. Guth claims, for example, to have had impressive success with the artful use of ridicule and embarrassment. "This may seem like a hazardous way of getting through to somebody," he told me, "but in my experience it works." Dr. Shew K. Lee, a Washington, D.C., optometrist, says he is kept running by the thought of all the medicines he no longer needs and the fact that not long ago his life insurance company placed him in a special low-risk category and reduced his premiums. Marilyn H. Nelson of Richmond, Virginia, admits to being motivated at least partly by vanity. "If I overindulge in a rich dessert," she says, "I can run it off." An elderly Atlanta woman told me, "Spending some time as a visitor in a nursing home is an incentive to run from that ol' rockin' chair." An Auburn, Maine, lawyer named John R. Linnell said simply that he got "sick of being fat," and a woman who for excellent reasons wanted to keep both her name and her address a secret told me, "I just found out that the 'other woman' is coming to town next month. She's a runner, too. I've increased my daily distance dramatically. So what if he loves her more? I love *me* better than before."

Like Philip Wilson, most professional physical fitness specialists, having searched in vain for a single technique that will motivate everybody, have reluctantly concluded that there probably is no such key. About all you can do, says Seth Chavez, who conducts adult fitness classes in Massachusetts, is instill confidence, create a pleasant atmosphere and have an understanding attitude. Maureen Bike, a women's fitness leader at the Fairfield, Connecticut, YMCA, says it is the obvious physical rewards that most often do the trick. Women, she points out, typically lose 1.5 percent of their body fat within the first eight weeks. "Such concrete evidence of success is usually all they need to continue," Mrs. Bike says. Dr. Ronald Converse, a California physician and lawyer, suggests that some people may be stimulated to exercise, as Dr. Lee was, once they realize that an increasing number of insurance companies offer lowered rates to policyholders who stay in good physical condition. Dr. Glenn M. Cosh, a Lakewood, Colorado, physician, finds he can occasionally motivate patients by saying, "If it's worth three or four minutes a day to save your teeth, surely it's worth twenty minutes of exercise a day to save your cardiovascular system and your life." For Dr. Richard L. Miller of Dayton, Ohio, however, such gentle persuasion is seldom enough. "I have found the only true motivator to be an actual disease process or illness," he told me. Finally, an Illinois college professor suggested that people who want to quit smoking without gaining weight may be lured into running once they realize exercise can help solve their problem.

More on specific motivational techniques in a moment. First, however, it is worth observing that just as some techniques may bring success, so others are almost certain to fail. Among them:

Bribery. Some time ago Jess A. Bell, who heads the Bonne Bell cosmetics firm, decided he wanted to encourage his employees to exercise more. A practical man, Bell devised what seemed to him a straightforward scheme. He offered a dollar for every mile run, fifty cents for each mile walked, and twenty-five cents for each mile covered on a bicycle. The program succeeded so well that, paradoxically, Bell was forced to rate it an utter failure. "We ran out of money," he says with dismay. "There were people running 200 and 250 miles a month. They obviously weren't out selling—they were out running. So we had to give that up."

Exaggeration. Partisans of running do a clear disservice to their cause when they call it a religion, argue in the face of the best medical evidence that it is a sure preventative of heart attack, and insist that runners stay young forever. It is one thing to acknowledge that running is good for us, quite another to say it is a genie that will miraculously improve any and all aspects of our lives. Although running can, it is true, do us a lot of good, there are distinct limits. When we let ourselves believe, or encourage others to believe, that such limits don't exist, we invite disappointment.

Overregimentation. One of the pleasures of running is that we're able to do it at our own pace. When a running program is so rigidly prescribed that it becomes overregimented, it is prima facie self-contradictory and interest in it is almost sure to fall off. Barry A. Franklin, an exercise physiologist and assistant professor of medicine at Case Western Reserve University, observes, "Participants in the Royal Canadian Air Force calisthenics program frequently become bored and fail to persist. Thus becomes apparent the need for variety and fun in any exercise program." A study by Michael L. Pollock and three associates at the Institute for Aerobics Research in Dallas lends weight to the message. The researchers assigned 272 men randomly to three groups that either jogged, did high-intensity interval training, or followed a combination of the two forms of exercise. Dropouts were 23 percent more numerous in the two groups employing the more rigidly codified interval training.

Overwork. Encouraged by weight loss, new energy and the pleasure of getting back into shape, some beginners try to do too much too quickly. Injury, mild or serious, is often the result. It's discouraging to run your first triumphant mile, then see your hard-won conditioning evaporate while you nurse a pulled muscle or stress fracture. Franklin advises beginners: "Intersperse a day of rest between days of activity and limit duration to twenty to thirty minutes."

Hypocrisy. Annette P. Sadowski of Detroit works for an endocrinologist named Charles P. Lucas. One day Lucas, a marathon runner, asked her, "When are you going to start running?" Her reply was prompt and unambiguous: "When hell freezes over." Lucas, a wily and patient man, bided his time. Finally, one brisk October day, he invited her to come along with him to a marathon. Though still skeptical of the whole sweaty enterprise, Ms. Sadowski agreed to go. "It was the first time I had seen anybody run just to run," she said later. "I still thought Dr. Lucas was crazy, but suddenly it was an acceptable form of craziness. I loved the excitement of the race and found myself seriously considering becoming a runner." Not long afterward she laced on her first pair of running shoes.

Few nonrunners, as Ms. Sadowski's experience suggests, can resist the persuasive effect of a friend or neighbor who runs and clearly benefits from the sport. Conversely, practically no one is influenced by authorities who give advice they themselves plainly violate. "Few things irritate me more," writes the same Betty Bones mentioned a few pages earlier, "than for a person who is fifty pounds overweight to tell me I shouldn't take a drink. Gluttony is gluttony." Whether for good or for ill, nothing succeeds like example. "A physician who is enthusiastic about his own exercise program can be successful in encouraging his patients," says Dr. Donald D. Volkmer of Lexington, North Carolina, who runs two miles every day. Dr. Terence Kavanagh, director of the Toronto Rehabilitation Center and a pioneer in using exercise to restore heart attack patients to health, says, "If a salesman believes in his product he will use it himself, and that goes for doctors, too. The public is too sophisticated these days to be taken in by a phony. The motivator must motivate from somewhere in the pack. It doesn't have to be from the front—just so long as it is not from behind the office desk." Jess Bell puts the matter simply: "Our company's program has been successful because of my own involvement, my wife's involvement, and my sister's involvement, plus that of the other executives. I think the example we are setting is the reason the program is working." Others agree. "My method of encouraging people to run," says Peggy Blount of Pulaski, New York, "is by running myself." A Milwaukee psychotherapist, Bill Falzett, says, "I have had good success in motivating people to do running or cross-country skiing because I do them myself and am therefore a role model." Jim Hershey of Robbinsdale, Minnesota, says, "To encourage others, I must be living proof of my convictions. I couldn't talk good health while being twenty pounds overweight with a cigarette hanging out of my mouth." A University of Iowa graduate student, Steve Becker, recently gave a persuasive demonstration of what example can accomplish after he encountered a thirty-two-year-old running dropout who was interested in starting again but feared he would not have the willpower to stick at it. Becker, realizing that a radical remedy was called for, rearranged his schedule so as to be able to run with his student every afternoon. Despite such initial difficulties as painful muscles and labored breathing, he continued to run, always in the company of his dedicated instructor. Eventually, as Becker had suspected would happen, self-motivation took over. At last report the student was running three miles a day and was talking about tuning up for his first marathon. George Murdock, a Provo, Utah, health-food manufacturer, offers a succinct summary of the power of example: "No amount of talking, cajoling or bragging will accomplish the task. Example does it all."

If, despite good examples and excellent intentions, you nonetheless have trouble staying with a running program, it may be comforting to know that even experienced runners run afoul of the problem. Fatigue, an overcrowded appointment book, travel or any of a hundred other reasons can make it seem impossible to exercise. The answer at such times is to counterbalance excuses with reasons for running persuasive enough to pry ourselves out of our inertia. The authorities I spoke with cited a number of weapons that have proved useful:

Understand What Exercise Does. Dr. Joseph Arends of Troy, Michigan, points out that while most of us are convinced we ought to exercise, few of us know precisely what exercise does. "The vast majority of people," he says, "do not understand the physiological, biochemical and personality changes that occur with endurance conditioning. Only when they understand these changes can they find any reason to maintain the life style we desire. Before you can motivate you must educate." Says Barry Franklin: "People are told they must exercise but are given little if any information on how and why they should exercise." As a start, therefore, reread Chapters 2 and 3 to refresh your memory about how exercise improves your health and makes you feel better. When you're pushing soggily along, feeling as if you're plodding through molasses, it helps to know exactly what you're accomplishing.

Make a Mental Commitment. Earlier in this chapter I mentioned the instructive case of Walter Guzzardi, who years ago pledged to run every day and doggedly kept his promise. If, like Guzzardi, you take promises seriously, making a serious commitment to an exercise program may be all that's required. Terry F. Masto, a staff member of the New Haven, Connecticut, YMCA, says, "I have seen many people over the years helped through exercise—once they make the mental commitment." One runner I spoke with, a New York City literary agent, told me that whenever he feels his zeal flagging he can usually revive it by silently dedicating a mile or two, or perhaps an entire run, to the memory of someone he has cared deeply about. "I'll tell myself, 'This one is for my beloved grandfather,'" he says. "That's usually enough to get me through a tough spell."

Acknowledge Running's Disadvantages. Many people, having been called to running by promises of painless, instantaneous miracles, become discouraged when they find that much of the time it's just plain hard work. Try, therefore, to remember that, as Maureen Bike puts it, "there are no shortcuts to fitness—you've got to work at it." Similarly, Terence Kavanagh told me, "The potential exerciser, whether jogger, cross-country skier, swimmer or what have you, has to be educated into not only the advantages but also the disadvantages of the hobby. It is pointless to expound over and over the 'highs' of

exercise without preparing the novice for the day-to-day ag-
gravations, even the more serious hazards. If you con someone
into an exercise program with promises of instant euphoria
(or even immortality), then don't be disappointed if he or she
becomes discouraged when the first three months result in
sore muscles, aching joints and stories from sedentary neighbors about the guy from the office who dropped dead jogging." A Massachusetts psychologist, Dr. Albert J. Kearney,
suggests that running's discomforts may be more easily endured if we reward ourselves afterward with something pleasurable. "I know of a group of graduate students who used this
method to get through an extremely hard textbook," he told
me. "They alternated chapters of *The Godfather* with chapters
of the text. In other words, people using this system don't get
their apple pie until they eat their mashed potatoes." Kearney
also mentioned another motivational technique. At the
beginning of each week the reluctant exerciser writes a number of checks, payable to organizations he can't stand. Kearney suggests the Ku Klux Klan, the American Nazi Party and
the like. The checks are held by a friend. As the runner completes segments of his appointed mileage the friend tears up
the checks. If, however, he fails to do what he set out to do, the
checks are mailed. "One or two cashed checks can work motivational wonders," Kearney said.

Identify Your Own Stumbling Blocks. Make an honest list of the
reasons you find it difficult to run. Then try to overcome each
objection. "For some who exercise at six A.M.," says Leroy H.
(Bud) Getchell, "the main obstacle is the need to go to bed
early. You probably have to refrain from watching the late-
evening news so you can get your proper rest." Unacknowl-
edged obstacles are, of course, the most insidious of all. Once
out in the open, however, they can be seen for the flimsy im-
postors they are.

Go Toward Good Health, Not Away from Ill Health. Nothing is
more discouraging to a twentieth-century human being, happily immersed in life's sedentary luxuries, than to be told he or

she should abandon smoking, drinking, overeating and the other pleasures and marvels of the flesh. To do so seems pure deprivation, with little if anything in return. If, on the other hand, we make changes in order to go toward good health, then the deprivations are likely to seem minor by comparison. When, a dozen years ago, I weighed 214 pounds, a daily full-course lunch seemed important. Today I enjoy food no less, but I'd rather have a good afternoon run than stuff myself at lunchtime. Odette Mulrooney, a New Jersey executive, had an experience similar to my own. Although she started exercising solely because of a bad score on a stress test, soon another, to-tally different form of motivation took over. "I feel so good now," she told me. Another runner, Linda S. Palter of Wash-ington, D.C., said she is motivated by similar, if more philo-sophically couched, concerns. "I know of no better way to mo-tivate a person to exercise for their health," she said, "than to appeal to his or her respect for the body. The truly aware individual is an evolutionary being of sorts. To be aware, we must meet the challenge of maintaining the perfection of our body. Those who fear fitness fear change. Those who seek health welcome evolution."

Exercise According to Need. Sometimes I think my marathon-ing friends and I must be an appalling and alarming sight to a novice runner, venturing out as we do every day to run ten or more miles. Novices, and for that matter everybody else, should remember, however, that it's not necessary to run nearly that much. As Dr. Ralph Paffenbarger has convincingly demonstrated, a mere half-hour a day is enough to confer a satisfactory degree of fitness. Running more than that is per-fectly all right if you're in serious training or if you simply enjoy doing it, but it is hardly essential. "Some people exer-cise beyond reason," says Dr. Ralph I. Fried of Shaker Heights, Ohio. "They run in spite of discomfort, pain, nausea, vomiting and even against the doctor's advice. This appears to be masochistic, a mortification of the flesh." Bob Spackman, a physical education professor at Southern Illinois University, points out, "Exercise must be prescribed for each individual according to his or her needs. People are then more apt to do the few exercises they need rather than many they do not need." James D. Kavaler, a Windsor, Colorado, physician's assistant, says, "I point out that we all don't have to start out with a mile run. To start by covering even a block may be too much for some people."

Set Goals. Then Periodically Evaluate Your Progress. Goals can be as idiosyncratically individual as we like. An adventurous Michigan runner named Sarah R. Weber made a Xerox copy of a county map and set out to run on as many of its roads as she could. Every time she ran on a new one she colored it yellow. Bridges were a special treat for Ms. Weber. "I confess a personal addiction to bridges," she told me. "Running over bridges is the most delightful running I know. I collect bridges and share them with my favorite fellow runners." Bud Getchell says it's fine for goals to be modest—perhaps to complete a five-mile race six months from now—but it's important to have them. "Without a plan based on goals," Getchell wrote recently in Ball State University's *Adult Fitness Program Newsletter*, "it is very easy to find some excuse to miss a day or more of training." It's equally important, of course, to check yourself from time to time in order to see how you're doing. In one women's program I know of, heart rate was lowered by an average of 15 beats per minute in only eight weeks—measurable proof that exercise had made the runners healthier. "Fitness testing of each participant at the start and throughout the program is invaluable," says Barry Franklin. "Reduction of fat stores, increased cardiorespiratory reserves, and a decreased serum lipid concentration are often powerful motivators."

Insist on Making Time for Running. You're not likely to have success with a running program unless you give it high priority. An overweight friend of mine, having decided he ought to lose weight, told me he planned to run "whenever I can find the time." It was no surprise to me that he quickly sank back into his old ways. "If individuals can get into the habit of starting workouts at a certain time every day, they will accept them as part of the regular daily schedule," Franklin points out. "Exercise will become habitual and the day won't seem complete without it." An increasing number of people, eager to exercise and at the same time save gasoline, have taken to running to and from work. A Boston physician, Arthur J. Siegel, has even coined a word for this form of commuting: *jogamuting*. "With the energy crunch," Siegel told me, "this approach seems even more relevant than ever."

Run with Others. Running with other people can be a powerful reinforcement to good intentions. "I encourage beginning runners to associate themselves with a Road Runners Club chapter or a jogging group," says Fred Schumacher. "Associating with people who have experienced what we are going through is an inspirational experience and serves to increase self-discipline." Says James Kavaler: "Running alone at the start is much like trying to play chess or tennis alone. It's not much fun." Experience demonstrates that it is possible to run with others even in some quite unlikely circumstances. Two years ago Donald F. Murphy, a four-mile-a-day runner, was appointed commanding officer of the Coast Guard cutter *Hornbeam*. Although the *Hornbeam*, a buoy tender, is only 180 cluttered feet from bow to stern, Murphy managed to keep running. Inspired by his example, nearly half the crew was soon running, too. "It is amazing," Murphy told me, "what an influence the person in the top position can have on subordinates. And he can accomplish this without written directives, arm-twisting or pep talks." An incidental benefit of spending time with other runners is that the practice has a subtly salutary effect on one's standards of fitness. If you're ten pounds overweight and all your friends are nonrunners, none of them is likely to mention the fact. Runners, on the other hand, are not known for restraint in such matters. They'll quickly bring you to your senses.

Remember that Running Is Fun. In our concern with losing weight and becoming healthier, it's all too easy to allow ourselves to be preoccupied with the physical changes running produces and to forget that running is a pleasurable activity, its effects aside. "When health is the only motivation," a sixty-year-old Florida runner named Al Iannone said, "great self-discipline is needed." If we run for the fun that's in it, fitness will take care of itself. Terry Masto told me, "I try to show my students that exercising is fun and feels good."

For most runners, such persuasive techniques and psychological ruses as I have been describing are necessary only at the beginning. It is part of the peculiar magic of the human mind and body that once set on the right course, however artificially, they tend to remain on course. As you first turn to running, therefore, you may find you have to lure yourself with feigned enthusiasms and temporary stratagems. Inevitably, however, your internal gyroscopes will take over. At that point you will find yourself irresistibly wanting to run. As I write these lines I have been at my typewriter most of a sunny spring day. From my window, through a halo of elm and oak leaves, I have seen several runners pass. Watching, I have wished myself with them but have waited, preferring to run as a reward rather than as an indulgence. Now, having written to the end of this chapter, I feel freed to lace on my running shoes and go. For me, running is not something I must do but something I want to do—pure, joyful play. No matter how difficult or unpalatable you now find running, it will become that way for you, too. That's a promise.

Rodgers Revisited

From the street, the Bill Rodgers Running Center, just around the corner from Cleveland Circle in Boston, is not what you'd expect. It's in a building that has unmistakably seen better days. In the window are several books that look not so much placed there as abandoned, their jackets long since faded by sunlight. Inside, the place is a clutter, albeit a cheerful one, of clothes, shoes and customers. On the walls are a lot of photographs—Bill Rodgers in running clothes; Bill Rodgers, triumphant, wearing a laurel wreath; Bill Rodgers running—and a good many framed newspaper clippings describing Bill Rodgers's racing achievements. Several posters are on display. One advertises the Third International Amsterdam Marathon, another Atlanta's Peachtree Road Race. A third poster is in Japanese. Three or four salesclerks, both men and women, are at work in the store. All wear running shoes, and one of them, a young man, wears bright orange running shorts and a mesh singlet.

The titular head of this purposeful chaos, a 128-pound wisp of a man with floppy blond hair and startlingly regular teeth, is the best distance runner alive today and quite possibly the best who has ever lived. I first met him in the fall of 1976 when, having decided to write a book about running, I hoped to discover what life was like for a world-class athlete. His achievements at the time, while impressive, were nonetheless limited. He had set a Boston Marathon record of 2:09:55 the previous year and had gone on, the following year, to win the New York City Marathon. Although it would have been ungracious to say so then, the Boston record seemed at least partly a fluke. For one thing, despite his undoubted natural ability, Rodgers was not yet a very consistent runner. In fact, one respected track writer, Jerry Nason of the *Boston Globe*, had told me he thought Rodgers had never reached his potential, and in fact might never reach it, because he wasn't tough enough mentally. For another, Rodgers had set his Boston Marathon record with the help of a howling tail wind that could not have failed to contribute significantly to his preternatural progress from Hopkinton to downtown Boston.

If there were doubts then, there were none now. Nagged, perhaps, by memories of that tail wind and the degree to which it detracted from the purity of his accomplishment, Rodgers had gone forth on a windless day in April 1979 and virtually flown over the course, finishing an astonishing twenty-eight seconds faster, in 2:09:27. Later the same year, bouncing back from a lackluster spell, he won his fourth consecutive New York City Marathon title. Furthermore, in the preceding year, 1978, he had lost only eight of the thirty-five races he entered, which included three marathons, three half-marathons and eleven 10,000-meter races, in the process leaving most of the world's top runners dejected in his wake. "It's the era of Billy Rodgers," said Tom Fleming, a world-class runner from New Jersey and a frequent Rodgers victim. "We've been through the Shorter era and now it's Rodgers's turn." There was no arguing with that ungrudging opinion. Rodgers, in his early thirties, was undisputed king of the roads. Other runners, such as Randy Thomas, Garry Bjorklund, Craig Virgin and Jeff Wells,

might occasionally threaten him, but for the moment Rodgers held sway.

These were good times in other ways, too. Rodgers had acquired not just his Cleveland Circle store but two others, one in Boston's trendy Faneuil Hall and one in Worcester, Massachusetts, thirty-five miles to the west. He and his wife, Ellen, were buying an impressive contemporary-style house in Sherborn, a half-hour southwest of Boston. With the help of Joe Concannon of the *Boston Globe*, he was writing a book. Finally, best of all, although the team was still to be selected, he was the clear favorite to bring a gold medal home from the 1980 Olympic marathon.

Rodgers and I sat in his office, back in the labyrinths of the Bill

Rodgers Running Center stockroom. Just outside were a profusion of racks hung with BR shorts, shirts and warmup suits. Nearby, too, was a machine intended for soft drinks but stocked instead with cans of cold beer. Rodgers had just showered after a run; his hair was wet. A few days earlier, having encountered him on a television talk show, I had been startled to see how unchanged he seemed despite his celebrity. I asked him now what psychological direction finder kept him so unnaturally sane.

He laughed. "I've had plenty of bad races to counteract the good ones," he told me. "There have been enough running disasters that nailed me. I've dropped out of Boston twice. I haven't won a gold medal in the Olympics. So those things are always in the back of my mind."

Admitting, however, that fame had had its effects, Rodgers got to talking about its vexations and rewards. "When I'm out running and I see a runner," he told me, "I feel I have to say hello. If I don't he'll say, 'Hey, what's the matter with *him*?' I feel, too, that these days I've got to win all the races I enter; second place is pretty bad. A lot of people want to know about me now. I've been interviewed a lot. I like interviews. To me an interview represents some fun. It's a reward, a little bit of ego gratification. What I don't like is when an interviewer doesn't respect what I've just done. Sometimes I've just finished a race and it's raining and I'm really tired, and someone will want me to do an interview the minute I cross the line. What I want to do first is go indoors and put on my sweatsuit and maybe take a shower. Then I'm glad to do the interview."

Rodgers smiled, reflecting on the paradox of being both a public figure and a distance runner, for distance runners are, after all, the world's most intrinsically reclusive breed of athlete. "It's weird," he said. "People come up to me for my autograph. I would never ask anyone for their autograph. Probably this is why Ellen and I are buying a house that's surrounded by lots of woods. We want to have plenty of land around us and be away from everything."

There are, however, compensations. For one thing, Rodgers said that by the end of 1979 his earnings were almost certain to have gone well into six figures. Three years earlier, when he and Ellen were still schoolteachers, they had to use food stamps when they went to the supermarket.

5 ////
Starting Out, Getting Better, Running Good Races
A Roundup of Research, Advice and Inspiration

During recent years few contemporary phenomena have enjoyed more diligent scientific scrutiny than running has. In laboratories, medical schools and athletic departments the world over, researchers have been busily searching out the most arcane secrets of the sport. A decade ago the typical athlete was largely on his or her own in ferreting out a training system. Today, by contrast, a great deal of information is available about how the body responds to various regimens. Moreover, as a result of a burgeoning array of journals, both lay and scientific (pages 204–207), much of this lore can be studied by any athlete with a modest curiosity. This chapter is based largely on what scientists are currently telling us about running.

On Starting from Scratch

When first undertaking a running program, don't assume that just because you're more active than some people you'll have an easier time of it. Rudolph H. Dressendorfer of the Department of Physical Education at the University of California at Davis tested a group of healthy men, twenty-five to thirty-eight years old, who regularly played tennis or golf, surfed, or went skin diving. They adapted to running exactly as if they had been totally untrained.

If you're over thirty-five, incidentally, be sure to get a doctor's approval before you start running. This is important because you can feel fine and nonetheless have cardiac or other abnormalities that may cause trouble when you're under physical stress.

The Uses of Patience

In the mind of the typical beginner, getting into shape is a simple matter. The muscles become stronger. Endurance increases. Breathing as you exercise becomes easier. What more could there possibly be to it than that?

There is quite a bit more. Profound and fundamental changes occur throughout the body. Since these changes can't be rushed, getting into good condition is likely to take longer than you think it will, especially if you're over thirty. This is particularly true because most such changes require not just exertion but rest as well; it is during the resting intervals that strengthening and rebuilding take place. Thus you may be improving at the very time common sense would suggest you are least likely to be doing so: when you are doing nothing.

How Far to Run at First

Beginning runners are sometimes puzzled about how far they should run. It's no wonder. Every coach, every book about running, and every YMCA and gym has its own program. The carefully devised progression outlined here has several advantages. First, it was designed by a distinguished exercise authority, Dr. Bud Getchell, author of *Physical Fitness: A Way of Life* and long-time director of Ball State University's highly regarded exercise program. Second, it is not at all experimental but has been in continuous use for some fifteen years. Third, it works for people of all ages and aptitudes. Finally, it can easily be adapted to your ability as you begin and can be changed readily as you improve.

Getchell's program consists of twenty steps, ranging from easy to strenuous. The single tricky part occurs at the beginning, when you must find the proper step to start with. In doing this, it's better to underestimate than overestimate your ability. Having discovered that a particular step is too easy for you, it's simple to move ahead. On the other hand, it's discouraging to have to move backward.

The first step in this program consists only of walking, while the last consists of a continuous two-mile run. All other steps consist of running a specific number of yards, always within the pulse range given in the table on page 71, with walking in between and, as a cooldown, at the end.

You should not, incidentally, walk for more than half the time the preceding run took, and you should always walk briskly.

Repeat each step for at least two days. If you don't feel uncomfortably tired an hour after the second day's workout, go on to the next step the following day. If, on the other hand, you still feel tired, continue at that step until you are able to recover completely.

STEP 1
Walk 1 to 1½ miles
Total distance run: 0

STEP 2
Walk ½ mile
Run 110 yards
Walk
Run 110 yards
Walk

Run 110 yards
Walk
Run 110 yards
Walk
Total distance run: ¼ mile

STEP 3
Run 110 yards
Walk
Run 110 yards

Walk
Run 110 yards
Walk
Run 110 yards
Walk
Run 110 yards
Walk
Run 110 yards
Walk
Total distance run: ⅜ mile

STEP 4
Run 110 yards
Walk
Run 110 yards
Walk
Run 110 yards
Walk
Run 110 yards
Walk
Run 220 yards
Walk
Run 220 yards
Walk
Total distance run: ½ mile

STEP 5
Run 110 yards
Walk
Run 110 yards
Walk
Run 110 yards
Walk
Run 110 yards
Walk
Run 110 yards
Walk
Run 110 yards
Walk
Run 220 yards
Walk
Run 220 yards
Walk
Total distance run: ⅝ mile

STEP 6
Run 110 yards
Walk
Run 110 yards
Walk
Run 110 yards
Walk
Run 110 yards
Walk
Run 220 yards
Walk
Run 220 yards
Walk
Run 220 yards
Walk
Total distance run: ⅝ mile

STEP 7
Run 110 yards
Walk
Run 110 yards
Walk
Run 220 yards
Walk
Run 220 yards
Walk
Run 220 yards
Walk
Run 220 yards
Walk
Run 220 yards
Walk
Total distance run: ¾ mile

STEP 8
Run 220 yards
Walk
Run 220 yards
Walk
Run 220 yards
Walk
Run 220 yards
Walk
Run 220 yards
Walk

Run 220 yards
Walk
Total distance run: ¾ mile

STEP 9
Run 220 yards
Walk
Run 220 yards
Walk
Run 220 yards
Walk
Run 220 yards
Walk
Run 220 yards
Walk
Run 330 yards
Walk
Run 330 yards
Walk
Total distance run: 1 mile

STEP 10
Run 220 yards
Walk
Run 220 yards
Walk
Run 220 yards
Walk
Run 220 yards
Walk
Run 330 yards
Walk
Run 330 yards
Walk
Run 330 yards
Walk
Run 330 yards
Walk
Total distance run: 1 ¼ miles

STEP 11
Run 220 yards
Walk
Run 220 yards

Walk
Run 220 yards
Walk
Run 220 yards
Walk
Run 440 yards
Walk
Run 440 yards
Walk
Run 440 yards
Walk
Total distance run: 1 ¼ miles

STEP 12
Run 220 yards
Walk
Run 220 yards
Walk
Run 440 yards
Walk
Run 440 yards
Walk
Run 440 yards
Walk
Run 440 yards
Walk
Run 440 yards
Walk
Total distance run: 1 ½ miles

STEP 13
Run 440 yards
Walk
Run 440 yards
Walk
Run 440 yards
Walk
Run 440 yards
Walk
Run 660 yards
Walk
Run 660 yards
Walk
Total distance run: 1 ¾ miles

STEP 14
Run 440 yards
Walk
Run 440 yards
Walk
Run 440 yards
Walk
Run 660 yards
Walk
Run 660 yards
Walk
Run ½ mile
Walk
Total distance run: 2 miles

STEP 15
Run 440 yards
Walk
Run 880 yards
Walk
Run 880 yards
Walk
Run 880 yards
Walk
Run 440 yards
Walk
Total distance run: 2 miles

STEP 16
Run 440 yards
Walk
Run 1 mile
Walk
Run 440 yards
Walk
Total distance run: 1 ½ miles

STEP 17
Run 1 mile
Walk
Run ½ mile
Walk
Run ½ mile
Walk
Total distance run: 2 miles

STEP 18
Run 1¼ miles
Walk
Run ½ mile
Walk
Run ½ mile
Walk
Total distance run: 2¼ miles

STEP 19
Run 1½ miles
Walk
Run ½ mile
Walk
Run 440 yards
Walk
Total distance run: 2¼ miles

STEP 20
Run 2 miles
Walk
Total distance run: 2 miles

The Next Big Step

Once you can run two nonstop miles, the next big hurdle is to continue for a full hour. Bill Mongovan, a coach whose training advice will be studied in greater detail in the next chapter, considers the ability to run for sixty minutes the mark of a bona fide runner. "What counts," he told me, "is time, not distance. I don't care how fast a person goes when he's trying to increase mileage." To prevent inadvertent cheating, Mongovan recommends running away from your house for half an hour, then turning around and heading back.

You'll probably have trouble running for a full hour at first. Try, therefore, running for a half-hour in the morning and another half-hour later in the day. When that has become fairly

THE PULSE TEST: HOW HARD TO TRAIN

WOMEN

Age	Minimum	Optimum	Maximum
25	130	157	185
30	126	153	180
35	123	149	175
40	119	145	170
45	116	140	165
50	112	136	160
55	109	132	155
60	105	128	150
65	102	123	145
70	98	119	140
75	95	114	135

MEN

Age	Minimum	Optimum	Maximum
25	137	166	195
30	133	162	190
35	130	157	185
40	126	153	180
45	123	149	175
50	119	145	170
55	116	140	165
60	112	136	160
65	109	132	155
70	105	128	150
75	102	123	145

easy, run for three twenty-minute periods with two ten-minute rest intervals in between. Within a few weeks you'll have no trouble skipping the rest intervals.

And the Next

When you can run for an hour, you're in shape to start working out harder if you want to. But don't try to run harder for a full hour. It's more effective to do most of your running at your accustomed pace; just toss in a brisk but not all-out quarter-mile from time to time. Bill Mongovan suggests doing your fast running on a track or level road rather than on hills. "It takes skill to run up and down hills well," he says. "It's much easier on the flat."

Under a hard-easy regimen you'll inevitably become faster because you'll increase the efficiency of both your muscles and your cardiovascular system. When Edward L. Fox and several other researchers put twenty-three Ohio State students on training programs, they found that aerobic power depended mostly on intensity, not distance. You can, in fact, run enormous distances without becoming appreciably faster. It is only speed that begets speed. "Specificity of training is one of the secrets of athletic success," Chris Neuhoff wrote recently in *Running* magazine. "To train the energy sources utilized at particular racing distances is the springboard to effective training."

Neuhoff's view is supported by recent scientific research. A Soviet sports specialist, O. M. Belakovsky, referred recently in a Russian athletics journal to "the significant increase in volume and intensity of training loads." He wrote: "Heavy training loads are a fact of life; they should not be feared."

On Not Overdoing It

Despite Belakovsky's observation, there *is* such a thing as overtraining. When you overtrain, you lose rather than gain ground. The same Dr. William P. Morgan whose views on running as an addiction were introduced in Chapter 3 put the matter this way in a recent issue of *The Physician and Sportsmedicine:* "Running should be viewed as a wonder drug.... It has profound potential in preventing mental and physical disease and in rehabilitation after various illnesses have occurred. However, just like other wonder drugs, running has the potential for abuse, and the runner who appears in the physician's office on crutches or in a wheelchair as a result of the crippling effects of excessive running can be compared to the hard-core drug addict who overdoses."

The Uses of Warmup

Before a race some runners warm up by running for a few minutes. Others don't. Recent research shows that a warmup really does help, particularly in short, fast runs. Bruce J. Martin and several other researchers at Indiana University's Department of Anatomy and Physiology tested trained runners in ninety-second treadmill runs with and without preparatory warmups. In the efforts following warmup, lactic acid production was lessened an average of 52 percent, creating greater efficiency. In addition, the temperature of the calf muscle was raised, also improving physiological function.

Presumably warmup is less important in longer runs, where the first few minutes can in effect constitute a warmup. Nonetheless, one top marathoner told me, "I always warm up plenty before a race. When you want to start right in moving at five minutes a mile, your body had better be ready to go."

To Stretch or Not to Stretch

Stretching is generally thought to contribute to a smooth, flowing style. A forward step is freer if the muscles at the back of the leg are as loose as possible, just as the leg's backward swing is more fluid if the quadriceps are well stretched. For this reason many if not most runners never undertake a workout without stretching first.

Not long ago, however, the Honolulu Marathon Association polled 847 marathon finishers. Its surprising finding was that injuries are nearly 40 percent more frequent among those who customarily stretch than among those who do not. It may be that many runners do not bother to take up stretching until they incur an injury.

Shoes Matter

Some runners wear lightweight racing flats in competition, while others use heavier training shoes. Does the difference in weight matter? Yes, according to the findings of M. J. Catlin and Rudolph Dressendorfer. When the two researchers tested a group of runners they found that while shoe weight had no discernible effect on stride length, an average of 3.3 percent more energy was required to run in training shoes than in racing flats. In races, wear flats.

Feeling Better Faster

Accumulated lactic acid contributes to the persistence of fatigue after a run. To rid the body of lactic acid, according to studies by Arend Bonen and Angelo N. Belcastro, the best remedy is gentle jogging. Movement, they report, is more effective than rest.

Ill Winds

The typical competitive runner pays diligent attention to his or her weight, diet and training, yet gives little thought to a factor that under some circumstances is just as important: the wind. Like jet pilots, top runners are aware of wind conditions and use guile, cunning and experience to make the most of them. It is no accident that in 1975, when Bill Rodgers set his first Boston Marathon record, he was pushed along by a friendly tail wind. (Nor, of course, is it an accident that four years later, when he set his second record on the course, his improved abilities required no such help.)

Studies show that in middle- and long-distance races from 15 to 25 percent of a runner's energy is used to overcome wind resistance. If, therefore, such resistance can be reduced, higher speeds can be attained with no increase in energy expenditure. As it turns out, the simplest way to lower wind resistance is to tuck in close to another runner. From 4 to 9 percent of your energy can be conserved in this way, according to calculations made by Chester R. Kyle of California State University at Long Beach.

Running in another runner's lee doesn't always mean, incidentally, running directly behind him. In a crosswind you'll have to run to one side.

And in a following wind, try not to stay directly in front of other runners. Get out in the open where the tail wind is strongest.

How to Breathe

Runners sometimes wonder how they should breathe while they run. Should they synchronize their breathing with their footsteps or what? Most authorities say breathing rhythm requires no thought; it takes care of itself without any deliberate attention. One suggestion some coaches, including New Zealand's Arthur Lydiard, make is that air be inhaled and expelled by using the stomach muscles. That way, breathing will be as deep as possible and the maximum amount of oxygen will be available.

Coffee Break

One researcher, Dr. David L. Costill, claims coffee can help athletes, including runners. He and his colleagues at Ball State University's Human Performance Laboratory gave trained cyclists caffeine before a two-hour ride and at fifteen-minute intervals during the first ninety minutes. The caffeine significantly increased the ability to perform work. Toward the end of the exercise session, fat oxidation was 31 percent higher than without caffeine.

Costill, a meticulous observer, is no doubt right. Nonetheless, in the interests of scientific balance I am bound to report on a cautionary experience of my own. Following his advice, I drank a cup of coffee just before the 1979 National Jogging Day twenty-kilometer race in Washington, D.C. An hour into the race the unaccustomed liquid ballast forced me to retreat to a secluded thicket for several seconds, thereby losing whatever advantage the marvels of fat oxidation might otherwise have bestowed on me.

Where There's Smoke

A Santa Fe woman wrote to express her disappointment in one aspect of *The Complete Book of Running:*

> You do not discuss marijuana and running. I run twenty to twenty-five miles per week. Marijuana enhances the sport in many ways, so I like taking a hit or two before leaving the house. It gives me a special kind of energy or power I don't experience otherwise. And it definitely increases my enjoyment of nature by heightening the senses. Those who equate marijuana with a sedentary lifestyle know only half the story. Do you have any information on the effects of marijuana on running?

Several researchers have looked into the question. Robert D. Steadward and Mohan Singh report that marijuana produces a marked reduction in work capacity and increases the resting heart rate; in one study heart rate averaged 73.7 when marijuana was not smoked, 105.8 when it was. Similar results were obtained in an experiment carried out at the University of California at Santa Barbara. Researchers there found that smoking marijuana didn't have any apparent effect either on blood pressure or on the body's oxygen-processing capacity. It did, however, increase the heart rate 34 percent while at rest, 18 percent during exercise, and 50 percent afterward. The increase had no appreciable effect during exercise of only moderate intensity. The researchers said it would, however, limit performance at higher intensities. Perhaps this is why, when I asked one top athlete about the incidence of marijuana smoking among elite runners, he told me he knew of none who used the drug.

Running with Jet Lag

If you're planning to race in a distant time zone, arrive early. So goes the advice of Dr. Joseph LaDou of the Peninsula Industrial Medical Clinic in Sunnyvale, California. LaDou says so many bodily functions are sent askew when you travel across time zones that it takes several days to readjust.

If you can't avoid doing so, however, you can race with no such adjustment period. Two other researchers, Irvin E. Faria and Bruce J. Drummond, report that a runner's aerobic capacity, probably the chief factor in running success, "appears to be an extremely stable function exhibiting no circadian periodicity." In other words, you can feel terrible but nonetheless race well.

A Bah to Biorhythms

Train diligently, eat lightly and get plenty of sleep if you want to do well in competition. But forget about choosing race days according to your biorhythms. When an Australian researcher, B. M. Quigley of the University of Queensland's Department of Human Movement Studies, studied 700 track and field records spanning more than six decades, he found no relationship between biorhythms and superior performances.

A Hoot for Hypnosis

Another Australian investigator, Dr. J. Arthur Jackson, looked into the effectiveness of hypnosis in improving running performances. He and two colleagues compared the treadmill runs of men who had been hypnotized and urged to do as well as they could with those of men who had been given a similar pep talk but had not been hypnotized. Jackson gave both groups instructions such as the following:

> If you realize in advance what things ordinarily make you think you have reached your limit, you will be able to keep on going

beyond the point where you are beginning to experience them. Most people use discomfort and fatigue as signs that they should stop what they are doing. They fail to realize that discomfort and fatigue are the first signs that they are approaching their maximum performance and that they can in fact keep going far beyond that point. Most people generally assume that when they start feeling uncomfortable this feeling will get worse, but as a matter of fact if you allow yourself to keep on going after you start to feel that discomfort, that feeling will actually diminish. . . . The thing that you really must keep in mind is the importance of noticing each sign of discomfort or fatigue and using it as a stimulus to keep going.

The results: Running after hypnosis was no more effective than having had Jackson's pep talk without hypnosis. Significantly, however, the pep talk, both alone and in combination with hypnosis, did improve performances. It pays to be psyched up for a race.

The Long and Short of Stride Length

It's a mistake to tinker with your natural stride length. When Dr. Peter R. Cavanagh of the Biomechanics Laboratory at Penn State studied runners on a treadmill, he found that their natural stride was most efficient. Any deviation required more oxygen and thus wasted energy.

Preparing for Hot-Weather Racing

If you're getting ready to race in a hot climate but the weather is cool where you train, you can nonetheless achieve partial adaptation, according to experiments conducted by Carl V. Gisolfi and Judith S. Cohen at the University of Iowa. It will, however, take several weeks. You can enhance the adaptation process by bundling up, thereby creating your own private tropics as you run.

Runners' Highs

If you go to the mountains to train, you will find that you can run faster when you return to a lower altitude. The best altitude for mountain training is 7,000 feet. Below that, the amount of oxygen is too close to the concentration found at sea level. At a higher altitude, oxygen is so scarce that training must be greatly curtailed. Dr. Lloyd Drake, John Walker's physician and training adviser, reports that it takes about three weeks of gradually intensified training to adapt to running at 7,000 feet. Once back at a lower altitude, you'll find that the benefits of high-altitude training last for a similar period.

The Doping Debate

The final word on blood doping, the controversial procedure in which blood is removed, stored and then replaced just before competition, still isn't in. When R. R. Pate and other researchers at the University of South Carolina's Human Performance Laboratory compared the efficacy of blood doping with that of sham procedures, no difference was detectable. At York University in Toronto, on the other hand, Fred J. Buick reports that blood doping increased the endurance of trained runners by 39 percent. Similarly, at the University of Pittsburgh, Robert J. Robertson, an exercise physiologist, found that blood doping increased the aerobic capacity and decreased the performance times of mountain climbers. Furthermore, even though they performed more efficiently, they didn't feel they were working harder.

Puddles: Theory and Practice

An analytical reader named John Oey takes issue with my recommendation in *The Complete Book of Running* that runners cool their feet on hot days by seeking out puddles. Oey's impeccable logic has won me over; I have not deliberately wet my feet in a puddle since reading his letter:

> In summer puddles exist under two conditions:
> 1) *When it's hot and humid.* If it is so humid that the rain on the pavement doesn't evaporate readily, the cooling effect on

the feet is minimized and the feet are going to stay wet for a long time. Hence the possibility of blisters. This gives us Rule No. 1: Don't run through puddles when they occur naturally.

2) *When it's hot and dry.* In this case, unless it has rained recently, the puddles were probably caused by a sprinkler or hose. Sprinklers and hoses are frequently used to cool runners in hot-weather races. It is more effective to cool yourself with the sprinkler or hose than a puddle. This gives us Rule No. 2: If puddles are caused by hoses or sprinklers, use them and not the puddles.

Combining Rule No. 1 and Rule No. 2 gives us: Don't run through puddles.

A Dozen Distinctive Races

Sooner or later, as your conditioning and skills improve, you may want to sample some of the nation's important races. Any race, even a minor one, is a memorable event. More perhaps than any other voluntary physical experience, races test your limits, your capacities and your willingness to push on in spite of discomfort. The big races, however, have another dimension as well: drama. To stand, after months of training, at the Staten Island approach to the Verrazano-Narrows Bridge as the helicopters rattle in the October winds off New York Bay is to enjoy a sweet and poignant anxiety that echoes in memory long after your muscles have forgotten the day's torments.

Like me, you probably have, or one day will have, a favorite race. Mine, for reasons of pure personal idiosyncrasy, takes place in an Eastern state on a national holiday. (Lest the hordes come, let its details remain a secret here.) It is an annual event. The hills in it would alarm a Sherpa. In the years since I first entered it, the number of runners who turn up on race day has grown from less than 100 to 1,000 or so, yet it remains, by today's swollen standards, a bucolically obscure event. Many of its competitors know each other, and it is not uncommon to hear a friendly jibe as one contestant passes another.

These days the really big races are seldom like that. Nonetheless, they, too, have their special rewards. The following dozen races are among those that are well worth going out of your way for:

Bay-to-Breakers, 7.6 miles, San Francisco, May. A combination race and masquerade party, Bay-to-Breakers could occur only in the tolerantly eccentric ethos of San Francisco. Run ever since 1912, it starts at San Francisco Bay, surmounts the formidable Hayes Street hill, works its snakelike way through Golden Gate Park, and ends at the edge of the Pacific. The 1979 race, the nation's largest, attracted 12,000 official and some 8,000 unofficial runners, among them two teams disguised as centipedes and two others dressed up as six-packs (Budweiser and Heineken).

Bloomsday, 8.2 miles, Spokane, May. Founded in 1977 by Olympic marathoner Don Kardong, the Lilac Bloomsday Run is not just the nation's third largest, with 10,000 entries in 1979, but its most literary, commemorating as it does the memory of Leopold Bloom of James Joyce's *Ulysses*. It has attracted the likes of Shorter and Rodgers, the winners in 1977 and 1978 respectively, but it's as much a people's race as Bay-to-Breakers.

Boston, 26.2 miles, April. Its newly instituted qualifying times (2:50 for all but women and over-39 men, for whom it's 3:20 and 3:10 respectively) make the Boston Marathon the nation's most elite running event, one worth watching even if you could no more qualify than run a four-minute mile. With a history dating back to 1897, Boston invariably attracts the top marathoners except in an Olympic year like 1980 or 1984, when most of them rest up for the trials a month later.

Charleston, 15 miles, Charleston, West Virginia, September. Founded in 1972 and won that year by Olympian Jeff Galloway, the Charleston Distance Run is gruelingly hilly at the start but generally flat for the last nine miles. Although it attracts relatively small fields (fewer than 1,300 in 1978), top runners invariably enter. The race is part of a ten-day civic celebration that includes bicycle races, magic shows, gymnastics exhibitions and a memorable sternwheeler race on the Kanawha River.

Cherry Blossom 10-Miler, Washington, D.C., late March or early April. The only major race with no entry fee, the Cherry Blossom starts at the Lincoln Memorial, passes the Jefferson Memorial and Tidal Basin, and circles Hains Point, a peninsula affording excellent views of the Potomac. All participants, including those in the two-mile run held at the same time, receive commemorative race patches. It's a practical way to get in a workout, tour the capital, and bring home a souvenir.

Falmouth, 7.1 miles, Falmouth, Massachusetts, August. One of the most difficult races to be accepted for unless your name is as well known in road racing as Rodgers, Shorter and Benoit, the run starts in Woods Hole and ends with a free meal in Falmouth Heights, on the south rim of Cape Cod. Although the atmosphere is that of a New England clambake, the race is among the most prestigious anywhere. The knowledgeable Amby Burfoot, a one-time Boston Marathon winner, has called it "probably the most important nonmarathon road race."

Honolulu, 26.2 miles, December. Although Hawaii's heat and humidity always make this a slow race by top standards, it is one of the largest, most festive and most glitteringly scenic. The course skirts Waikiki Beach, circles Diamond Head, visits Kapiolani Park and finishes in a blaze of band concerts and picnics. For slugabeds, a drawback is the 6:00 A.M. start. Still, there's something to be said for getting your agonies out of the way early.

Mardi Gras, 26.2 miles, New Orleans, February. The race was pure improvisation in 1979 after a police strike forced officials to move it from downtown New Orleans to the 24-mile-long causeway spanning Lake Pontchartrain. It was a last-minute emergency measure, but it couldn't have turned out better. A lashing rain mercifully stopped as the starter's gun went off, a gusty following wind buffeted the runners, and practically everyone's time was accordingly spectacular. Indications are that the changed course, though it started as a mere fluke, is now as permanent as the Mardi Gras, with which this marathon coincides.

New York City, 26.2 miles, October. The New York City Marathon isn't just a race but a gala tour that meanders through all five boroughs. Now that Boston (see above) has chosen to turn elitist, many runners argue that this is the nation's premier marathon. It's a plausible view. New Yorkers are peerless marathon spectators, and their encouragement is as knowledgeable and spirited as anything ever encountered between Hopkinton and the Prudential Center. Moreover, the changing urban scenery is without parallel in American athletics. Miraculously, the New York City Marathon, despite some 12,500 competitors in 1979, is as impeccably organized as any race in the nation.

Peachtree, 10 kilometers, Atlanta, July 4. One of the most meteorically popular racing events, the Peachtree Road Race attracted 110 runners in 1970, its first year. In 1979 more than 20,000 competed. Run along famed Peachtree Street, the race invariably attracts runners such as Shorter, Rodgers, the perennial hometown favorite Jeff Galloway, and anyone else who wants to look into the combined effects of heat, humidity, hills and Southern hospitality.

Pikes Peak, 28.2 miles, Manitou Springs, Colorado, August. Devised a quarter-century ago as a contest between smokers and nonsmokers. Pikes Peak is one of the world's most arduous athletic events. Ascending a rocky trail, participants stop climbing only when they stumble onto the 14,110-foot summit. They can either collapse there, at 14.3 miles, or run back down as well. One fact alone suggests the difficulty of Pikes Peak: The record holder for the uphill portion, a world-class athlete named Chuck Smead, averaged nearly nine minutes a mile instead of his customary five or so. "It is not a race for the faint of heart," said one laconic observer.

Virginia 10-Miler, Lynchburg, September. The course is forbiddingly hilly and the day is likely to be muggy, but participants agree that when it comes to making out-of-town runners feel at home, there's no race like this one. To discourage the overexuberant, organizers have instituted a modest entry requirement: you should be able to run ten miles in fewer than 100 minutes.

6

Breakthrough

Their Long Warmup Ended, Women Finally Come Into Their Own

Bill Mongovan stands in a clover patch near the edge of the gray asphalt running track encircling the football field at Greenwich High School, in southwestern Connecticut. A slight, weather-bronzed man with an angular face and an omnipresent stopwatch, he studies a half-dozen young women as they run swiftly by, leaning hard into a curve. Mongovan (the accent, fittingly, is on the second syllable) purses his lips but says nothing. When the runners have passed, he turns to me and remarks, "I try not to do too much coaching. If a girl isn't eager to run without my telling her to, I'm beating my head against a wall."

Mongovan has coached some five hundred women since he started specializing in women's track and field a dozen years ago. Intractable motivational problems have been rare. Just

west of the field a wooded hillside slants toward the sky. Beyond a stand of ancient elms the sun has already set, yet Mongovan's charges push on as if they planned to run right through the dinner hour and into the night. He tells me, "Women are more highly motivated than men, especially when they're young. They improve so quickly they can't help being full of enthusiasm."

Mongovan has witnessed the burgeoning of women's running at close hand. Besides his coaching duties he is a member of the Amateur Athletic Union's women's athletics committee and of five of its women's subcommittees. He is the AAU's regional chairman for women's track and field, responsible for all athletic events in New England, New York and the northern half of New Jersey. He is the founder of the Gateway Track Club, which came into being a few years ago to allow more young women to enjoy track and field. He told me with mixed pride and dismay that in one recent year he participated in two hundred running-related activities, ranging from AAU meetings to track meets. In calculating the total he did not count phone calls, curbstone coaching sessions and impromptu pep talks.

Over the years Mongovan's attitudes toward women athletes have changed. When he started coaching he was wary of asking too much of them. In keeping with the prevailing prejudices about women's athletic potential, he let his athletes run far shorter and less tiring training sessions than were customary for men. Then, a few years ago, it struck him that since some of the women he coached were able to run faster and farther than many men, it was illogical to prescribe less rigorous workouts. Today, as a result, it is not unusual during certain phases of training for young women to run twelve miles at a time under Mongovan's tutelage. Nor are hard interval sessions foreign to them. "When they finish," he told me, "you can be sure they feel as if they've done a lot of work."

The evolution of Mongovan's expectations parallels a widespread revision in the way knowledgeable observers view women athletes. Until a few years ago almost everyone assumed that arduous running, in ways both specified and unspecified, was almost certain to be harmful to women. Their breasts would surely droop, their reproductive systems dislodge or malfunction, their femininity dissolve in sweat. Even when these misfortunes did not materialize, a feeling prevailed that it was, well, unseemly for women to bestir themselves vigorously. The medieval view of woman as an ethereal, ineffably otherworldly species, too pure for the earthly concerns that trouble their brothers, was a long time in dying. In the past decade its throes have, however, been hastened by the discoveries of researchers who have reported that women are no more subject to athletic injury than men are, that their reproductive systems, even during pregnancy, are no less durable, and that the biomechanical aspects of their running, while different from those of men, are no less efficient.

Much of this had been known, at least in a general way, for decades. The earliest studies correlating athletic ability with the menstrual cycle, and revealing that menstruation had no discernible effect on athletic prowess, took place more than half a century ago. To most people, however, the available information had an unsatisfyingly theoretical cast. After all, if women were capable of outstanding athletic achievements, why did they perform so poorly compared with men? It was all very well for researchers to report, as five did at a medical conference in 1976, that women would one day cover a marathon course in two hours and thirty minutes or even less. But where were such women?

As it happened, they—or more precisely, she—was at that very moment busy training in Oslo, Norway, where she lived. She was twenty-two years old, her name was Grete Waitz, and two years later almost to the day, in the 1978 New York City Marathon, she was to cover the course in 2:32:30, more than two minutes faster than any woman had ever before run 26 miles, 385 yards and only seven minutes slower than the winning time for men in the 1956 Melbourne Olympics. Furthermore, the following year she covered the same course nearly five minutes faster. By so decisively breaking the existing record and then her own, Ms. Waitz, a schoolteacher, lifted

women's running into an orbit inconceivably remote from anything most people had thought possible. "Can you believe it?" one male runner said in astonishment. "I run a 2:30 marathon and get beaten by a *woman*." Now that Grete Waitz had run that epochal marathon, anything could happen. Excellent as she was, after all, it was unlikely that she was athletically unique. Still more impressive performances were bound to be on the way.

The only question was how long the extraordinary improvements in women's running would continue. When men break records these days, they typically do so by tenths of a second. In some events, records have not been broken for several years. It is only among women athletes that vast chunks of time are still being chopped off. Plainly the quantum jumps will not continue forever.

For one thing, unless we are hopelessly unregenerate wishful thinkers, we are bound to acknowledge that women have several well-documented handicaps.

They are not as strong as men. When Terrence Hoffman, Robert W. Stauffer and Andrew S. Jackson studied sixty West Point cadets, evenly divided by sex, they found that differences in body size were insufficient to account for men's superior strength, particularly in the upper body. "Male cadets," said the researchers, "are stronger than female cadets."

Women are, furthermore, less willing than men to endure discomfort in order to increase their strength. In a second experiment, also conducted at West Point, Colonel James L. Anderson, the academy's physical education director, enrolled twenty women, all of them former high school athletes, in a weight-lifting class. He reported that, compared with men, the women were hampered "by their inability to push past a perceived level of pain for a greater strength gain. . . . Society tells women they are frail and if an exercise hurts, they shouldn't do it."

In an experiment at Wellesley College, other researchers reported similar findings. Young women were asked to report how hard they felt they were exercising as they ran four times a week for progressively greater distances. These women, particularly if they had never previously engaged in heavy exercise, invariably underestimated their capacity for physical activity. Dennis Kowal, one of the researchers who conducted the experiment, commented, "Women can perform well above previous expectations, even their own."

Women have proportionately smaller hearts than men.

Their cardiovascular systems are therefore less efficient in transporting oxygen to muscles.

Women have proportionately more body fat. By analogy with the metabolism of migrating birds, some medical authorities theorize that women's fat gives them an advantage in long-distance running. Not all researchers agree. When I talked not long ago with Dr. David L. Costill, director of the Human Performance Laboratory at Ball State University, he told me his experiments had yielded no evidence to support the fat-as-fuel view. It may turn out that excess fat, in women as in men, is little more than dead weight.

Women experience more injuries when they start running. Although these are thought to result from muscular weakness and athletic inexperience rather than inherent delicateness, such mishaps can nonetheless be discouraging.

Women are more likely than men to be timid about taking up running. "For a woman who has not run a step since childhood," says Dr. Peter D. Wood of Stanford University, "initial embarrassment can be a problem. 'What will I look like?' 'What will the neighbors say?' The first step is the most difficult this woman will ever take as a runner, but once committed, slimmed down, toned up and confident—what a difference."

Faced with the foregoing catalogue of frailties, even a Gloria Steinem might conclude that, whatever their undoubted abilities in such sports as tennis and gymnastics, women simply are not meant for running. This is hardly the case.

First of all, a similar list might readily be drawn up for men: excessive body weight, susceptibility to injury through overtraining, and so forth. What do such lists prove? Only, perhaps, that a more benevolent deity could in his (or her) farsighted wisdom have designed us all like Bill Rodgers.

Second, women runners do enjoy a number of advantages.

They sweat more efficiently than men. In one hot-weather comparison of the sexes, only half the men were able to complete a four-hour work session. By contrast, 92 percent of the women were successful. The researchers concluded that women achieve proper thermoregulation with less sweat, perhaps because they are capable of a more precise sweating response. "The male . . . ," said one of them, "is a prolific, wasteful sweater."

Women, whatever injuries they suffer, seem to be no more subject to them than men, particularly when they are in shape. Not long ago Drs. Barry A. Franklin, Louis Lussier and Elsworth R. Buskirk reported on a study in which thirty-six sedentary women, aged twenty-nine to forty-seven, volunteered for a twelve-week conditioning program consisting of flexibility exercises, calisthenics, walking and running. The types and frequency of injury, according to the researchers, almost precisely paralleled those reported in earlier studies of male runners. A study at Annapolis, furthermore, showed a significant reduction in injuries as women's conditioning progressed. "Differences in performances between men and women," says Dr. Norbert Sander, "are far more the result of cultural sexual bias than physiological difference."

Other studies have shown that similarities between men and women runners are considerably more striking than the differences.

When, for example, Edmund J. Burke and Florence C. Brush evaluated the aerobic power of thirteen women runners, all of them members of the Charger Track Club of Syracuse, New York, they found that it was virtually identical to that of young men of equal ability.

Similarly, when Jack H. Wilmore and C. Harmon Brown compared top women distance runners with male runners of comparable achievement, they found that even differences in body fat were considerably less than had been expected. Well-trained women runners, it appears, do not carry nearly the fat handicap that had previously been reported. "The results suggest," said the researchers, "that the large differences observed between normal males and females in previous studies . . . are at least partially socially-culturally determined as opposed to being strictly of biological origin."

Finally, H. Harrison Clarke, editor of the *Physical Fitness Research Digest*, says psychological tests show that "male and female athletes are more alike than different in personality traits." Compared with nonathletic women, women who participate in athletics are more self-confident, better adjusted, and have greater self-control and psychological endurance.

Many writers on running, even otherwise enlightened ones, make a great to-do about the cosmetic benefits women derive from running, as if women as a sex were uniquely interested in how they look. It is true, of course, that vigorous exercise makes people, men as well as women, look better. It is, however, just as true that less visible benefits are equally important and equally valued. The typical woman, for example, finds unsuspected pleasures in athletic competition. At first she may hesitate to enter a race. "Women," writes Nancy Anderson in the newsletter of the New Orleans Track Club, "have been conditioned to be supportive and cooperative rather than self-seeking and competitive. Many women equate competition with aggression and stressful battle for victory, qualities which they may feel are incompatible with the female personality and with the pleasure they find in noncompetitive running." Eventually, however, they find that races are not the snarling, antagonistic enterprises they once seemed. Ms. Anderson continues: "Racing *is* aggressive, but we all, male and female, have aggressive impulses which can better be satisfied in honest, direct activities rather than more indirect, sometimes invidious ways. . . . So much in life seems inflexible and unchangeable, and part of the joy of running and especially racing is the realization that improvement and progress can be achieved."

Most women find, too, that running changes their attitudes toward themselves and even, for that matter, toward being women. Phoebe Jones, who in 1979 helped organize a conference on women's running, told the gathering, "Running is a statement to society. It is saying 'no' to always being on call, to sacrificing our daily runs for others' needs, and to the poverty and overwork so many of us face. When we run we are doing something for ourselves, and that is not in society's game plan. We regain control over our bodies and our lives through running." Should that seem an overpugnacious view of an essentially gentle sport, Dr. Gerald Besson's observation in *The Complete Woman Runner* is somewhat less so: "It is the female that bears an age-old burden of the subservient role in our culture. . . . Who does she see when she looks in the mirror but a reflection, not of self but of someone who is easily recognized by how well she plays the role she has accepted. She is someone's wife or sweetheart. Someone's mother. Someone's cook. Someone other than an individual in her own right. Running strips away all these sociocultural impositions and leaves the female runner quiet and alone with her true self." In a deft summary Janice Kaplan writes in *Women and Sports*, "The trouble so far in women's sports is that the athletes have been busy explaining, 'I do this *even though* I'm a woman,' while few have been wise enough to claim, 'This is *what it is* to be a woman.' "

Despite running's growing list of physical and psychological benefits, one old wives' tale persists with particular tenacity. It is that physical stress acts adversely on the female reproductive system, inflicting undesirable and even dangerous effects on both the menstrual cycle and pregnancy. Current research, not to mention the experience of thousands of runners, suggests that this is simply untrue.

It is curious that exercise enjoys such a bad reputation in this respect, for there is plenty of contrary evidence. A half-dozen years ago, having reviewed much of the research on the gynecological ramifications of physical activity, Dr. Allan J. Ryan reported that sports participation usually produces no significant changes, either favorable or unfavorable, except that painful menstruation is less common among athletes than among nonathletes. More recently, Dr. Edwin Dale of the Emory University School of Medicine conducted a thorough inquiry into the effects of hard training on the menstrual cycle. In Dale's experiments volunteers, both athletes and nonathletes, were tested for the presence of a wide range of body chemicals during each phase of their cycles. Invariably, at some level of training intensity the menstrual period became irregular or infrequent. Dale quotes one runner as saying, "My periods are absent now that I run more than four

FOUR HORMONES ASSOCIATED WITH THE MENSTRUAL CYCLE

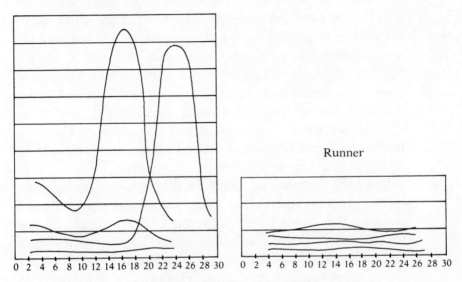

Nonrunner

Runner

Days of Menstrual Cycle

miles per day." Another said, "Since I have increased my mileage to 120 miles per week I have only three periods per year." When he compared the presence or absence of menstrual periods with the hormones associated with ovulation and menstruation, Dale produced graphs like those above. (The one at left shows hormone levels in a healthy nonrunner, while the one at right shows levels in a runner who, presumably because of her training regimen, had not had a period in fourteen months.) Such changes might appear ominous for the childbearing futures of athletes if it were not for one fact: as soon as training is lessened, says Dale, normal hormone levels and physiological function can be expected to return.

So it is, too, with pregnancy. Running has nothing but excellent effects on healthy pregnant women. Coreen Nasenbeny of Fort Defiance, Arizona, told me how, despite neighborhood skepticism, she ran throughout her pregnancy: "Everyone in our community of well-educated professionals would ask in wide-eyed disbelief, 'Still running, Coreen?'—as though my activity were unnatural." The skepticism turned to awed admiration and even, she suspects, to a few conversions when, two weeks after her baby's birth, the same neighbors saw Mrs. Nasenbeny out running again. Medical authorities suggest that pregnancy is not the best time to start a running program, since it may impose unnecessary strain on a woman who has long been sedentary. If, on the other hand, a woman is already a runner when she becomes pregnant, most experts say there is no reason not to continue. They do, however, suggest running slowly and comfortably rather than trying to improve at that time.

Research suggests, incidentally, that hopes of giving one's offspring a head start on becoming an Olympic champion are not a good reason for running when you're pregnant. To see what might happen, researchers at the University of Iowa's Stress Physiology Laboratory required rats to exercise regularly during pregnancy. Their workouts did nothing, alas, to improve the aerobic capacity of their young.

As women more closely approach the running performances of men, the evidence grows that the training of women should probably not differ greatly from that of men. A few years ago Gail Campbell, having sent questionnaires to the fifty leading women marathon runners in the United States, compared the results with the findings in a similar survey of top men runners. The differences suggest one reason why until recently women ran more slowly than men:

	WOMEN	MEN
Average miles for 8 weeks before fastest marathon	533	805
Minimum miles per week	46	74
Maximum miles per week	87	121
Average distance of longest run	20	23.6
Number of runs greater than 20 miles	2.29	3.8

Today the signs are abundant that such differences in training are diminishing. Bill Mongovan, who was introduced at the beginning of this chapter, told me he is convinced women should do more interval work and, after appropriate conditioning, should run greater distances than most of them currently do. Similarly, Dr. Joan Ullyot, an accomplished marathon runner and the author of *Women's Running*, wrote in *Runner's World*, "My feeling is that men and women can train along virtually identical lines . . . , since the physiological principles that underlie training apply to both sexes." Bob Glover, co-author of *The Runner's Handbook*, agrees. "Women runners," he says, "do not need to be treated differently from their male counterparts. . . . It is not unusual to see a woman progress . . . faster than a man." Finally, a top runner named Patti Lyons, reflecting on the achievements of Grete Waitz, said, "She's making girls realize they can't work out like girls. They have to work out like athletes." Eventually, perhaps, even the International Olympic Committee will join the fold. Currently it permits women to compete at no distance greater than 1,500 meters, a little less than a mile. In the 1980s a more unnecessary restriction is scarcely imaginable. One respected researcher, Dr. E. C. Frederick of the University of Montana, recently predicted, on the basis of mathematical and physiological analysis, that by 1987 a woman will run a 2:17:17 marathon.

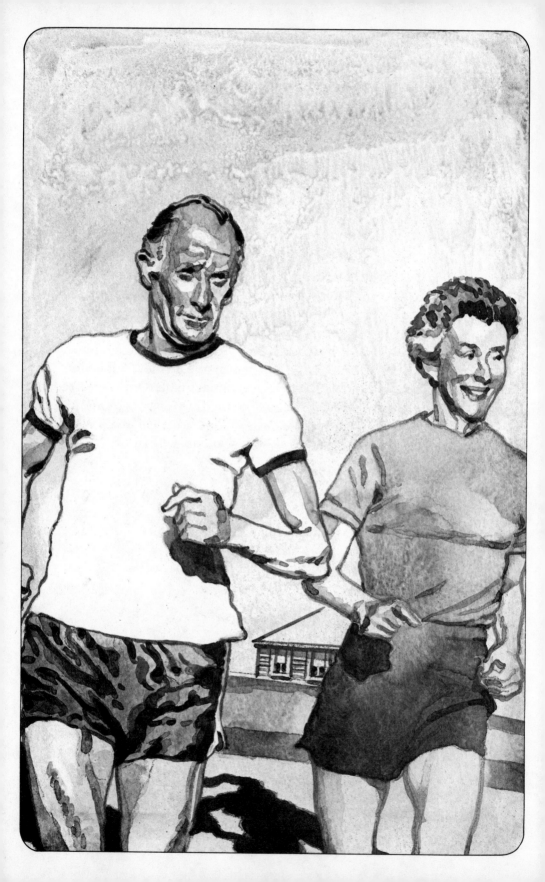

7 ////
Countering the Rocking Chair Argument

What To Do When You're Past Forty

A day or two after President Carter ignominiously collapsed in a hilly 10,000-meter race near Camp David, *New York Times* columnist James Reston suggested that maybe the nation's leader should abandon such sweaty foolishness, "which scrambles the brain," and take up fishing instead. "What was he doing in this six-mile race in the first place?" Reston asked unsympathetically. "Why didn't he just go fishing? Is all this physical exercise really good for him or the country?"

Reston's questions and others like them were being asked with increasing frequency as the first euphoric flush of the running movement began to flicker toward the end of the 1970s and most runners settled down to quietly reaping the benefits of the sport rather than boring each other to distraction with it. Until then, a determined optimist could persuade himself to believe, as at least one California doctor still insists, that covering the 26.2 miles of a marathon bestows, with iron-clad certitude, several years of immunity to heart attack and other bodily ills. Yet as the relationship between athletics and health enjoyed progressively more rigorous scrutiny, including that of such unimpeachable students of the subject as Dr. Ralph S. Paffenbarger, Jr., of Stanford University and Dr. Tim Noakes of the University of Cape Town, it became clear that the statement was probably more wishful thinking than fact, and that runners are much like ordinary mortals. They can, sad to say, get sick. They can even die.

Realizing this has led some observers to conclude, with more timidity than logic, that running is bad for people. In late 1979, on the Public Broadcasting System's *MacNeil-Lehrer Report*, a Washington, D.C., physician argued that because runners occasionally encounter cardiovascular, orthopedic and other problems, no one should run. He himself, he told the audience, did a little walking and, in proper moderation, some swimming. He seemed unimpressed by the arguments of fellow panelists who agreed that, yes, runners do sometimes get sick but in far fewer numbers than nonrunners.

These arguments and counterarguments have their strongest relevance for people beyond life's midpoint. Until about age thirty-five or forty both men and women are largely protected by youth alone, and women enjoy the additional protection, presumably hormonal, associated with the decades preceding menopause. By the forties, however, heart attacks become more common in both sexes. In the study of Harvard graduates cited in Chapter 2 the death rate from heart attack per 10,000 alumni rose relentlessly as they aged:

AGE	DEATH RATE
35–39	24.5
40–44	26.8
45–49	39.4
50–54	101.4
55–59	210.0
60–64	309.1
65–69	394.5

Other analyses, including those based on nationwide statistics and not merely on limited populations, show the same pattern. If, therefore, exercise can reduce the incidence of heart attacks or otherwise improve health, it is well worth finding out about.

As it happens, the evidence is strong that exercise is able to do exactly that. Among the same Harvard graduates, the overall incidence of first heart attacks for those who exercised only lightly or not at all was 57.9 per 10,000 man-years, while among those who exercised the equivalent of twenty miles of running per week it was only 35.3. The reduction attributable to exercise alone was thus a full 39 percent.

It is, moreover, simply untrue, despite James Reston's sense of propriety, that strenuous exercise is inappropriate for older men and women. Not long ago I talked with John A. Kelley, who won the Boston Marathon in 1935 and again, putting his juniors to shame, a decade later. Now in his seventies, Kelley, who remains as energetic as any teenager, continues not just to run but also to race. "I'm more serious about it today than I've ever been," he told me. "Now that I'm retired and have time to train, I'm trying to improve again." Two or three times a week Kelley does a hard workout on a golf course across the street from his house on Cape Cod. "I'll do three or four hundred yards at just under top speed," he said. "Then I'll jog a bit, then do another three or four hundred yards fast. I'll keep doing that until I've gone a total of about six miles. My times are getting good. I'm racing ten thousand meters in forty-three minutes. In an average race I beat half the field."

Accomplished older runners are of course nothing new. The legendary Clarence DeMar, who competed in thirty-four Boston Marathons and won the event seven times, trained and raced until just before his death at age seventy. What is new today is the realization, solidly supported by research, that almost anyone of any age can benefit from the sport and, given enough dedication, run with distinction. At the age of forty-six, for example, Jack Foster finished sixth out of 11,000 contestants in the 1978 New York City Marathon. No longer is it safe to assume that just because a runner has a few gray hairs or a few grandchildren, he or she will be straggling along at the back of the pack.

Consider, as further cases in point, these runners and their achievements:

Mavis Lindgren, who in her seventies continues to set marathon records. Mrs. Lindgren, who started running only a decade ago, trains six to eighteen miles a day.

Alex Ratelle, who at the age of fifty-two ran a 2:45 in Boston and then, the following month, cut his time by ten minutes in the Wisconsin Mayfair Marathon in Milwaukee, setting a record for Americans over fifty.

Don Dixon, who at the age of fifty-one ran a 2:39 in the 1979 Boston Marathon and at the age of fifty-two a 2:43 in the New York City Marathon.

Fritz Mueller, who in his forties covered the Boston Marathon course faster than any runner his age had ever done it: an improbable 2:20.

Monty Montgomery, who has set marathon records for sixty-five-year-olds (2:53) as well as, more recently, for seventy-one-year-olds (3:07), and who at the age of seventy ran a record-setting 5:22 mile and an 880 in 2:42.6.

Miki Gorman, who at the age of forty-one ran the New York City Marathon in 2:39 and the following year finished a 10,000-meter cross-country race in 35:28.

Such runners as these, like thousands of others with lesser gifts, are currently demonstrating that age alone need be no impediment to athletic performance. Nor need it be an impediment to the strenuous, sustained workouts required to produce superior racing times. In less than a decade at the sport my neighbor Stephen Richardson has become one of the world's fastest over-fifty marathoners. In his early running years he and I often trained together. Now, unless I want to scourge my body with cramps, side stitches and burning lungs, I run with him only on days when he pledges that he doesn't plan to push.

A runner beyond his or her thirties need not, of course, compete with the distinction of Ratelle, Mueller, Dixon et al. in order to profit from the sport. There is, nonetheless, growing evidence that running confers its maximum benefits only when some of it is done at a fast enough pace to cause mild muscular discomfort and hard breathing. Research, in particular the Paffenbarger studies cited earlier, suggests that while slow running produces indisputable benefits it is only fast running that brings a man or woman to full fitness. This is not to say that a fifty-year-old marathoner should try to imitate the regimen of Bill Rodgers. He or she will do well, however, to include an occasional brisk quarter-mile or half-mile in training runs.

A word of caution, though: Fast running puts greater stress on the body than slow running and is therefore more likely to bring to light latent cardiovascular and orthopedic weaknesses. It is important, therefore, to 1) see a doctor before you start running, 2) do several minutes of stretching exercises before as well as after each workout, 3) slow down if you start to hurt, and 4) intersperse hard workouts with enough easy days to allow full recovery. As for the specifics of training, most of the techniques described in Chapter 5 and in *The Complete Book of Running* are as applicable to senior citizens as to college track stars.

Beyond such caveats as the foregoing, doctrinaire prescriptions have little place in running, a sport that derives much of its value and practically all of its pleasure from the fact that each of us can run with whatever degree of exertion suits our goals and moods. If, therefore, you prefer never to run faster than a relaxed lope, you will nevertheless be far better off than someone who does not exercise at all. It is only recently, however, as researchers have begun to look into the effects of exercise on the aging process, that we have begun to realize exactly how much better off.

Every runner knows he or she feels better than nonrunners. An English author, Robert Heller, wrote not long ago in Britain's *Jogging* magazine, "I have one highly personal reason for rejoicing in running. Without it, my book *Superman* . . . would never have been written. This isn't because my daily two or three miles have sharpened my intellect, improved my concentration or even reinforced my will power. . . . No:

I owe *Superman* to the discovery, through running, of how far my own performance . . . fell below its potential."

Such testimony is common. Persuasive though it may be, however, it is anecdotal rather than scientific. It is only when we turn to the work of trained researchers that we discover, sometimes to our astonishment, what vigorous exercise can accomplish for those well along in life.

These days such researchers are spending increasing amounts of time studying older runners. One reason is that while everyone knows that a well-trained twenty-year-old is likely to be capable of prodigious athletic accomplishments, we still know little about what older athletes can do when properly trained and highly motivated. Not long ago Dr. Michael L. Pollock examined William Andberg, a sixty-year-old veterinarian who in a single track meet set three world records for runners in his age category, running a mile in 5:19, 5,000 meters in 17:47 and 10,000 meters in 37:12. (As if to demonstrate the diversity of his talents, he has also run a marathon in 2:51.) Pollock found that Andberg's resting heart rate was 42, exactly what might be encountered in a top athlete half his age, and that his maximum was 173, well above the 150 or 160 that medical authorities cite as typical at his age. On another occasion, when Pollock investigated the oxygen-processing ability of athletes in their seventies, he found it to be, on average, 30 to 40 percent greater than in nonathletes the same age. He also recorded cholesterol levels well below normal values. Both oxygen-processing ability and cholesterol concentrations are key indicators of fitness.

Despite such convincing evidence of the value of exercise, some older people, particularly those who have become accustomed to sedentary living, are wary of undertaking exercise programs. A few years ago C. Carson Conrad, writing in a U.S. Administration on Aging publication, pointed out that many older people mistakenly think that with age their need for exercise diminishes and eventually disappears. Furthermore, he went on, they exaggerate the risks of exercise after middle age and, perhaps most significantly, underrate their abilities and capacities. Unfortunately, their misapprehensions are often buttressed by doctors. A Mayo Clinic staff member, Dr. Donald J. Erickson, says, "Physicians' admonitions usually are not accompanied by realistic prescriptions.... At least three half-hour sessions are required each week to promote a satisfactory level of physical fitness." That, of course, is only a minimum. Many older men and women, even those who do not think of themselves as serious athletes, exercise at least twice that much, while those who are serious athletes are in another class altogether (see "Training with an Over-Fifty Champion" on page 108).

If you are past forty, how much running you do and how hard you do it is best governed by both your interests and your abilities. The *Physical Fitness Research Digest*, published by the President's Council on Physical Fitness and Sports, said not long ago:

> While the nature, extent and significance of physical and motor differences have been demonstrated for younger ages, the same situation is found at older ages throughout the life span.... Yet, despite the obvious, society clings to chronological age as a criterion for many things, the most obvious of which for older people is the age of retirement, usually 65 years. Just what does elderly mean? It certainly should mean different things to different people. Older Americans should be discouraged from equating infirmity with chronological age.

Numerous studies demonstrate that such an equation is, as the publication suggests, entirely unnecessary. When Dr. Herbert A. deVries of the University of Southern California put 112 men, ranging in age from fifty-two to eighty-eight, on a physical fitness program that included running, he found improvements in such important measures as blood pressure, endurance, vital capacity and oxygen-processing ability.

Nor are such beneficial changes limited to men. When the same researcher and a colleague, Gene M. Adams, enrolled seventeen women with an average age of sixty-six in a three-month exercise program they recorded similar improvements. The training capacity of the cardiovascular system, deVries and Adams reported, was demonstrated by the improvement in resting heart rate and an increased ability to do hard work.

A researcher named Alan J. Barry reported in the *Journal of Gerontology* on a study in which men and women in their early seventies were encouraged to exercise three times a week for three months. Heart rate and blood pressure decreased. Endurance, agility and oxygen-processing capacity increased.

Still another researcher, Bryant A. Stamford, enlisted volunteers from among geriatric patients. They worked out five days a week for twelve weeks, gradually increasing the duration of exercise from six to twenty minutes. Both heart rate and blood pressure decreased.

In Finland an investigator named Harri Suominen recruited twenty-six men and women, all of them sixty-nine years old, for an eight-week program. The men and women did exercises, including running, for an hour a day five times a week. Despite the brevity of the program, Suominen was able to detect significant improvements in both oxygen-processing ability and muscular efficiency.

Not only physical but psychological improvements have also been reported in exercising older people. In one study R. John Young and A. H. Ismail found that those who are physically fit, when compared with those of lower fitness, are emotionally more stable, more secure, more easygoing and more adventurous, as well as, for reasons that can only be guessed at, more inclined to pursue intellectual activities.

This profusion of research all points to the same central fact: that exercise, including running, can help keep us young. Even if it could not, however, most runners would no doubt argue that it is nonetheless worth doing. In what other way, after all, can we achieve such close kinship with those many years our junior? And in what other way can we continue, despite all the incontrovertible signs of aging, to be bona fide athletes? As I write this paragraph I have just come home after running a fifteen-kilometer race in Harrison, New York. For much of the course I trailed two young men. One had a blond ponytail. The other reminded me, with his beard and wondrous explosion of hair, of Bjorn Borg. They were no more than half my age; I despaired of overtaking them. Finally, in the seventh mile, a steep hill confronted us. There I passed them both. I looked, or at least tried to look, appropriately modest. But need I tell you what unpardonably exuberant pride filled my aging heart as I went by?

Training with an Over-Fifty Champion

The leader of the over-fifty runners in the 1979 Boston and New York City marathons was a 130-pound producer of television documentaries named Don Dixon, who ran 2:39 and 2:43, respectively. He was fifty-one years old for the first race, fifty-two for the second. Dixon's daily regimen illustrates how slight the differences may be between the training of young and older runners.

Back in the 1940s Dixon ran for his high school cross-country team. He admits, however, that he wasn't very good at it. "Even on my best day," he says, "I often came in last." After graduation he gave up running and didn't take the sport up again until he was almost forty. Waiting for a handball court at a YMCA one day, he decided to pass the time by circling the track a few times. "One day," he says, "I ran three miles. It was the farthest I had ever gone. I felt very satisfied." On a whim Dixon entered the 1971 Yonkers

Marathon, which passes not far from his home in Hastings-on-Hudson, New York. He finished in 3:35. Later the same year he ran the New York City Marathon. This time he ran a 3:25. Encouraged, he started working out harder. In his eleventh marathon, the Earth Day on Long Island, he finally broke three hours.

Dixon does most of his training at a 7½-minute-per-mile pace, practically never going any faster except in the dozen or so races he enters each year. He covers four to twelve miles a day and averages sixty miles a week, with a buildup to seventy in the six or eight weeks before the New York and Boston marathons. "I'd like to do more," he says, "but I don't have the time."

As a correspondent for International News Service during the Korean War, Dixon and two other Americans took a sailing holiday near Hong Kong. They were captured by a Chinese gunboat and spent eighteen months in prison, six of them in solitary confinement in Canton. A lifelong exercise enthusiast, Dixon did pushups and other exercises in his cell. His fellow prisoners did not. "I came out in much better shape than the others," he says.

Dixon professes to be mystified about the reasons for his continuing athletic improvement. "I train less than a lot of people," he says, "and I don't do much speed work. I guess I'm just stubborn. And I have to admit I do like to run long distances."

8

How Much
How Early?

Reflections on the
Youth-and-Distance Debate

*I*n Anchorage, Kentucky, according to what may be the season's most precocious piece of journalism, a three-year-old boy named Nick Roskelly not only entered the local Run for Arts race but sat down later and, with a little help from his father, wrote a full-page article on the experience for *Runner's World*. ("Mom," he quoted himself as having said, "I need to potty so I don't wee-wee in the race." And later, while waiting for the starting gun: "From my vantage, I could see nothing but a flock of prepubescent fannies.")

In Lawrence, Kansas, five-year-old Bucky Cox gets up at five-thirty every morning to run six miles under the tutelage of Ray Foster, of the University of Kansas Bureau of Child Research. As psychological inducement Foster dispenses nickels in return for good performances. Apparently the rewards work. In the Sundown Salute Marathon, run in 94-degree heat, Bucky covered the course in 5:29:09, setting an unofficial world's record for runners his age.

In Overland Park, Kansas, barely an hour to the east of Lawrence as State Route 10 meanders, nine-year-old Wesley Paul sets out for a daily dawn run. The only differences between him and Bucky Cox, other than Wesley's more advanced years, are that he runs ten miles rather than six and that, having posted a 2:55:59 in a recent New York City Marathon, he has begun to muse about someday winning an Olympic gold medal.

There is no longer any doubt that children as young as Nick Roskelly, Bucky Cox and Wesley Paul are capable of prodigious athletic performances. Countless thoroughly trained adult marathoners have suffered dismay as youngsters not yet in possession of their six-year molars have bounced buoyantly past them. What is, on the other hand, in considerable doubt is how much good or harm running does them, particularly when it takes the form of mile upon grueling mile of serious training rather than merely brief, playful runs of the sort children most often choose when left to themselves. The question is particularly resistant to easy answers because there is thus far practically no evidence about the long-term effects of the sport when started in early childhood. Nor, to cite a related but different issue, has any researcher compiled data to show how much running is appropriate at various ages of childhood. If you should decide today to start training your infant son or daughter for next year's 53½-mile London-to-Brighton race, the neighbors will no doubt mutter darkly about your parental qualifications. Yet not even the most sourly critical among them is likely to come up with a single documented reason for their not running ten or fifteen miles a day. When, recently, I consulted several standard texts on sportsmedicine, I discovered that not one offered even the flimsiest shred of guidance on the question.

The lack of evidence has, however, hardly inhibited the growing debate about how much and what kind of running is appropriate for children. Not long ago, for example, *Runner's*

World, largest of the nation's running magazines, announced that in order to discourage excessive running among the young it would no longer recognize marathon records for anyone under twelve and went on to suggest a minimum age of eighteen for marathon running. No sooner had the magazine announced its decision than the American Medical Joggers Association took it to task, arguing that "if we are to wait till age eighteen we will be too late; the kids will already have early atherosclerosis, and they will have the wrong life-style pattern set."

For a debate that is at best a matter of earnest fears and learned guesswork rather than reliable information, it has elicited no end of strong opinion. Dr. Kenneth H. Cooper, the author of *Aerobics* and a close student of the effects of exercise, told a reporter for *The Runner*, "I can't medically endorse a distance of more than two or three miles for kids up to puberty. . . . I am afraid of the potential damage and trauma to the epiphyseal joints. I can't document this in the literature, but it's a medical feeling that I have." Concern about injury to the epiphyses, soft plates that contribute to the growth of long bones, is frequently expressed by authorities opposed to prolonged running for young children. So, for that matter, is concern for purely hypothetical injuries that have not yet been identified as having an athletic origin but that one day, as increasing numbers of children take to running long distances, may be attributed to the sport.

Unlike Cooper and the editors of *Runner's World*, some medical authorities are unconvinced that running is any more harmful to young people than it is to adults. Dr. Gabe Mirkin, co-author of *The Sportsmedicine Book*, has compared the current anxieties about children's running with the worries a few years ago about women's running. Those worries, of course, have almost entirely subsided as thousands of women have emerged unscathed, so far as anyone can tell, from marathons and even ultramarathons.

If one is troubled by forebodings about an activity's potential for harm, it is easy simply to avoid that activity or to impose suitably conservative limits. When, for example, the now-defunct publication *The Marathoner* asked six medical experts how much training a thirteen-year-old should under- take in preparation for a marathon, all six counseled modera- tion and one said flatly, "I don't think thirteen-year-olds should run marathons." That, however, is scarcely an accept- able solution if you are searching not merely for safety but for athletic excellence. Many authorities argue that an athlete will reach his or her adult potential only if training is started in childhood. This view gained support not long ago from studies conducted by Frank H. Fu at Springfield College. Using laboratory rats, Fu found that if the animals were made to swim regularly during the second month of their lives, the growth of alveoli, the lungs' air sacs, was greater than if they were permitted to live sedentary lives during their youth. A greater alveolar density lets more oxygen pass from the lungs to the bloodstream, thereby presumably increasing muscular efficiency. Fu's experiments suggest that there may be periods in the life spans both of animals and human beings when physiological development takes place most readily. Once these uniquely favorable periods are past, growth can perhaps never again be as complete.

Even if one's goals are not athletic superiority at all but sim- ply good health and development of a balanced personality, there is much to be said for running in childhood. Consider the weight problem alone. When Dr. H. Verdain Barnes of the University of Iowa College of Medicine undertook a ten-state study, he found that no fewer than 39 percent of boys and 33 percent of girls aged eleven to eighteen weighed more than they should. Barnes cited the value of exercise for such people. "Exercise," he said, "not only helps burn calories but aids in taking away in-between-meal hunger pains." One might, inci- dentally, also cite the value of exercise for the adults who are among their most persuasive examples, their teachers. Re- cently David N. Aspy and Flora N. Roebuck studied the health practices of 1,000 teachers. They found that 90 percent were overweight and did not exercise regularly. "Teachers as a group," they concluded with forgivably unscientific disdain, "are not physically fit."

Research has demonstrated that athletic participation brings young people not just physical but psychological benefits as well. One of the most persuasive bodies of evidence emerged from a twelve-year study conducted in Medford, Oregon, under the direction of the University of Oregon's H. Harrison Clarke. Clarke, a respected researcher who serves as a consultant to the President's Council on Physical Fitness and Sports, tested a group of boys annually from age seven until they graduated from high school or left the Medford school system. Predictably enough, he found that boys who engaged in athletics were stronger and more physically adept than those who didn't. Less predictably, he found that all active students tended to have similar psychological characteristics ·and that those characteristics were detectable in the earliest elementary school years. Specifically, regular athletes formed closer personal relationships, showed more interest both in other people and in school subjects, and were more inclined toward social participation.

By the time they were in junior high school, Clarke found that athletes had developed greater leadership qualities, social initiative and maturity, and intellectual capacities. They also did less complaining and suffered less from self-doubt.

In high school, Clarke's research showed, athletes were more likely than nonathletes to form close personal relationships. Moreover, their grades showed greater improvement. When, furthermore, Clarke made differentiations for various sports, he found that track athletes accepted themselves more completely than students in other sports.

Although there may be a self-selection factor in Clarke's research, it nonetheless seems to reinforce the view that sport, rather than being merely a pleasant but insignificant pastime, is in fact an activity of considerable importance. In its exploration of sport's psychological dimensions, it also suggests that the age-and-distance debate may thus far have been waged largely over issues that are not the crucial ones at all. Rather than wondering what running does to children's epiphyses, hearts and lungs, perhaps we should be wondering what it does to their minds.

One of the few other authorities to have addressed this question publicly is a San Diego child psychiatrist, Thomas P. Johnson. Asked by Dr. Allan J. Ryan, editor of *The Physician and Sportsmedicine,* whether he thought it a good idea to let very young children run marathons, Johnson replied, "Children's self-esteem is based on what they think their parents think of them. Consider the subtle parental pressure on a child just by having him enter such a competition. Parents often say the child 'wants to,' but why would a five-year-old want to enter formal competition unless he got the message from his parents? Suppose a four-year-old sets a record and his parents are ecstatic. What about the child at another time when he loses? Do his parents seem as happy with him, to value him as much? The message can be subtle, but powerful. At that age self-concept is too fragile for that kind of stress." Johnson, let it be noted, is scarcely opposed to athletics for youngsters. He serves on the Little League's national board of directors.

A similar anxiety was expressed not long ago in a thoughtful letter to *Running Times.* Questioning the magazine's policy of publishing reports on the achievements of young runners, Richard A. Schultz wrote, "I fear that many children may be pushed into competition or rigorous training by their parents. It may be overt parental pressure, or it may come from the child's desire to please a parent's unspoken wish. . . . I see many cases in which the children are pushed too hard by aggressive, competitive parents. . . . Is not childhood meant for play?"

Stephen Richardson, an accomplished runner as well as a specialist in childhood mental problems, told me he perceived a less subtle danger in parental pressures. It is, he said, simply that the child will become so sick of running that he'll turn away from it forever.

Twice recently I have had occasion to spend time with outstandingly accomplished young runners. One was an eleven-year-old girl, the other a boy the same age. Both are widely known in the sport. Magazines have published articles about them; they have appeared on television. When I talked with them, they had just run full-length marathons at speeds that would have been creditable at any age, and were receiving, as a result, considerably more attention than most of the adult runners who had participated in the same events. News reporters were recording what they had to say; television interviewers were questioning them. Almost anyone, having run well, would have relished, as they were doing, the well-deserved limelight. Yet I could not chase from my mind a dark thought: What if these were the high points of their lives? What are the next six, seven or eight decades like when your most celebrated accomplishment was at age eleven?

Probably few people, no matter how wary of pushing their children, would want to decree that youngsters should never, under any circumstances, try to excel. The urge to excellence is, after all, part of the evolutionary principle, and is no doubt as strongly rooted in children as in adults. Who would want to deny young people its expression? The solution, plainly, is not to prohibit children from running. What are needed are principles that will provide, if not definitive rules, at least some guidance. Some time ago, in its quarterly publication, *Physical Fitness Research Digest*, the President's Council on Physical Fitness and Sports set forth several such principles. Among them:

1. Exercise should be based on the individual's tolerance.
2. An exercise plan should provide for progression.

Seemingly straightforward, those two principles are in fact a philosophical Scylla and Charybdis. What if a child's tolerance is so low that he or she cannot possibly improve? On the other hand, what if the desire to improve is so great that a child continually risks exceeding his or her tolerance? More guidance is plainly required.

Or less. For it may be that the dilemma is not as insoluble as it seems. There are, first of all, clear danger signals in excessive running: recurrent injuries, chronic fatigue, a lack of interest in running or in anything else. There is, however, an even more revealing danger signal: a parental will to excel. Not just a strong will, *any* will. A parent of a young runner might well ask: What do I value most, good races now or overall physical and psychological development? The minds and bodies of young athletes, like those of their elders, give unmistakable complaint if running is too tiring. Provided adult pressure is not irresistible, most young people will respond to those complaints by making appropriate adjustments. Adults should never, therefore, prod young athletes toward more running but should give them the room and trust they need to search out what is most satisfying. Some, perhaps the majority, will decide to run only short distances, and why shouldn't they if that's what they enjoy? Others may turn toward longer runs.

Dr. Harry DuVal, who is associated with the University of Wisconsin's noted La Crosse Exercise Program, recently offered some sane advice. "Let the child be a child," he said. "Let [children] set their own limits. They are very well attuned to their body signs. It is only as we become adults that we allow our 'higher' brain centers to rule over telltale signs of fatigue. Finally, don't push the child. If he has a natural desire or talent for running, encourage him, and compliment him often. If he comes home one day and says that he no longer enjoys running, let it be. Perhaps it is time to invest in a tennis racquet or a violin."

While he was still in high school one of my teenaged sons, John, accompanied me to the New Orleans Marathon. Because his cross-country season had long since ended and he had been running only a few miles a week, he planned to watch rather than participate. On the morning of the race, however, he asked what I would think of his running the marathon slowly, as a workout. I said it was up to him. He covered the entire distance, never developed so much as an ache or blister, and felt fine afterward. That night, when his exhausted father fell into bed, John was going strong. My most zealous sense of parental concern can to this day summon up no reason why running that marathon was a bad idea. Nor can that concern argue me away from the conviction that the childhood running problem is most often an adult problem.

9 ///

The Equipment Explosion

The Gear Runners Need (and Don't Need)

*T*he entrepreneurial inventiveness of the American busi-
nessman was never more arrestingly in evidence than at
the vast exposition of runners' equipment held in Boston during the weekend of the 1979 Patriots' Day marathon. For several hours one afternoon I wandered through the exhibits, surveying with wonder and occasional dismay the fruits of the
national genius for creating a need where none, or at least very
little, exists. Here were runners' trampolines, runners' wrist
radios, runners' vitamins, liquids and dietary supplements.
Here were beeping metronomes to tell us when to place our
feet on the ground as we run, a profusion of arch supports, foot
powders and heel protectors, and so many varieties of shoes,
warmup suits and rain outfits that if you or I owned a thou-
sandth part of what was on display we would never again

need to supplement our wardrobes by so much as a single shoelace. A friend, beholding this array, shook his head and said in wonderment, "It's as if someone had turned a mad inventor loose."

For a long time afterward I meditated on the experience. It was an epiphany. For a runner, I suddenly realized, ours could easily be bewildering times. An anonymous writer for England's *Road Runners Club Newsletter*, fresh from having his mind boggled by a visit to our shores, put the matter concisely: "The crowd at the starting line of the Boston Marathon is spare compared with the crush of capitalists trying to cash in on running." Study the ads in *Runner's World* or *The Runner*. From among their offerings, what do we really need? Do I need a plastic waistband to carry water or Gatorade in? Bee pollen tablets for extra strength and endurance? A license plate that reads "Runnin"? Despite the current hype and hoopla, the answers are, fortunately, not much more complex than they were in those halcyon days before America's industrial might was brought to bear on runners and their previously innocent world. For the essentials of running are still mercifully few. There isn't much we need other than good shoes and enough clothing to keep us warm when it's cold outdoors.

Most of the principles outlined in *The Complete Book of Running* are still true:

In shoes, look for a variety that is well padded and flexible and has a stable heel. For most runners, a shoe should be higher at the heel than at the ball of the foot, so that the rear of the shoe lands first and absorbs most of the body's weight. A fairly thick heel also minimizes stretching of the Achilles tendon, an important consideration if you're a woman and wear high heels much of the time.

In shorts, nylon is best because it's light and dries quickly. On the other hand, when the weather is cool but not cold enough for long pants, cotton gives a touch of warmth.

In long pants, traditional sweatpants are the least satisfactory because they're so bulky and weigh so much. Most runners find warmup suits, despite their extra cost, more comfortable. I'll confess they once seemed to me an expensive way to keep warm, but they do look nice and feel good, so I recently caved in like just about everyone else I know.

In gloves, white cotton gardening gloves of the sort Bill Rodgers wears on cold days are the most practical and the cheapest. They cost only $1.00 or so a pair, unless you choose the kind with an official Bill Rodgers emblem on them; in that case you'll pay about $1.50.

In hats, a simple wool one, the kind you can roll down over your ears, is best. When it's bitterly cold outdoors, you can cover most of your head with such a hat. When it's warmer, you can roll it up or take it off and stuff it into your waistband.

Two or three years ago it wasn't necessary to know much more about equipment than that. So much new gear has recently come on the market, however, that some additional notes are in order.

Women's Gear

Most running equipment can be worn by either sex. So long as the size is right, T-shirts, rain suits and winter hats fit men and women equally well. Increasingly, however, gear is being designed especially for women. There's a reason. First, women's feet are likely to be narrower than men's; hence the popularity of shoes like Saucony and New Balance, which are manufactured in varying widths. Second, women's torsos are typically different from men's, not just in the obvious ways but also because women tend to be wider and longer in the rear and longer from waist to crotch.

In the past two or three years these differences have prompted at least four firms, all of them run by women, to start producing running clothes exclusively for women. They are Gobelle, Pantera and Moving Comfort, which offer shorts, shirts and other clothing, and Jogbra, which sells a specially designed brassiere that has no inside seams or metal hardware. In addition, a company called Lady Madonna offers sportswear for pregnant women, while several manufacturers of ordinary clothing market special sports brassieres. One woman marathoner, Christine Steinmetz, told me, however, that she is not enthusiastic about the sports brassieres currently on the market. "No one has yet made the perfect running bra," she told me. "Most of them work for short distances, but when I get back from running fifteen miles there's always a scrape or abrasion somewhere." Mrs. Steinmetz says the Lily of France Sport Bra is the most satisfactory she has found and the Formfit Rogers Running Bra the next best. (Formfit's more recently introduced You Can Do It Running Bra is, I was told by a company official, "functionally similar.") She finds the Jogbra tight and hot.

For any manufacturer that wants to make an impressive dent in the market, guidelines are close at hand. After a recent marathon in Minneapolis the magazine *The Physician and Sportsmedicine* asked twenty-seven women finishers what they would like to see in a runner's brassiere. They wanted, the magazine reported, "a soft and stretchy cotton bra that 1) gives firm support on the sides, 2) has no seams or metal parts, 3) comes in a variety of sizes, 4) has an all-elastic back, 5) has no lace, padding or underwires, and 6) gives lots of support."

Dr. Gale Gehlsen, director of the biomechanics laboratory at Ball State University, considers the last characteristic most important. When she recently tested various sports brassieres to determine their ability to resist bouncing, she rated the following three most effective:

1. Warner's Get Moving brassiere ($9; available at department stores)

2. The Runderwear brassiere ($15.95 from Athletica, Inc., Box 13357, Philadelphia, PA 19101, or in sporting goods stores)

3. The Henson Winner's Bra ($12 and $13, depending on size; specialty stores)

Shoes

Among runners, there are few more controversial subjects than the selection of shoes. Recently *Running Times*, in an effort to make sense out of the complexities of footwear, offered some useful guidelines. First, said the magazine, it's a good idea to narrow your choices to companies that specialize in running shoes and don't look on them just as a sideline. Chief among such companies are the following:

ADIDAS	LYDIARD	PONY
BROOKS	NEW BALANCE	PUMA
CONVERSE	NIKE	SAUCONY
ETONIC	OSAGA	TIGER

Second, be wary of ratings. Instead, select a shoe that matches your own biomechanical idiosyncrasies. Some shoes, for example, fit narrow or wide feet better than others; some are more comfortable for runners with flat feet or with exceptionally high arches; and some have heels that, because of their thickness, suit some runners better than others.

If you don't find exactly what you want among the leading companies' shoes, there are dozens of others you can investigate. Richard O. Schuster, a knowledgeable podiatrist who frequently treats runners, has observed, "Some of the most poorly rated shoes are usable—if not uniquely suited for—some segment of the running population." I myself have worn various models from such lesser-known companies as Ambi, Autry and Bob Wolf with complete satisfaction. My Autrys, in fact, although not as durably lined as they ought to be, are among my favorites.

A number of other runners apparently feel the same way. While waiting for the starting gun at the 1979 New York City Marathon I studied the shoes some of my fellow competitors were wearing. The enormous variety they had chosen made it plain that there was anything but a consensus. Nonetheless, a pattern of sorts later became distinguishable. Curious about what the top runners were wearing in the race, a shoe-company representative whose testimony I have no reason to mistrust recorded the brands worn by the first fifty men and the first twenty-five women to cross the finish line. They were as follows:

MEN	WOMEN
20 Adidas	11 Adidas
19 Nike	8 Nike
4 Tiger	3 Brooks
3 Brooks	1 Karhu
3 Karhu	1 Lydiard
1 Puma	1 Reebok

The results may, of course, have been skewed by the fact that some leading runners have contractual arrangements that require them to wear only specific brands of shoes.

Rain Suits

Several manufacturers have recently begun marketing two-piece weather-resistant suits that are useful when it's wet and foul outdoors. Excellent ones are offered by Bill Rodgers, Frank Shorter, Brooks, Devaney, International Sports, General Universal Training Supplies, Adidas and Sub 4, among others. In addition, I particularly like the lightweight K-Way rain jacket and pants, available from Northsport USA Ltd., Box 100, Richford, VT 05476. The K-Way is cleverly designed with a built-in pocket that holds both the jacket and pants; it straps around your waist when not in use. It's the best solution I've found for days when you want to be prepared but aren't sure about the weather. Some varieties of rain suits, incidentally, keep the rain out better than others, so you may want to make some inquiries before you finally settle on one.

Night Gear

When you're running in the dark it's important to be seen easily by automobile drivers. At the very least, therefore, wear white clothing. Even more effective is to wear apparel especially designed to reflect light. The best I've found, and among the most brilliantly reflective, is sold by Jog-a-Lite (Box 125, Silver Lake, NH 03875). In addition to its vests, Jog-a-Lite offers reflective headbands, leg bands, sashes and backpacks. I've tried them all; they work well.

If you don't mind looking like the Concorde coming in to Orly, you can buy battery-operated flashing lights that clamp to your upper arms. They're called Runner's Beacons, are marketed by P&M International (Allston, MA 02134) and cost about $7 apiece. Their only drawback is that when the temperature falls much below freezing the batteries fade out.

Identification

Ever since a medical journal urged that runners carry identification in case of accident, manufacturers have been offering bracelets, necklaces and tags of various kinds intended to serve that purpose. A recent issue of *Runner's World* carried advertisements for no fewer than seven such devices, ranging from Professional Charms' solid gold Jog Tag at $200 to others costing only a few dollars. One of the cheapest I've heard of is available at $2 from Run-I-Dent, Box 144, 8 Main Street, Francestown, NH 03043. It's much like a military dog tag, fastens to your wrist with an elastic band, and has embossed on it your name, telephone number, blood type, and other information. If you can get along without solid gold, the Run-I-Dent will serve the purpose just fine.

You can also keep identification, as well as keys and emergency money, in an ingeniously designed quarter-ounce pocket called a Ripper that fastens to one of your shoelaces. Available from Ne-Toe Products (Box 829, Silver Spring, MD 20901), they cost $3.50 each and come in a choice of blue, green, yellow or red nylon.

Chronographs

When you're racing or training it's often useful to have some method of measuring elapsed time. That way, you can record your own finishing time without having to wait for race officials' computations, which are often hours in coming. In a training run, if you know your customary pace you can try unfamiliar courses for variety and still calculate how far you've gone. A runner's chronograph, which is nothing more than a stopwatch that can be worn on your wrist, is the most convenient way to keep track of elapsed time. Two principal types are available. One looks much like a conventional watch, but in addition to the customary large dial with a second hand, it has two or three smaller dials that keep track of minutes and hours. The second type is digital. It gives a direct reading of elapsed time and is easier to read while you're running. The kind I use is a Microsel LCD Wrist Chronograph, available from Microsel, 699 East Brocaw Road, San Jose, CA 95112. Among other advantages, it is significantly lighter than the conventional Breitling chronograph I have owned for many years. In rating electronic chronographs, *Running* magazine found the Microsel, which costs $79.95, somewhat more expensive than most of the others, but added, "Since it has the best controls, it is worth its higher price."

Not Recommended

Some running gear is purely a matter of taste. If, for example, you prefer a Bill Rodgers rain suit to a Frank Shorter model, no one is likely to care except Rodgers and Shorter. There is, however, some equipment that almost always brings disappointment:

Runners' radios. I have tried every type of radio advertised as being designed especially for runners. None has worked adequately. Whether worn on your wrist, strapped to your head or chest or clamped to your waistband, such radios give intermittent or just plain awful reception. If you get bored running without sound, buy a regular transistor radio and carry it in your hand. Dr. Alan Clark of Atlanta brought one along when we ran together not long ago; it worked fine.

Mail-order orthotics. At least one manufacturer offers orthotics by mail. Upon receipt of your order the firm sends two rectangular blocks of plastic foam into which you press your feet to create imprints. From these he molds the inserts. My son John and I tried them and could detect no advantage, although it is possible in principle that a pair might help in specific cases. The chief problem, I suspect, is that while conventional orthotics are specifically shaped to correct problems, mail-order orthotics are likely only to mirror the problems. One well-known West Coast podiatrist, Steven I. Subotnick, even told me he thought such orthotics were dangerous. "I have my share of problems right here in the office," he said. "I have to watch my patients run on a treadmill. I have to make many fine adjustments. How can that be done by mail? Then, too, you may have some problem that won't respond to orthotics."

If you think inserts might help but you hesitate to spend the $50 or more that podiatrists charge, you might first try Dr. Scholl's Flexo Foam Arch (about $4) or the same manufacturer's model 610 (about $14). If your heels need more cushioning than your running shoes provide, try Tuli's heel cups (Box 1363, Glendale, AZ 85311). They are made of wafflelike latex and cost about $9 a pair. They have significantly eased the pain of a runner friend who had been troubled by painful heel spurs.

Metronomes. Several firms offer electronic devices that emit rhythmic beeps and thus, the manufacturers claim, help a runner maintain his correct training pace. Such instruments might, I suppose, work for a track athlete. Most of us, however, train mainly on roads where varying terrain necessitates frequent changes in tempo that render a metronome worthless. Bill Rodgers told me he didn't know of any top athlete who used one. Do you suppose the top athletes know something?

Pedometers. These are unnecessary simply because there's an easier and cheaper way to calculate how far you've run. Wearing a watch, run a mile at your usual pace on a track or other measured course. Thereafter, when you go running, figure that you're moving at that speed. As you improve, you'll want to recalibrate yourself from time to time.

10 ///
What to Eat

*With Runners' Foods,
Staying Both Healthy and Thin
Is No Problem*

S everal years ago, when I first got the idea for a book on
running, it seemed sensible to devote separate chapters
to the related subjects of how to lose weight and how to eat
properly. In most writings, after all, even though dieting and
nutrition both have to do with eating, they are for good
reasons treated as more or less distinct. Such a distinction
may have made sense when *The Complete Book of Running*
first appeared, but recent nutritional studies suggest that such
a division would be a mistake today. The main reason is that
both scientific research and the experience of thousands of
runners show clearly that these apparently separate subjects
are more closely related than most people suspect. The evidence is strong, in fact, that a runner who eats sensibly is unlikely ever to become overweight and, furthermore, that a fat

nonrunner who takes up the sport will in all probability turn without any particular effort to a better diet and become thinner in the process. An Auburn, Maine, lawyer, John R. Linnell, told me how, weighing 300 pounds, he started running and lost 75 pounds in the first six months. Similarly, 340-pound George Mize, mentioned in Chapter 1, lost 85 pounds in the five months after he bought his first pair of running shoes and 132 pounds in the first year. Needless to say, both Linnell and Mize kept a close eye on what they ate, but when I was in touch with them recently neither complained about ever having felt uncomfortably hungry. On the contrary, running provided a pleasure that entirely compensated for the abandoned rewards of overeating. "I'm actually beginning to look forward to each day's run instead of dreading the thought of the drudgery," Mize told me. The shift in his expectations was predictable, since without exception the thinner a person is, the better he runs.

Having spoken with any number of runners whose experiences parallel those of Linnell and Mize, I wanted, in the present book, to try to demonstrate the often overlooked relationship between diet and dieting. I also wanted to be much more specific about what to eat and not eat. In a study of running this seemed particularly appropriate. For reasons not fully understood, running provides at least a partial refuge from contemporary dietary pressures that make it difficult to eat wisely and sparingly. The same 1979 Harris survey mentioned in Chapter 1 showed that, once having taken up running, people tend to eat more fruit, green vegetables, wholewheat products and other healthful foods. On the other hand, increased consumption of salt, beer, hard liquor and junk foods is uncommon.

That the dietary pressures on us are well known makes them no less difficult to resist. From infancy most of us were unwittingly guided toward obesity and poor nutrition. Babyfood manufacturers added unneeded salt and sugar to their products, thereby accustoming us to using too much of those substances. The typical school served lunches that contained too many calories and too much fat. Dairy interests encouraged us to use products made of high-fat whole milk. A recent survey of 21,000 boys and girls aged twelve to fourteen showed that as much as 60 percent of their diets consisted of fat, compared with the 30 percent recommended in 1977 by the U.S. Senate's Select Committee on Nutrition and Human Needs. Is it any wonder that one in five of the youngsters was overweight?

As adults, we don't do much to amend our childhood habits. Most of our meals are too rich, a throwback, perhaps, to earlier periods of poverty when only the wealthy ate juicy red meat, heavy cream and the like. Moreover, Americans currently eat about one-third of their meals in fast-food restaurants, which emphasize high-calorie meats and deep-fried foods at the expense of more healthful fruits and vegetables, and it has been estimated that within the next fifteen years half of all our meals will be eaten in such restaurants. The following sampling of the caloric content of various fast foods, as itemized in *Physical Fitness: A Way of Life* by Bud Getchell, suggests one reason our dietary practices are hardly consistent with staying thin:

Burger King Whopper	606
Colonel Sanders' three-piece special	660
McDonald's Big Mac	557
McDonald's Quarter Pounder	414
Pizza Hut ten-inch pizza	880–980
Dairy Queen medium-sized cone	339
Dunkin' Donuts plain doughnut with hole	240
Baskin-Robbins sugar cone with one scoop	180–230
French fries, one serving	200
Milkshake, average size	300

A government survey a decade ago showed that the United States led the world in obesity. Matters have improved little since then. When researchers recently studied 13,600 Americans aged eighteen to seventy-four, they found that the average man weighed at least twenty pounds more than was desirable, while the average woman was at least fifteen pounds above her ideal weight. Part of the blame can be attributed to the height and weight charts prepared by life insurance companies. Almost without exception, these charts give "normal" weights that are several pounds above what the weight of a healthy man or woman should be. Furthermore, by encouraging the idea that normal people weigh more as they get older, they no doubt inhibit some of us from staying as thin as we could so easily be.

Other researchers have reported another disturbing fact, one reflecting a trend not even the complacently sedentary would want to applaud. Comparing figures obtained in 1959 with those gathered twenty years later, they found that the average man in his fifties was two and a half pounds heavier than his counterpart two decades ago, while the average man in his twenties was a full nine pounds heavier. Women in their early twenties were five pounds heavier than women of the same age in 1959. The one encouraging aspect of the study was that women thirty and older had shown consistent declines in weight during the twenty-year period.

Clearly, our customary living patterns constitute a powerful counterforce to the way runners ought to eat if they hope to perform well. True, Bill Rodgers, the most consistently fleet marathoner the world has ever known, has a reputation for being a prodigious consumer of junk foods, and Randy Thomas, a 2:11 marathoner, is said to revel in pizza, ice cream and chocolate candy and even to munch cupcakes during his classes at Boston University. It is nonetheless doubtful that either Rodgers or Thomas would urge their diets on others or argue that such foods are the key to their speed. It is more likely that such runners excel in spite of their diets, for research has consistently shown that good nutrition and staying thin correlate irrefutably with running well. Dr. Marvin Brooks, an assistant professor of clinical medicine at the University of California at San Francisco, has calculated that a 150-pound 3:30 marathoner might improve his time by some 21 minutes if he lost 15 pounds. The reason is that, health hazards aside, fat interferes with good running in at least three ways:

1. Fat is pure dead weight. To be eighteen pounds over-weight is exactly like carrying a case of beer along on every run.

2. Fat is insulation. It prevents the body from ridding itself of the heat that running creates. Retained by the body rather than dissipated into the surrounding air, excess heat slows you down and, not incidentally, increases the risk of heat exhaustion and heat stroke.

3. By lowering the body's efficiency in using oxygen, fat reduces the speed of which a runner is capable. Scientists measure the body's oxygen-processing ability in milliliters per kilogram of weight per minute. If, therefore, a 165-pound runner has an oxygen capacity of 60 milliliters per kilogram, he can increase his efficiency some 10 percent merely by losing 15 pounds.

Losing weight is never easy, but the task is less arduous if you understand a few elementary facts. The body of the average American man of college age consists of 15 percent fat, while that of the average woman of the same age is 25 percent fat. Top male distance runners average 6 to 8 percent fat, and top women runners average 8 to 12 percent. Although an occasional runner is even leaner, it is ordinarily a mistake to try to reduce beyond that point, since a certain amount of fat is needed for the proper functioning of the brain, nerves and other tissues. One reason that lowering your body's fat content, however slightly, invariably requires considerable willpower is that long-term overeating appears to condition the brain's hypothalamic satiety center to send hunger signals even when no physiological need for food exists. Another is that overweight men and women, according to recent studies, have not just bigger fat cells than other people but more of them. Even after such people have reduced their weight, therefore, the sheer number of their fat cells prompts a continuing hunger alarm. Like former alcoholics who never consider themselves finally cured, a man or woman, once overweight, is never totally free of his or her obesity. Dr. Joseph Arends, who was quoted in Chapter 4, uttered a profound truth when he recently told dieters: "It must be clearly understood that weight control is difficult and will continue to be difficult forever. It is a day-to-day war."

In addition to well-known dieting hazards such as the sheer availability of fattening foods, Arends cites four others that have ambushed more than one runner:

First, the fact that dehydration, particularly when water loss exceeds three or four pounds, increases not just thirst but also appetite. One theory is that the brain's thirst and appetite centers are so closely related that thirst and hunger are readily confused. The lesson is clear: When you're exercising, drink frequently.

Second, the fact that during the evening, when there may be little to draw our minds away from thoughts of food, we often think we're hungry when we're really not.

Third, the fact that, through a mechanism not yet fully understood, dog-tired fatigue often stimulates appetite. Thus runners who have wearied themselves by a sudden increase in training are particularly subject to overeating.

Fourth, our fixation on eating three full-size meals a day. Our three-meal pattern developed in an agrarian culture when a daily expenditure of 4,000 to 5,000 calories was common. Today, when most of us expend little energy at work, two meals, supplemented if necessary by low-calorie snacks, are plenty.

Whatever eating pattern you choose, staying thin is easiest if you avoid high-calorie foods as far as possible. In *Nutrition and the Athlete* Joseph J. Morella and Richard J. Turchetti list the number of minutes of running you have to do to metabolize common foods. It does not require a statistician to see the difference between, say, carrots and hamburgers:

Apple, large	5 minutes
Banana, small	4 minutes
Cake, layer, average-sized piece	18 minutes
Carrot, raw	2 minutes
Chicken, fried, ½ breast	12 minutes
Doughnut	8 minutes
Egg, fried	6 minutes
Egg, boiled	4 minutes
Malted milk	26 minutes

Milk, 1 glass	9 minutes
Milk, skim, 1 glass	4 minutes
Pizza, cheese, ⅛	9 minutes
Hamburger	18 minutes
Spaghetti, 1 serving	20 minutes
Strawberry shortcake	21 minutes

Exactly how thin is thin enough? Some authorities say a male runner should weigh two pounds for every inch of height. For the average runner, however, the most reliable way to determine your correct weight is to forget your bathroom scales, take off your clothes and simply look at yourself in a mirror. If your waist is at all puffy and the skin is not stretched tight across your chest, ribs and abdomen, you are fatter than you should be. If you want to be scientific about it, you can measure the thickness of your skin at various sites with calipers and, by consulting specially prepared tables, compute your percentage of body fat. An inexpensive instrument for this purpose is available from Health and Education Services, 2442 Irving Park Road, Chicago, IL 60618. The cost, including postage, is $9.95.

Thus far we have been discussing quantitative nutrition. What about quality? What, exactly, should we eat and not eat? As I write these words I have at hand a dozen or more volumes on nutrition, all of them reasonably describable as authoritative, plus a foot-thick pile of magazine articles, tear sheets from scientific journals, and documents from organizations whose purpose is to persuade us to drink more milk or eat more beef. All purport to be based on scientific research of one sort or another, yet the advice they offer is startlingly divergent. One book recommends that our diets consist of 15 percent protein, 30 percent fat and 55 percent carbohydrates; another urges markedly different proportions: 10–10–80. One book insists that runners should avoid caffeine, yet a respected researcher, as was seen in Chapter 5, recommends it before races. Most writers urge us not to touch alcohol, yet a well-known heart specialist praises the physiological benefits of beer. One doctor urges us to shun all vitamins, minerals and other dietary supplements; another recommends that runners take Vitamin C.

The chief reason for the variety of opinion is simple: no one, not even the most august nutritionists, knows everything there is to know about nutrition. Despite millennia of experimentation, no one is certain what human beings should eat. Within broad limits we know, of course, that we need some carbohydrates, some proteins, some fats and so forth. But we don't know how much. A few years ago four distinguished British nutritionists wrote in *Nature* magazine: "The energy requirements of man and his balance of intake and expenditure are not known." It is widely believed, they went on, that 70 percent of the world's population is undernourished, but it may just as easily be that 30 percent is eating too much. The ignorance cited by the British nutritionists is partly attributable to the fact that multi-generational human studies, unlike multi-generational animal studies, are difficult if not impossible. In cases where human volunteers have been used in nutritional studies, the experiments have occupied only a fraction of the subjects' expected life spans. It has thus been impossible to assess the long-term effects of varying diets.

The uncertainty surrounding human nutrition has given rise to all manner of myths. Americans have long been told, for example, that a good diet includes protein from both meat and dairy sources. In fact, however, there appears to be no such physiological requirement; protein from vegetable sources is, it appears, just as good for us. It is the same nutritional uncertainty that permits so many radical dietary theories to flourish. Dr. Albert Creff, chief nutritionist for the French Olympic teams, takes his fellow nutritionists to task for isolating single phenomena in the digestive process and building whole theories around them. Creff writes, "It has been seriously argued . . . , by men with medical degrees and other credentials, that because the human gut is quite long, like that of fruit-eating monkeys, human beings are therefore biologically fruit-eaters." In an earlier era it was nutritionists of the same pragmatic bent who argued that athletes who wanted to excel at the hurdles should eat kangaroo meat.

Less bizarre myths and theories also abound. Many runners, for example, believe extra vitamins and minerals are essential. Once or twice a week a pleasant and persistent gentleman telephones me to report on the racing successes of certain runners, all of whom, as it happens, regularly ingest bee pollen, said to contain sixteen vitamins, sixteen minerals, eighteen enzymes and eighteen amino acids. Is it mere coincidence that my caller is a bee-pollen distributor? (A young friend named Todd Benoit may have had the final word on the pollen question. Suggested Benoit: "Bee pollen won't make you run any faster, but you'll buzz while you're doing it.") While it was once thought that vitamins and other dietary supplements were useful, most doctors and nutritionists now believe that for most people, including athletes, they are worthless. In *Run for Your Life* Dr. Art Mollen writes, "Protein supplements and vitamins have their value for certain people, but they are unnecessary for most. If you exercise a great deal, then increased amounts of vitamin C can be beneficial. Iron is excellent during women's menstrual periods. But excessive amounts of vitamin dosages are equivocal: that is, they certainly do not harm you, but there is no evidence that they help you either." Dr. Elsworth R. Buskirk, director of Penn State's Noll Laboratory for Human Performance Research, agrees. "No requirement for extra vitamins appears to exist," he writes. Nor, for that matter, do athletes who eat a balanced diet need extra salt, no matter how much they sweat. In *The Sportsmedicine Book* Dr. Gabe Mirkin and Marshall Hoffman write: "Never take salt tablets! Let your taste buds tell you when to salt your food. If you are low on salt, you will crave salt. Salt tablets bypass your taste buds, which are nature's protection against eating too much salt."

There is even a question, despite Mirkin's observations on the usefulness of iron supplements, whether for most women they are necessary. Russell R. Pate, of the University of South Carolina's Human Performance Laboratory, and two other researchers reported recently that "there is no basis for recommending that all women athletes routinely ingest oral iron supplements." Rather, they suggest monitoring the iron levels of women athletes and administering extra iron only if a deficiency exists.

Some runners believe fasting is beneficial, chiefly because it reduces body weight and supposedly lets the system cleanse itself of impurities. Even if it did purge unwanted substances, however, its adverse effects might well outweigh any advantages. In fasting, blood acidity can become abnormal. Muscle and body organs can be broken down in the body's continuing search for glucose. Excessive amounts of minerals can be lost. Finally, glycogen supplies can be reduced below desirable levels. "A runner who flirts with fasting may be making a bad mistake," reports *Running Times*.

In a sport in which seconds may make the difference between success and failure, it is probably inevitable that participants will explore unlikely dietary byways in their search for speed and endurance. Recently such explorations have led increasing numbers of runners to include beer, mentioned a few paragraphs earlier, in their training regimens. The conventional wisdom is, of course, that expressed by Buskirk in *Sports Medicine:* "Alcohol deserves no consideration as a food to be consumed by athletes.... With consumption of fairly small amounts of alcohol, coordination, judgment and consequently performance are all impaired." At least two prominent runner-physicians, Dr. Thomas J. Bassler and Dr. George Sheehan, take issue with the conventional wisdom, arguing that beer, among its other alleged benefits, is an excellent electrolyte replacement. Not long ago Jeff Darman, who at the time was president of the Road Runners Club of America, offered a rebuttal to the views of Bassler and Sheehan. Said Darman:

> There is no scientific evidence that runners need to drink large amounts of alcohol to be successful.... It makes as much sense to say that, because Bill Rodgers used to smoke cigarettes, to be a good runner you should smoke for a year. So go ahead and drink beer if you want to, but don't try to rationalize that you do it because it is a great electrolyte replenisher or that it is necessary for good health.... Whatever benefits, if any, are in beer, in terms of aiding the metabolism, can no doubt be duplicated in other, nonalcoholic substances.

During competition I myself once received incalculable help

from beer. The race was the 1977 Thanksgiving Day 25-kilometer Turkey Trot in Poughkeepsie, New York. I had been pursuing a runner for ten or twelve miles and, unable to gain a yard, had despaired of catching him. Without warning he stepped off the road, rummaged in a pile of leaves, withdrew a can of beer he had apparently secreted there earlier, popped open the top, and stood drinking it as I passed. I never saw him again until he came across the finish line a minute or more after I had arrived.

Like alcohol, caffeine has long been thought to inhibit athletic performance. Wrote Buskirk in 1974: "Although caffeine ostensibly improves attention and alertness and delays fatigue, there is no known evidence that it improves the performance of athletes." Since then Dr. David L. Costill, director of the Human Performance Laboratory at Ball State University, has conducted experiments that suggest coffee before competition may increase the blood's concentration of free fatty acids and thus delay fatigue by helping to conserve the body's supply of stored carbohydrates. The Costill findings were reported so recently, however, that few if any other researchers have had time to confirm or refute them. Until we know more about the effects of coffee on runners, it would seem fairly safe to drink it in moderation but risky to rely on it for improving performances.

In sum, rather than experimenting with problematical adjustments that may or may not increase athletic ability, it is more sensible to eat a properly balanced diet in general. The same Select Committee on Nutrition and Human Needs whose findings were cited earlier recommended seven shifts in the American diet. All are as applicable to runners as to nonrunners. They are:

1. To avoid becoming overweight, consume only as many calories as you expend.

2. If you are already overweight, consume fewer calories than you expend and exercise more.

3. Eat more complex carbohydrates, such as fruits, vegetables and grains.

4. Limit consumption of refined and processed sugars to 10 percent of energy intake.

5. Limit consumption of fats to 30 percent of energy intake.

6. Reduce consumption of saturated fats such as those found in meats.

7. Reduce consumption of salt.

Following these rules may seem complicated to those unfamiliar with nutritional intricacies. One of the most readily understandable translations is that offered by Dr. John W. Farquhar in *The American Way of Life Need Not Be Hazardous to Your Health*. Farquhar, a cardiologist who directs Stanford University's Heart Disease Prevention Program, has devised a chart (see page 142) that divides foods into three types, those of high caloric density (Column 1), those of medium caloric density (Column 2) and those of low caloric density (Column 3). The chart is further divided into two subgroups, those foods currently common in the U.S. diet (top) and those recommended as improved substitutes (bottom). Farquhar recommends that, over a period of two or three years, we move down the chart toward foods low in saturated fats, cholesterol, salt and sugar, and if weight is a problem, to the right of the chart, toward foods of lower caloric density. For those who think such a dietary shift would be unsatisfying, Farquhar has an answer: "In my view, people only *think* that they eat what they like; in truth they eat what they have *learned* to like."

If we followed Farquhar's recommendations we would, it is clear, eat less meat and more vegetables. Is this an argument for vegetarianism? Perhaps. Studies have shown that vegetarians are leaner, have less cholesterol, and experience a lower rate of cardiovascular disease than nonvegetarians. It is, moreover, indisputable that many excellent runners, including Amby Burfoot, winner of the 1968 Boston Marathon, are vegetarians, while many others eat little meat. For what it may be worth, I find myself eating progressively less meat and neither miss it nor can discern any unpleasant effects.

Farquhar's chart does not prescribe precise proportions of protein, fat and carbohydrate, nor would such a prescription

EATING THE RIGHT WAY

Use Less of These Foods . . .

HIGH CALORIC DENSITY	MEDIUM CALORIC DENSITY	LOW CALORIC DENSITY
Commercial baked goods and cakes made from mixes (SF, C, Sa, Su)	Buttermilk (SF, C, Sa)	Bouillon (Sa)
Frankfurter (SF, C, Sa)	Egg yolk (SF, C)	Consommé (Sa)
Bacon (SF, C, Sa)	Whole milk (SF, C)	Canned vegetable juice (Sa)
Luncheon meat (SF, C, Sa)	Granolas with added salt and sugar (Sa, Su)	Most canned garden vegetables (Sa)
Ham, sausage (SF, C, Sa)	Shellfish (C)	A few frozen vegetables (peas, succotash, lima beans) (Sa)
Most regular cheeses (SF, C, Sa)	Turkey franks (Sa)	Pickles (Sa)
Ice cream, ice milk (SF, C, Su)	Roasting turkey injected with salt (Sa)	Sauerkraut (Sa)
Creamy peanut butter (SF, Sa)	Canned soups (Sa)	Melba toast (Sa)
Red meat (SF, C)	Canned corn, beans, or peas (Sa)	Salted popcorn (Sa)
Organ meat (SF, C)	Frozen fish (Sa)	
Butter (SF, C)	Canned tuna (Sa)	
Snack crackers (SF, Sa)	Biscuits, muffins, pancakes (Sa)	
Palm oil, coconut oil (SF)	Instant cereals (Sa)	
Hardened margarines (SF)	Dehydrated potatoes (Sa)	
Candy (Su)	All-Bran, bran flakes, corn-flakes (Sa)	
Fruit in heavy syrup (Su)	Soda crackers (Sa)	
Sherbet and frozen yogurt (Su)	Soft drinks (Su)	
Salted nuts (Sa)		
Potato chips and other chips (Sa)	*Low in fiber, but otherwise "heart healthy":*	
	White bread, English muffins	
	White rice	
	Spaghetti and other pasta made from white flour	
	Fruit juice without pulp	

. . . And More of These

All vegetable oils (*including* olive oil) except palm and coconut	Breads, lightly milled or whole-grain	Alfalfa sprouts and bean sprouts
Avocado	Brown rice	Artichokes
Honey	Canned fruit (no syrup)	Beets
Mayonnaise or salad dressing	Chicken without skin	Broccoli
Natural peanut butter (no salt)	Common potato and corn	Brussels sprouts
Sesame butter	Egg whites	Cabbage
Sesame seeds	Fresh fish	Carrots
Soft margarine	Fresh or dried fruit	Cauliflower
Sunflower seeds	Fruit juice with pulp	Celery
Unsalted nuts	Granolas without salt or sugar	Chard
	Legumes (beans, lentils, peas, soy beans, garbanzo beans)	Cucumbers
	Low-fat cottage cheese	Fresh vegetable juice
	Nonfat milk	Green beans
	Puffed rice	Lettuce
	Shredded wheat	Mushrooms
	Spaghetti and other pasta (from partial whole-wheat varieties)	Radishes
	Turkey	Spinach and other greens
	Yams and sweet potatoes	Squash
		Tomatoes and most other garden vegetables
		Most frozen vegetables

KEY: SF = saturated fat; C = cholesterol; Sa = salt; Su = sugar

Chart adapted from *The American Way of Life Need Not Be Hazardous to Your Health.*

be easy to arrive at with certainty. Although most nutritionists recommend proportions of 15–30–55 or thereabouts, one widely read authority, Nathan Pritikin, author of *The Pritikin Program for Diet and Exercise*, recommends a 10–10–80 mixture. If you have a cholesterol or weight problem, it would probably make sense to lean toward the Pritikin end of the scale by adopting a diet high in carbohydrates and low in proteins and fats.

Thus far we have been discussing diet in general, the foods to be eaten day in and day out. Before a race smart runners deviate from their customary diets by avoiding proteins and fats, both of which are digested slowly, and eating instead a high proportion of carbohydrates in order to supply the liver and muscles with as much glycogen as they can hold. In addition, runners subject to stomach cramps or diarrhea learn, often the hard way, to avoid fresh fruits, leafy vegetables and other foods high in roughage. If digestive upsets are a severe or persistent problem, a liquid diet for eighteen hours before a race will probably help. You may get hungry, but at least you'll be able to keep running.

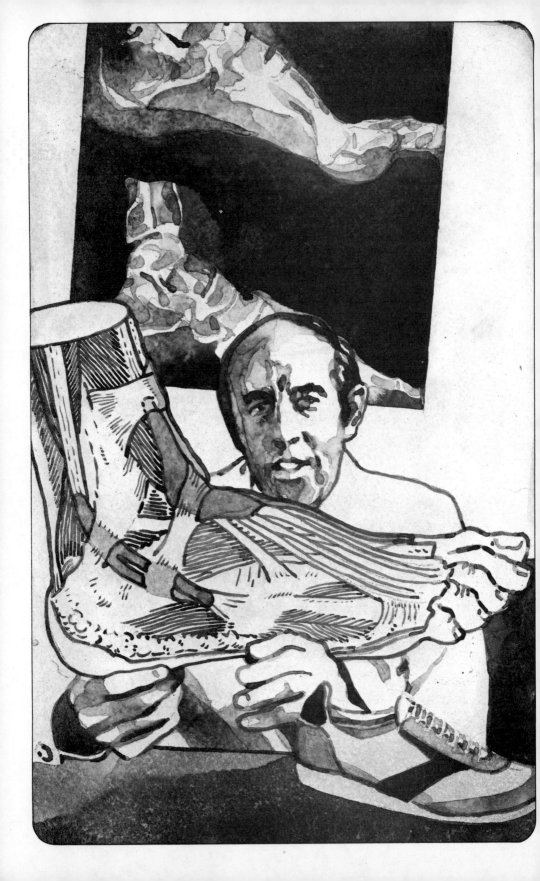

11

When Feet Fail

For Runners,
It's the Dawning of
the Age of Podiatry

Not long ago, while running in a 10,000-meter race, I felt a sudden sharp pain in the ball of my left foot. For some time I had been bothered by intermittent discomfort, but this was something else altogether. It was exactly as if, each time my foot landed on the pavement, an acetylene torch were applied to it. Nonetheless I finished the race, certain that as soon as I stopped running the pain would stop. To my surprise, it did not. On the contrary, even when I walked as gingerly as I could, the acetylene torch continued to blaze away at the ball of my foot. Further running was out of the question.

It was then that I reluctantly decided to see a doctor. Until that time I had been lucky. Other than shin splints a decade or more earlier, a mercifully brief bout of Achilles tendinitis and an occasional blister, I'd had no injuries worth mentioning.

Nor, physiologically fortunate as I had been, had I missed more than a dozen or so running days during the preceding five or six years. Now, I told myself, both I and my running record were in trouble. Any doctor was sure to tell me not to run until whatever had gone wrong with my foot healed.

A runner friend recommended a local podiatrist, or foot doctor, and I limped to his office. He studied the painful spot. "It's only a callus," he said finally, "but it's a bad one. You don't usually see this sort of callus except perhaps on workmen who spend all day standing on hot tar." The podiatrist said he would try to relieve the pain by shaving the callus down with a scalpel, a quick, painless procedure. With my foot raised and a bright lamp shining on it, he began to whittle away. I felt like Pinocchio.

As he worked he asked me, "How did you get this callus?"

I told him it came from running.

He smiled knowingly. "That puts a different light on your problem," he said. "I had planned to do this procedure in such a way that you'd have to baby the foot for several days. But I know you runners too well. You're like ballet dancers. I could tell you not to run for a week, and fifteen minutes after you were out of my office you'd be on the roads again."

He finished carving, applied moleskin and taped the foot. That afternoon, on a day when the possibility of running had been as remote from my mind as being chosen for the Olympic marathon team, I ran three miles.

More significantly, however, I had my introduction that day to a new breed of doctor, one who understands that for a runner to be told he can't run is to be offered an appalling and unreasonable form of medical treatment.

In increasing numbers, podiatrists understand that. Although there are fewer than 10,000 in the United States, one for perhaps every 2,500 runners, they have rapidly become our most indispensable medical specialists. Almost every world-class runner, including Bill Rodgers, has consulted one.

Podiatrists have, in fact, become so trendy that some of their names are as celebrated as those of top athletes. Among runners, California's Steven I. Subotnick, John Pagliano and Harry F. Hlavac, New York's Richard O. Schuster and Boston's Rob Roy McGregor are as well known as Rodgers, Bjorklund, Virgin and Wells. Subotnick and Hlavac have written books on feet and the misfortunes that befall them. McGregor is currently at work on one and also regularly discusses physical fitness on a Boston television program. Schuster is so heavily booked that when one ailing runner sought to make an appointment with him he was told he might have to wait as long as two months. The public appetite for podiatry these days is all but insatiable.

It was not always so. The modern podiatrist, or doctor of podiatric medicine, traces his lineage back to the chiropodists of the mid-nineteenth century, healers who made arch supports, treated corns and calluses, and knew how to look convincingly sympathetic when ladies in tight shoes complained that their feet felt terrible. Following World War II, in a quest for greater etymological purity, chiropodists decided they preferred to be called podiatrists, but neither that change nor the steady increase in professional standards did much to bring widespread glory. In ordinary circumstances the foot is, after all, not one of the human body's more glamorous appendages.

Podiatrists finally began to come into their own when two related events occurred. First, the early wavelets of the running tide began to lap at America, creating a vast army of people worried about their feet. Second, an iconoclastic New Jersey cardiologist named George Sheehan took to arguing in his *Runner's World* column that most conventional doctors, including orthopedic surgeons, don't treat runners as artfully as a good podiatrist does. The two concurrent developments, fanned by a flair for self-dramatization and vivid public relations on the part of a few entrepreneurial podiatrists, were enough to create the boom.

In principle, what podiatrists do is easily described. As doctors specializing in feet, they are licensed to do practically everything except amputations. They can reconstruct deformities, do plastic surgery, devise corrective shoes, prescribe medicines and physical therapy, and relieve biomechanical problems by using shoe inserts called orthotics. It is the latter function that they most often—some insist far too often— perform for runners.

An orthotic looks much like a conventional arch support. Depending on which podiatrist it comes from and what its purpose is, it can be thick or thin, short or long, and made of rigid plastic, leather and rubber, or some other material. Orthotics do not correct foot abnormalities; they compensate for them by persuading the proper part of the foot to bear weight in the correct sequence. If, for example, because of a congenitally short Achilles tendon a runner characteristically lands on some part of the foot other than the heel, a simple lift might be enough. Many problems treated by podiatrists are not, however, that simple. For this reason it is often necessary to fit the bottom of an orthotic with raised surfaces, called posts, that place the foot in correct sequential relationship to the ground as it moves through its gait.

Uncomplicated in theory, positioning such posts can be awesomely complex. Each foot is, after all, a formidable mechanism consisting of 26 bones, 107 ligaments and 19 muscles, plus, just to confound nature's symmetry, an occasional supernumerary bone for good measure or bad. Furthermore, the foot does not perform a single function but a whole array, ranging from going as floppy as a Raggedy Ann doll when it first strikes the ground to becoming as rigid as a crowbar when the toes finally push off. Analyzing exactly how your feet or mine behave when we run may become slightly more scientific as a result of a new $3,500 instrument called Footprint, which uses pressure transducers to describe a foot's weight-bearing characteristics, but devising an effective orthotic is nonetheless likely to remain as much an art as a science.

Orthotics, which can cost less than $50 and as much as several hundred dollars, are currently much in vogue. In at least one sense it is a curious vogue because, as Charles Steinmetz, a knowledgeable runner-physician, recently observed, orthotics technology does not yet match the strength of the running explosion. Most orthotics are too heavy. Many are too cumbersome. Leather doesn't hold up well. Plastic breaks. Under the repeated pressure of running, surface cushioning slips across the underlying structure. "The materials leave a lot to be desired," Steinmetz told me.

Despite the drawbacks, many runners view orthotics almost as talismans. Bob Hensley, a 2:16 marathoner, uses them even though he is convinced that the ones he owns don't perform any identifiable function. "I'm just used to them," he said when I asked why he wore them. Orthotics do, however, bring relief in many cases. Furthermore, they do so not just with foot problems but often with problems as far afield as the knee, hip and back. The reason, as podiatrists explain it, is that imbalances in the feet are likely to radiate throughout the body, much as an earthquake's shock waves are detectable far from its epicenter. One doctor familiar with athletes' problems flatly advised a runner, "Accept no treatment directed at the knee."

It is probably inevitable, given their emergence as virtual cult figures, that podiatrists should currently be receiving their share of criticism. Fred Lebow, president of the 15,000-member New York Road Runners Club, has spoken out against overcharging by podiatrists who have suddenly found their services in uncharacteristically high demand; some in the New York City area, he said, ask as much as $400 for examination, treatment and construction of orthotics. Orthopedic surgeons, medical doctors whose purview includes the biomechanics of the feet and legs, have not typically been overgenerous in their praise of podiatrists, whom they are inclined to look on as upstart rivals. And many runners themselves wonder whether all the orthotics being prescribed today are really necessary. At least one podiatrist, Rob Roy McGregor, wonders, too. "There's a good basis for the suspicion that too many orthotics are being prescribed," he told me. "For knee problems a doctor will recommend exercises to strengthen the muscles. But by tradition problems of the feet have been managed with a mechanical device, anything from a special shoe to a pad in the shoe to an orthotic. Why should the foot and ankle joints be treated differently from the knee joint? You can be sure there are a lot of unnecessary orthotics being worn today."

McGregor, a graduate of the Temple University School of Podiatric Medicine, is an associate in orthopedics at the University of Massachusetts medical school and staff podiatrist at Sports Medicine Resource, Inc., a group of twelve Boston doctors who banded together in 1977 in an effort to offer, under one roof, all the medical services an athlete was likely to need. McGregor has a face that has been described, more or less accurately, as turtlelike, and a sense of humor that is describable, with complete accuracy, as puckish. Passing an acquaintance in the twenty-second mile of the 1979 Mardi Gras Marathon, he deadpanned, "Do you experience a lot of pain running with such an ungainly style?" Because McGregor is currently one of the nation's half-dozen or so best-known podiatrists, has a solid reputation among runners and other athletes, and holds views about sportsmedicine that have attracted considerable attention, I decided to visit him at his office in Boston.

Sports Medicine Resource is on Boylston Street in Chestnut Hill, a suburban enclave of proper Bostonians. The building that houses it is set well back from the road and has a broad, sloping lawn. In the lobby are several large posters depicting athletes in action. On the day I stopped by, McGregor was wearing chinos, a yellow sweater and a pair of orange-and-blue Etonic Stabilizers, a running shoe that, as a consultant to the manufacturer, he helped design.

McGregor is exuberant and articulate, and in the best tradition of New England characters he enjoys sounding both quirky and, if he can manage it, shocking. "If you're getting along without pain, no matter how bad your feet look, that's fine," he says. "I don't want to see you. And even if you do develop pain I am going to argue, long and fervently, that you should experiment on yourself first. I'm not opposed to people doctoring their own feet any more than I am to their tuning their own engines."

He examines a patient, Susan Williams, thirty years old,

who has driven four and a half hours from Colchester, Vermont, to see him. Leaning against a windowsill at the end of a hallway, he watches her as she walks. "Look at that!" he says with utter fascination. "Bing-*bang*, bing-*bang*, bing-*bang*." I see nothing unusual. McGregor, however, is mesmerized. He takes Ms. Williams to an examining room and has her lie first on her stomach and then on her back. Without warning he seizes her by the feet and shakes her as if he were getting ready to pitch a sack of potatoes out of a barn door. "To measure strength, flexibility and the ranges of motion of joints," he explains. When he finally stops, although her hair has fallen somewhat awry, she looks wonderfully relaxed. "As soon as you get home," he tells her, "I want you to send me a left running shoe. Right away. I'm going to put a lift in it. Send it immediately."

A thirty-two-year-old lawyer, Roger E. Hughes, of Norwell, Massachusetts, comes in. He tells McGregor he has had pain in his left arch for ten weeks; he developed it when, having just been elected town moderator, he celebrated by leaping too vigorously from a curb. McGregor watches him walk, shakes him much as he had Ms. Williams, and listens gravely as Hughes says he has tried everything he could think of, including a heel cup.

"That's what I want to hear!" McGregor exults. "I want you to experiment! Try anything! If that doesn't work, try something else! Don't come to me until you can't think of anything else to do."

He tapes Hughes's foot. "A lot of problems," he tells me, "will go away by themselves. Most people don't need orthotics. Thirty percent of the people only need stretching exercises. I give orthotics to maybe 30 or 40 percent of my patients. The only reason it's that high is that so many of them these days are runners."

McGregor sees two more patients, a thirty-three-year-old woman named Jacqueline Lindsay who runs five miles a day and has a pain in her left heel, and Jackie Patterson, a twenty-three-year-old dance teacher who developed pain in his arch while doing stretching exercises. He prescribes orthotics for neither. He does, however, crack the same joke with both, a play on the words *body* and *bawdy*, which because of his Boston accent sound identical. Neither Patterson nor Ms. Lindsay laughs very heartily, or for that matter seems to understand quite what McGregor is getting at.

"The patient buys my services," McGregor explains later as we sit in his office. "He doesn't buy an orthotic. I charge forty dollars for soft orthotics, eighty dollars for rigid ones. That's exactly what they cost me, so there's no profit and no temptation to prescribe them needlessly. Where orthotics are concerned, what we've tried to do is eliminate the human factor. If I see a way to make a buck I may want to make a buck. What would happen if Blue Shield didn't pay so well for some surgical procedures? Would you see as many of them done?"

I ask McGregor if there is any way a runner can tell when he needs orthotics. He launches into an imaginary conversation:

"I have a short leg, Doctor. Should I put something under it?"

"Not until you need to."

"Well, how will I know if I need to?"

"You'll hurt."

McGregor, who seems genuinely pleased to prescribe as unelaborately as possible, insists on preserving the distinction between findings and symptoms. "If you're getting along without orthotics," he tells me, "regardless of the findings, that's great. Johnny Kelley has bunions and he's run almost fifty Boston Marathons. You shouldn't use orthotics unless you start hurting. Anyone who says we can prevent problems hasn't lived long enough. We don't know if we're going to prevent a damn thing."

Many runners, he goes on, find their way to podiatrists' offices when time alone would heal them. He says medical help should be sought only when at least two of the following four symptoms are present:

1. Redness
2. Swelling
3. Pain
4. Heat

"There's only one type of patient I know I can't help," says McGregor. "That's the person with the high-impact foot, the foot that doesn't roll in. The rigid foot can't dissipate shock. That's the guy who grinds his joints to dust, who will need a hip replacement when he's sixty. There's nothing I can do for him except send him to Tahiti and tell him to walk on the sand."

McGregor leans back in his chair and muses about the direction sportsmedicine is taking. "Marathons and long-distance running aren't for everyone," he tells me, "any more than tennis or skiing is. The better a person understands his own body and the demands a given sport puts on it, the better he can cope not just with physical problems but also with the medical community, which needs to catch up to such an approach. My sense is that medicine in the 1980s must inevitably move toward self-understanding and self-care."

Sooner or later most runners discover that McGregor's point about self-care is both sound and thrifty. Many have found relief by using nothing more complicated than a pair of Dr. Scholl's arch supports bought for $4 at a drugstore. Others have found that simply losing ten pounds lessens jarring and strain. Neil M. Scheffler, an Arbutus, Maryland, podiatrist, told me, "For many of my patients who have foot pathology and obesity, I have suggested weight reduction programs." In cases of Achilles tendinitis, a simple quarter-inch heel lift may relax the tendon enough to let healing start.

Some runners, feeling that podiatry has recently become steeped in an excess of hyperbole and hocus-pocus, continue to experiment on their own, hoping that hit-or-miss methods will eventually lead them to a solution. Often, of course, it does. But sometimes it does not. This is when podiatry can seem a kind of miracle. In Florida recently, I talked with an active seventy-two-year-old woman who suffered from Morton's neuroma, a painful but benign nerve tumor, and had been told that surgery was the only answer. Why not, a friend suggested, try a podiatrist first? After all, she had nothing to lose. Acting on the suggestion, she visited Michael H. Katz, D.P.M., in nearby Venice. Katz made two recommendations:

1) give up street shoes and wear only sandals or New Balance running shoes, which are softer and more flexible than many others and lace farther from the toes, and 2) use orthotics. When I talked with her recently she was free of pain for the first time in a year. Similarly free of pain were two of McGregor's four patients whom, without telling him I was going to do so, I managed to track down for progress reports. One of them, Roger Hughes, told me, "I can't believe that what McGregor did took away the pain. It's amazing. I can't understand it."

12

Beyond the Marathon

When 26.2 Miles Is Only the Beginning

*I*t is a gray October dawn. A cold northwest breeze blows down from the Irish Sea, roughening the face of the Thames into oily cat's paws. Not far from Big Ben, ninety-six men shiver under the bemused eye of a helmeted London bobbie. At the first toll of seven o'clock they break into a run and head methodically across Westminster Bridge, bound for far-off Brighton, an English Channel resort some 53½ miles to the south. Five hours and thirteen minutes later Don Ritchie, a formidably fleet Scotsman with a red beard, heaves himself across the finish line. He is followed at intervals by seventy-three other competitors in various states of distress and bedragglement. The whereabouts of the missing twenty-two has never been officially ascertained, though it is presumed that in one way or another they all made their way home.

Surveying the human wreckage at Brighton, one observer declared such races "a lunatic hobby." Perhaps. Nonetheless, the lunatics have been coming out in force for some thirty years now, lured by the optimistic hope of proving that the human body can accomplish what any sane person knows it ought not to be able to accomplish. Nor is the London-to-Brighton race the oddity it might seem. Every May in South Africa a 56-mile race, the Comrades Marathon, snakes its hilly way between Pietermaritzburg and Durban. And in the United States there are so many 50-mile, 100-kilometer, twenty-four-hour and 100-mile races that the mind winces just contemplating the agonies they visit on those who are drawn to enter them.

Such ultramarathons, as runs longer than 26.2 miles are called, can be traced to ancient Greece, where specially trained foot couriers called *hemerodromoi* routinely covered distances that are impressive even by today's standards. Plutarch, for example, mentions one such courier who not only ran nearly 300 miles but carried a lighted torch much of the way. The modern revival of long-distance running began in the 1880s when an Englishman named Charles Rowell stayed on the move for five full days. Thereafter, such feats became all but routine. In 1927, at the age of forty-five, another Englishman, Arthur Newton, set a 100-mile record of fourteen hours and forty-three minutes, and two years later ran 152⅓ miles in twenty-four hours, a record that endured for twenty-two years. An athlete named Al Monteverdi ran the 96 miles between Milwaukee and Chicago in fourteen hours and fifty minutes. A twenty-two-year-old Londoner, Peter Gavuzzi, ran from New York to Los Angeles in seventy-eight days and won $10,000 for the feat, but discovered that because of the promoter's tax problems his check was worthless. In the years since Gavuzzi's achievement so many other people have made transcontinental runs that even the running press scarcely bothers to mention them any more.

Ted Corbitt, the former Olympian, probably knows as much about ultramarathons as anyone alive. He not only points out that we are in the midst of an explosion of such races but predicts that the trend will continue. "Many marathoners finish a race and have too much left," he says, "so they speculate about how much farther they could have run."

Ultramarathoning has been helped along by the increasing amounts of spare time most of us have. The reason is that, if you plan to train for 50- or 100-mile races, time is the vital ingredient. Max White, a Philadelphia schoolteacher who in 1973 set a London-to-Brighton record for Americans, routinely runs 120 miles a week and adds an extra 30 miles during vacations. Don Choi, a San Francisco mailman who has covered 62 miles in seven hours and forty minutes, runs his entire delivery route carrying a heavy mail sack. And Ted Corbitt, when in serious ultramarathon training, has on more than one occasion started running at dawn and not come home till suppertime.

Why do people like Corbitt do what they do? Certainly in the ordinary 26.2-mile marathon can be found challenge and suffering aplenty for any but a certifiably masochistic competitor. Yet runners by the thousands enter ultramarathons, not just once but repeatedly. Nor are these runners necessarily the haunted, driven souls you might expect. Some, in fact, are very much like you and me.

Consider Dr. Charles Steinmetz, who was mentioned in the preceding chapter. Until recently he ran mostly races of ten miles or less, with an occasional marathon like Boston or New York City thrown in as a treat. Then one day curiosity got the better of him and he entered a 50-kilometer (31-mile) race. Before long Steinmetz, who is in his early fifties, was an ultramarathoner. Recently he ran a 50-mile race one weekend, a 100-kilometer (62-mile) race a few Saturdays later, and, as a warmdown, a marathon the next day. He described one of his races as "a blur of pain and fatigue" but told me he plans to persist at ultramarathoning. "I like finding out what my body can do," he said.

These days more and more runners are searching out the limits of their physical abilities. "Ultra runners," writes Jim Shapiro in *On the Road: The Marathon*, "are the cutting edge that extends the ordinarily accepted boundary of human endurance."

For example, Max Telford, a New Zealand runner, covered the 5,198 miles from Anchorage to Halifax in 106 days, an improbable average of 49 miles every twenty-four hours. Though thwarted by Moscow's bureaucracy from running across the Soviet Union as he had hoped to, he was undiscouraged. When I talked with him not long ago during a workout in Auckland's Cornwall Park, he was cheerfully trying to arrange a run along the entire 2,000-mile length of the Great Wall of China.

Bruce Tulloh, an English runner and author, averaged 44 miles a day in covering the 3,200 miles between Los Angeles and New York.

If runs like that seem excessively ambitious, there's always the more modest Western States 100-Mile Endurance Run, held each June in California's Sierra Nevada. Contestants traverse terrain ranging from craggy trails to river bottoms to punishing highway pavement. Anything under twenty-four hours is considered an excellent performance, and you are an oddity if you aren't sobbing and mumbling to yourself by the time you reach the finish line.

In almost every part of the world today, there are plenty of 50-kilometer, 40-mile, 50-mile, 100-kilometer and 100-mile races. How to train for such events has recently been the subject of considerable debate, largely because their popularity is so new that not much lore has been amassed. Some participants insist that gruelingly long training runs are required, while others argue that routine marathon training is enough. I talked recently with an ultramarathoner in his early thirties who takes a comfortable middle ground. He is a real estate salesman named Paul Fetscher, and when we spoke he was on the eve of his thirteenth ultramarathon, a 100-miler. Fetscher, who has won 40-mile and 50-kilometer races and has placed creditably in others, customarily trains 100 miles a week, or slightly more, and does not bother to increase the distance when preparing for an ultramarathon. "I don't think you can get in much better shape than a hundred miles a week will give you," he told me. "The only thing running farther will do is to get your head right by giving you the confidence to run for a long time."

A typical training week for Fetscher looks like this:

Sunday: A ten-kilometer race, preceded by a two-mile warmup and followed by a two-mile cool-down. Four more miles in the afternoon.

Monday: Eight miles in the morning, four in the afternoon, both slowly.

Tuesday: Six moderately hard miles in the morning, eight to ten miles slowly in the afternoon.

Wednesday: Six moderately hard miles in the morning, eleven or twelve miles slowly in the afternoon.

Thursday: Six miles slowly in the morning, eight to ten hard miles in the afternoon.

Friday: Six hard miles in the morning, ten slowly in the afternoon.

Saturday: Thirteen to fifteen miles slowly in the morning, followed by an optional four to six miles in the afternoon. If, however, he is planning to run an important race the following day, Fetscher runs only six miles. Furthermore, he does it in the morning in order to put as much time as possible between his training run and the race.

Should he be planning to run an ultramarathon, Fetscher typically rests by running only sixty or seventy miles during the preceding week, most of it packed into the first four days. Three days before the race he runs six or eight miles, two days before the race six miles, and the day before the race only four or five miles.

As for the race itself, Fetscher, like most ultramarathoners, insists that mental preparation is the most important factor. "When your blood sugar gets low," he told me, "you're going to feel depressed. If you don't have a very convincing reason for being out there, you're just going to quit." Fetscher's view of the motivation problem derives scientific support from a study conducted not long ago by George L. Parrott, Jim Mansoor and Abe Underwood. They found that the second most reliable predictor of running time in a fifty-mile race, after one's best marathon time, is the time in which one expects to finish the race.

Ultramarathoners point out that their races are not merely extra-long marathons but unique ordeals that must be run in an entirely different spirit. "In a marathon," says Fetscher, "I'll go out and run hard from the very start, red-lining it all the way. But in an ultramarathon it's important to start out with a very laid-back attitude. The main thing is to plan to keep moving. What usually counts is who's most determined at the end. A lot of ultramarathons have been won by some guy who can just keep banging out eight-minute miles no matter how bad he's hurting."

For you, as for me, a mere 26.2-mile marathon may offer all the challenge and agony we need for the time being. But isn't it cheering to know there's more awaiting us if we should ever decide to find out what we're really made of? After all, if you're a mountain climber a day hike may be pleasant enough. Still, it's nice to know Everest is there, too.

13

Running Away

*Faraway Places
Give the Sport a
Special Zest*

Addled and fatigued by jet lag, I was pushing myself through a ploddingly dutiful ten-mile run beside the race track at Ascot, a town thirty miles southwest of London. It was sunrise. I had arrived in England only the day before, so as far as my body knew it was still midnight, not exactly its favorite time for vigorous exertions. Nonetheless, having scheduled a full day of appointments, I could be sure of squeezing in a run only at this hour. Coming over a rise in the thicketed terrain near the track, I saw a man in tweeds striding briskly along as he exercised a hunting dog. We drew closer to each other and he heartily called out, "Good morning! Are you training for the Olympics?" The day's weary sourness vanished. My unknown companion had conferred on me a distinction, no matter how spurious, that miraculously lifted my spirits. Feeling light and strong, I flew through the remaining miles of the run in strange, irrational joy. We were, of course, both utterly mad, he for imagining me an Olympic athlete, I for seizing at his improbable suggestion. But what did a little madness matter so long as it cheered the day for both of us? There are worse ways of feeling wonderful than by momentarily playing catch as catch can with reality.

What happened that morning was less an event than a brief frolic of the imagination. Yet for all its insubstantiality, it illustrates one quite palpable aspect of running while we are away from home: we never know what will happen. Over the past dozen years I have run the equivalent of once around the equator and then halfway around again. Most of my running has been on the roads and paths near my home, but much of it has been in places I had never before seen. For the best of reasons, three such places stand out most prominently in my mind. This chapter offers some notes on the qualities of each that continue to tug at my memory. Sometimes, I am prepared to argue, insubstantiality is as real as anything that exists.

Hawaii: Adrift in Aloha Land

From almost anywhere in Honolulu the wooded cone of Diamond Head, climbing 761 precipitous feet from the Pacific's edge into the unnaturally blue Hawaiian sky, is a mesmerizing presence. Although the final wisps of smoke rose from its crater farther back than human memory reaches, it continues to radiate power, like a great beast asleep. I was walking one day along a noisy Waikiki street, feeling as mauled by urban America as if I had been in Detroit or Chicago, when I turned a corner and suddenly caught sight of Diamond Head's gray-green hulk, hovering in majesty and menace just beyond the city. It was as startling as if, visiting Manhattan, I had gazed on King Kong.

During my first couple of days in Hawaii I kept a respectful distance from Diamond Head. Several times, it is true, I drove past in a rented car, and once or twice my runs took me not far from its base. But nothing more. I'm a sensible fellow. I would no more have thought of assaulting its formidable presence in only nylon shorts and running shoes than I would contemplate trying to jog up the façade of the World Trade Center.

Then, unbidden, so far as I could tell, a vagrant notion took root in my brain. I would try to run to the summit of Diamond Head. I have no idea why. Perhaps it was simply that the great cone was there, and that that, to my jet-befuddled brain, was reason enough.

The next morning I laced on my running shoes and ran east along a thoroughfare called Monsarrat, which meanders gently upward, flirting with the north wall of Diamond Head. Soon a blacktop road branched away, turning more steeply uphill. Following it, I found myself in a few minutes on the face of the cone. The road was steep, even for a runner accustomed to New England's hills. Suddenly, to my surprise, a tunnel appeared, wide enough for two automobile lanes. Inside, a cool wind whined. I ran through it and found sunlight again. There was no mistaking where I was. This was the crater itself, its mile-wide floor an improbably Oz-green lawn of grass and shrubbery that was alive with doves and white-tailed shore birds.

Diamond Head's rim lay above. In windless heat I clambered upward along a trail of flaked lava, moving across the crater's west wall. Finally, breathing hard, I stumbled over the top. Below me was all Honolulu, its concrete high-rises glowing in sand-white miniature in the sun. To my left a school of surfers carved calligraphy into the azure Pacific's surface. To the right the heart of Honolulu slept in mysterious silence, too far away to make a sound.

Sprawled on the rim's thin edge, resting, I thought what an excellent and appropriate way this was to spend a few minutes of a Hawaiian morning. For it was already plain that this was one of the half-dozen or so most spectacular runs I had ever taken. What better place to celebrate it than here, looking

down on the principal city of a state whose runners, per cap-
ita, far outnumber those of any other, and whose running
vistas have no rival anywhere?

Part of Hawaii's distinction among runners, I knew, is quite
accidental, a happenstance of geography and climate. Part,
however, is entirely man-made, the product of guile and diligent goading, calculated to suggest that making running the
cornerstone of your life is not the aberration a sedentary skeptic might so easily imagine it to be.

Hawaii's natural appeal for runners is described easily
enough. Temperatures are kindly the year around, rarely
straying from the 70s and 80s. Topography offers anything a
runner could want, from table-flat Waikiki to the unforgiving
Mount Tantalus route favored by serious competitors. And,
should you overheat on a run, a good beach is seldom more
than a few yards away; there are fifty on Oahu alone. One day,
near the island's northern bulge, I felt hot. Seeing a surf-
washed strip of sand just off Route 72, I plunged in and stayed
until I was restored. It was only later, when I consulted a
guidebook, that I discovered the venue of my dip to have been
Sunset Beach, officially classified, because of its frequently severe waves, as "dangerous."

Hawaii's salubrious natural benefits are scarcely enough,
however, to account for the irrepressible exuberance of the
running phenomenon as it manifests itself there. One
morning, my biorhythms still askew from a flight across five
time zones, I awoke at three. Restless, I dressed for running,
slipped quietly from my room, and headed for Waikiki's Kapiolani Park, supposing at that hour I would have the place to
myself. It was then that my education into the ways of Hawaii's runners began in earnest, for I came upon so many of
them that by comparison Central Park on a summer weekend
is like Death Valley.

Later that day, a copy of the *Honolulu Advertiser* having
been slipped under my door, I turned to the sports pages.
Though the baseball season was in full cry, here in the islands
you would have thought running was the only sport worth
mentioning. One story reported the imminent start of a clutch

of jogging clinics. Another described a YMCA seminar on something called "Beyond Jogging," intended to teach runners, for what reason I cannot guess, such skills as "structural patterning, visualization, energy awareness and concentration." There is, in fact, so much running going on in Hawaii that one property owner, impatient with the sweating platoons of exercisers that regularly jounced along an adjacent hiking trail, erected an official-looking sign reading "Beware of the Bears." It had little effect.

Had the hapless property owner been disposed to assign blame, he could have laid much of it at the feet of two Honolulu cardiologists, Jack H. Scaff, Jr., and John O. Wagner. Nearly a decade ago, long before such innovations were medically fashionable, Scaff and Wagner started experimenting with the rehabilitation of cardiac patients through running. Discovering that perhaps 90 percent of men and women who have suffered heart attacks can be coaxed back to full health by a sensibly prescribed exercise program, they began to attract modest local notice. Not long afterward, when the idea of holding a marathon in Honolulu first came up, they gave birth to an innovation that was to help transform Hawaiian running into something never before witnessed anywhere.

Called the Honolulu Marathon Clinic, it was a nine-month training program that would, if scrupulously followed, turn the most sedentary mound of human flab into a full-fledged marathon runner in time for the 26.2-mile race the following December. That promise was enough. In its first six years the number of entrants in the Honolulu Marathon multiplied by forty-three-fold.

In retrospect, the reason is clear. Scaff's and Wagner's program stresses the fun and the social pleasures of running, not just the health benefits. "There's no better way to meet people," Scaff told me when I dropped by his office one afternoon. "Look at all the unattached men and women who run in Kapiolani Park. Believe me, there's a lot of action there." He cited the case of one couple who met in the park one day. They showed up to run, got to talking, liked each other, and simply, in Scaff's words, "disappeared into the woods."

Even a dedicated nonrunner could scarcely fail to notice running's impact on Hawaii. On my way in from the airport I saw swarms of lithe, sun-bronzed runners in Ala Moana Park and thought it some special gathering place. It was only later that I came to realize that everywhere is a special gathering place. There is, in fact, hardly a patch of sand on the islands that is not imprinted with the distinctive sole marks of Adidases and Nikes.

One day, while running in Kahala, a quietly elegant beach-front community that numbers Clare Boothe Luce and Doris Duke among its residents, I met two young nurses, Marie Pine and Ann Marie Daunt, out training for a marathon. As we ran they told me about their running club, S.A.T., which formed almost by accident after several puzzled women asked Mark Cockrill, the proprietor of a sporting goods store, if it would be possible for them to complete a 10,000-meter race. Cockrill, an obliging sort, offered to coach them. Before long they were meeting early on Saturday mornings and had christened their group, fittingly enough, Saturday at the Track. Soon a few members took to running full-length marathons, and eventually eight S.A.T. runners entered the Hilo Marathon, on the nearby island of Hawaii. To Cockrill's and their own delight, seven posted their best performances ever, averaging twenty-seven minutes faster than they had ever before covered a marathon course.

Another day, on a popular 4.8-mile loop encircling Diamond Head, I met a forty-eight-year-old runner named Al Dalton. Dalton, who works as an air traffic controller at an installation tucked into a corner of the Diamond Head crater, told me he had recently been part of a team that competed in a 133-mile round-the-island relay race. I asked what his friends had thought when they heard what he was doing. "Nobody said a thing," he shrugged. "When it comes to running, everybody in Hawaii is crazy."

I soon came to see his point. Passing a neatly clipped front yard one afternoon, I noticed a garden hose with a hand-lettered sign nearby: "For Thirsty Joggers." And when I visited Scaff and Wagner in their suite in the downtown Kukui Plaza business complex, they handed me the official schedule of local races. I counted nearly seventy, enough to keep the most exacting runner in a state of cardiovascular distinction year-round.

There's trouble even in paradise, though, so I should probably mention that running in the islands has its hazards, too. Because Scaff and Wagner know exactly how to lure the unwary into the athletic life, some of the Honolulu Marathon Clinic's practice runs end at the doors of the Primo brewery. There, magnanimous brewery executives simply open the spigots and let everyone drink his or her fill. An injudicious hour can undo a week's training.

Despite the local pitfalls, there are always runners aplenty at such popular sites as the Ala Wai Canal footpath, the Pearl Harbor bicycle path, Ala Moana Park, the Mount Tantalus and Hawaii Kai loops (10.5 and 4 miles long, respectively) and Kapiolani Park. It is at the latter place, however, that the spirit of running reaches its fullest and finest flowering. Here an abandoned trolley station, rococo to its roof beams, has been turned to use as a joggers' rest stop, complete with benches and a drinking fountain. Here, when Honolulu's offices let out at five, swarms of secretaries congregate, warming up in preparation for the nightly run around Diamond Head or the park's 1.8-mile perimeter. And here, at any hour, runners ranging from fleet twenty-year-olds to overweight matrons may be found training, visions of the Honolulu Marathon dancing in their heads. The park is also, naturally enough, one of the sites where Honolulu Marathon Clinic participants gather on weekend mornings.

All this running activity explodes to a boisterous climax with the marathon itself. One recent winner, a reed-thin Olympian named Don Kardong, said, "Everyone comes here because it's a fun race to run." Contestants gather long before dawn in order to be ready for the 6:00 A.M. bark of a howitzer that signals the start of the long trek to and from Koko Head. The slowest runners will not be seen again for nearly nine hours. Not to worry, though. No matter how long it takes them, they are sure to be back in plenty of time for the revel that fills Kapiolani Park for the rest of the day, turning it into a vast Woodstock for triumphant runners.

Much else is also likely to come to a climax that day. In 1978, to cite only one example, two San Diego participants named Sherri Lee and Jerry Stowe had themselves joined in holy matrimony an hour before the starting gun by a cleric in yellow running shorts. To celebrate their marriage, the Stowes ran the course together, holding hands as they finished.

Only, perhaps, in Hawaii.

New Zealand: A Run with the Multitudes

Saturday, March 17, 1979, dawned bright, warm, windless and silent. In the streets of downtown Auckland, on New Zealand's North Island, no person stirred except an insomniac American writer. Queen Street, Quay Street, Customs Street and Fort Street were empty. At the water's edge a ferry, moored to an ancient pier, made one of daybreak's few sounds, a raspy creak where steel gunwale ground against wood piling. Otherwise, an alert listener might have heard a cat's footsteps.

As the sun climbed over Waitemata Harbor, a growing sound filled the streets of Auckland, a hushed scuffle of many thousands of feet, all of them moving toward the grassy rectangle of Victoria Park. All their owners wore running clothes, and all, within a few hours, would become part of the most prodigious run the world had, until then, ever known. By midday, 32,000, by the most scrupulous count, were to have covered the 10.3 kilometers between the starting line at Victoria Park and the finish line at St. Heliers Bay.

From the beginning it had been plain that the race, officially designated the Round the Bays Run, would be an unprecedented event. The previous year some 25,000 people had participated, and the sponsor, the *Auckland Star*, was pushing for a record. Moreover, everyone in town seemed to be talking about the race, and most, to judge by their anxious conversations, were planning to run in it.

If the Round the Bays was an extraordinary athletic occurrence, New Zealand as its locale was not. One can plausibly argue, in fact, that New Zealand is the land that invented running as it is known today. Long before the boom visited America, New Zealanders by the thousands were running. Some of the world's great runners, among them a world record-holder in the mile, John Walker, have been New Zealanders. One of its most influential coaches, Arthur Lydiard, is a New Zealander. One of its most inventive and indefatigable long-distance prodigies, Max Telford, lives in Auckland. New Zealanders are, in short, old hands at doing remarkable things in the sport.

Even for New Zealand, however, Round the Bays was something different. An hour before Rob Muldoon, the Prime Minister, was to start the race with a 105-millimeter howitzer, the streets near Victoria Park were clotted with humanity: supermarket clerks wearing T-shirts with their store's name stenciled on the front; gaunt young athletes leaning against trees to stretch gastrocnemius muscles and Achilles tendons or sitting on the grass to do hurdlers' stretches; middle-aged men and women, their midriffs swollen by New Zealand's overgenerous standard of living, trying to look convincingly purposeful as they jogged in place or checked to see that their shoelaces were properly tied.

A crowd of 32,000 is no longer individual people at all. The race was to start at 9:30, but six full minutes before that, perhaps in a demonstration of one of the inexplicable laws of humanity-at-large, runners simply began to flow northward like lava. Prime Minister Muldoon, a man who plainly accepts life's realities, fired the howitzer and bellowed merrily through a loudspeaker, "All I can do is say goodbye." Aerial photographs in the *Star* next morning showed a vast curling ooze, like a serpent coiling its way along the waterfront.

It hardly mattered that, given the sweaty crush, finishing times meant little. What mattered was that it was a perfect morning for running past the harbor's blue-gray waters, that at St. Heliers Bay there were fresh watermelons, cold beer, and a swim, and that on that Sunday, on an island between

the Pacific Ocean and the Tasman Sea, running history was
made.

England: Runner's Highlands

The mountainous fells of Britain are like mountains nowhere
else in the world. They are not notably high as mountains
elsewhere go; the highest, Ben Nevis, reaches a mere 4,406
feet. They are, however, so craggy and unruly that they are
comparable to mountains two or three times their size. I remember my astonishment the first time I drove northward
out of the Lake District and after only a brief ascent found myself in country so steep, rocky and bare of vegetation that I
was reminded of the treeless wasteland that surrounds Mount
Washington in New Hampshire. Mount Washington towers
6,288 feet high, nearly half again the height of Ben Nevis.

The fells, one would think, are best suited for viewing from
afar, or at the very most for stumbling awkwardly over if we
are in a particularly intrepid mood and the weather is excellent. They are emphatically, one would suppose, not the place
to go when the wind howls, the mists roll in, and the rains turn
the trails to watery mud.

It is, however, the unfathomable paradox of the fells that at
precisely such times they attract their most passionate aficio-
nados, an indomitable breed of athlete known, though not as
widely as it deserves to be, as the fell racer. Fell racers are
not like you and me. Poised to hurl himself down a 45-degree
rocky slope, a fell racer does not meditate on the barked shins
and broken bones that would spring to the mind of a more
earthbound sort. No, he beholds pure challenge, and he revels
in it.

Fell racing is a peculiarly British sport, one that flourishes
in the north of England and in Scotland, with occasional man-
ifestations in Wales and Ireland and on the Isle of Man. Races
range in distance from less than ten miles to a hundred miles.
In difficulty they range from a gentle romp across a moor to a
jarring, twisting, terrifying clamber over countryside no pru-
dent mountain goat would willingly visit.

Although fell racing can be dauntingly competitive, its adherents like to cite its friendly and democratic spirit. It is not uncommon for a fell racer, passing a checkpoint, to be offered a pint of beer by an official, and on at least one occasion a participant who is an automobile salesman offered a rival a good bargain in a used car. Some fell racers compete occasionally in track and cross-country, but only when they can find nothing better. For them, life is fully lived only in the harrowing, hard-breathing world of the fells.

Fell racing was flourishing in the Lake District as early as the 1850s. The annual Grasmere Guides race was first held in 1868. The Burnsall race dates back to sometime before 1881. The Ben Nevis race was solidly established by the turn of the century. Despite the prodigious problems involved in running such races, it is not difficult to see why they have been so long-lived. Bill Smith, the reigning historian of fell racing, writes: "The atmosphere of a fell race is very informal and down-to-earth. There is none of the pompous officialdom which is to be found in track running, and most of the runners are on friendly first-name terms with the organizers, helpers, checkpoint marshals and mountain-rescue team members. If there's a pub handy, there's usually a session after the race, where the top men drink and joke with the scrubbers."

Almost all fell racers enjoy living close to the land. Says Smith: "Everyone who is seriously involved in fell racing is a lover of mountains, fells and moors. Many are also fell walkers, rock climbers and all-round mountaineers. There are no posers or outrageous extroverts. No one goes around blowing kisses to the crowd."

A few years ago the secretary of the Fell Runners' Association, Eddie Leal, was speculating about why his sport remains so undeservedly obscure. Leal mused, "One point which may well be contributory to a lack of information on the fell running scene is the utter modesty which prevails throughout the whole fraternity. Perhaps it has something to do with the vast majesty of the high and lonely places in which the fell runner performs."

All sorts of people seek out that vast majesty. One of the

most admired, Jos Naylor, is a sheep farmer. Others are stone masons, plasterers, schoolteachers, clerks. Another is an Outward Bound instructor and tester of mountaineering equipment. In 1977 women were at last permitted to participate in this most hazardous of all running sports. Thus far, happily, they have failed to confirm the fears of the faint-hearted that, confronted with the mist-shrouded rigors of the fells, they would collapse into helpless exhaustion.

Entering a fell race is simplicity itself. The Fell Runners' Association publishes an annual schedule that lists seventy or so races and includes descriptions of each. Some are so simple that a child would be unlikely to stumble or get lost. Others require advanced navigational skills, unless you want to spend half the day scratching your head on some desolate moor.

Training for the fells, on the other hand, is not so simple. More than once, runners who are acclaimed on the track have swaggered to their first fell race, only to be publicly humbled as their muscles turned to tapioca under the awesomely relentless punishment of the high places. Like runners everywhere, the best fell runners have their training secrets and superstitions. But there is at least one incontrovertible principle: to race well on fells you've got to do lots of training on them. Mike Short, who won the Fell Runner of the Year award in 1975, takes a 2½-hour moor run every Sunday, even during the off-season.

Curiously, however, not all fell runners feel a need for formal coaching, an aid considered indispensable by many athletes. Rather, they prefer to let their bodies tell them how they're doing. "I've got a mind of my own," says Martin Weeks, a Bradford engineer who was Fell Runner of the Year in 1976. "I don't think I would ever let a coach organize me. We pool our ideas among all ranks of athletes and do the best we can from that. We all discuss our ideas and theories, usually in a pub after a training session." (The topic of pubs, one quickly notices, comes up often in the free-and-easy world of the fell runner.)

During such discussions one name is sure to be prominent:

that of the incomparable Jos Naylor, mentioned a few paragraphs ago, who in his early forties still runs the fells with such speed, precision, and navigational cunning that more than one athlete half his age has had to look twice to be sure his eyes were not deceiving him as the ageless wonder plunged by, arms and legs flailing. During the past decade Naylor has set a dozen or more fell records. His most celebrated achievement was to visit no fewer than seventy-two Lake District peaks in twenty-four hours, an achievement made doubly remarkable by the fact that it was accomplished during a heat wave. While standing around with his fellow competitors before a race, Naylor hardly looks the part of history's most preternaturally gifted fell runner. Lean and compact, with the high cheekbones and deep-set eyes common to well-trained runners everywhere, he has been described as "an unspoiled, down-to-earth man of the hills." Only when the race starts and one sees Naylor's crisply efficient style does it become clear why he is so much at home in the rocky highlands. It is a style that has frequently left the most sober of observers, the knowledgeable Chris Brasher among them, in open-mouthed wonder. When, a while back, Naylor covered the 271½ miles of the Pennine Way in an astonishing three days, four hours and thirty-six minutes, Brasher summed it up in one phrase: "The greatest long-distance performance ever seen in these islands."

The most popular fell race in Britain is not, however, an improbable test like the Pennine Way run but a more manageable course that starts in a place called Horton-in-Ribblesdale and snakes its twenty-three-mile way over three summits. Held every April and known as the Three Peaks race, the event attracts four hundred or so participants, but is by no means as easy as its popularity might suggest. In one recent year some 10 percent of the field, dazed into submission by the hardships of the fells, simply gave up and hobbled dejectedly back home. Clearly, fell racing isn't for everyone. But if you enjoy the idea of testing your limits it's one of the best ways to do it—especially if you can persuade yourself to be philosophical about scraped shins and bruised elbows.

14 ///
Running and Writing

An Evaluation of the Major Magazines and Books

*T*hink for a moment about carbohydrate loading. Every marathon runner knows what it is and more or less how to do it. Although in diet as in much else we all respond uniquely, the general outlines of carbohydrate loading are sufficiently clear so that with a modest amount of experimentation you can easily discover what pre-race eating sequence works best for you. Why is it, then, that during a recent twelve-month span the running press carried no fewer than twenty articles on the subject? What could there possibly have been to say that was new?

The answer, sad to relate, is that there was very little. Writers write and publishers publish all those repetitious articles about carbohydrate loading, interval training, running shoes and a hundred other familiar aspects of the sport because of an irksome little secret. The secret is that, aside from covering races and doing personality pieces, for the most part there isn't that much new to say about running, particularly when it must be said precisely on schedule every month. The most fruitful sources of fresh material, the laboratories where running research is conducted, offer only a meager trickle, far too anemic to keep the scores of national and regional running magazines supplied with fresh articles. Journalistically, running is a tough beat.

It has become even tougher with the arrival of a couple of ambitious upstarts that are irreverently challenging the long-held supremacy of *Runner's World*, the first and during its infancy the only national magazine devoted primarily to long-distance running. The field has also become a lot more interesting to watch, for while at one time we had no choice but to accept whatever *Runner's World* offered us, now there are alternatives. *Runner's World* is still perched at the top, but its position is no longer quite so impregnable as it once was, particularly since recent suggestions in such publications as the *Wall Street Journal* and *New West* magazines that its highly publicized running-shoe ratings may be tainted with conflicts of interest. The unaccustomed competition is producing not just a scramble for readers but also some scrappy skirmishes and, at least once in a while, a bit of lively reading.

Much the same is true of the books about running. As of late 1979, according to *Books in Print*, no fewer than 140 hardcover running books were available in the United States, and scores, both hardcover and paperback, were due to be published within the next several months. It is plain that at the very least there must be an occasional overlap or redundancy, and of course there is. There is also a notable unevenness of quality. Happily, however, there are also some books well worth reading, and even owning.

In this chapter I plan to examine briefly the literature of running, both magazines and books, indicating what I find most provocative, inventive or useful.

The Magazines

Runner's World, Box 366, Mountain View, CA 94042. $13 per year, $24 for two years. It was *Runner's World* that, a decade or more ago, first introduced me as well as hundreds of other fledgling runners to the complexity and wonder of the sport. At the time there was little else to read about running, and even though the magazine was thin, unevenly edited and not particularly attractive, its cumulative effect was enormous. One of its chief assets at the time was its editor, Joe Henderson, a writer of subtlety, insight and taste and one of the first people to insist publicly that running was something more than just sweat and hard breathing. In retrospect, in fact, it is clear that what *Runner's World* was saying through Henderson and its iconoclastic medical writer, George Sheehan, was little short of athletic heresy. For at a time when the prevailing attitude toward sport was that it was chiefly and properly a test of aggressive dominance, and an exclusively masculine test at that, Henderson and Sheehan were arguing that, on the contrary, running could be exactly what you, either man or woman, wanted to make of it.

Henderson's role has diminished over the years, and not long ago he finally left the staff. But Sheehan is still a regular contributor, as are Amby Burfoot, winner of the 1968 Boston Marathon, and Arthur Lydiard, one of the world's most highly regarded coaches. Furthermore, the magazine has demonstrated a consistent ability to attract some of the most significant names in running: the physiologist David L. Costill, the podiatrist Steven I. Subotnick, the biochemist Peter D. Wood and the apparently ageless marathoner Alex Ratelle. To read *Runner's World* is to stay well abreast of what's what and who's who in the sport. It is also to read at least an occasional piece of vivid and workmanlike writing. Amby Burfoot, who joined the staff in 1978, stands out as the contributor of a succession of memorable articles. His report on the 1979 Boston Marathon was the most imaginative account of that race to appear anywhere, and the only one to do full justice to its sustained drama.

Over the years, however, the stock in trade of *Runner's World* has been its basic instructional articles. This is the reason the magazine currently has something of a problem. For the fact is that there are only so many ways to tell people how to run uphill, so many ways to describe carbohydrate loading, and so many ways to tell a beginner how to get in shape for his or her first marathon. The result is that, while the magazine may seem as lustrous as ever to new readers, long-time subscribers invariably find much that is overfamiliar and repetitious. Bob Anderson, who founded the magazine in 1966 and today serves both as its editor and publisher, told me he thought the repetition was more apparent than actual. "We don't try to put everything on a subject into one article," he said. "There are different types of carbohydrate loading and different ways to train, so there's room for different articles on the same subject. On the surface people may think we do a lot of repeating, but if they get into it they'll find new information." Anderson may be right. Nonetheless, the sense of *déjà vu* persists.

Runner's World has grown impressively, from a circulation of 65,000 in early 1977 to nearly 400,000 two years later. Anderson says he attributes the magazine's success to its deep involvement with running itself, and not just with running as journalism. "We cover the scene for people in the scene," he said. "All along we've been putting out a publication that helps the sport grow." He cited the magazine's so-called fun runs, currently held in some 400 cities, its twenty-four-hour relay races, and its Corporate Cup races, the latter open only to teams recruited from business firms.

Anderson and his staff have responded to the competitive thrusts of rivals by improving the magazine's appearance and by adding features, columns and listings of races. Despite such efforts, however, the quality of *Runner's World* remains somewhat below top professional standards. As *Runner's World* continues to improve and as the competition's aim becomes surer, it will be interesting to see what the struggle produces.

The Runner, 1 Park Avenue, New York, N.Y. 10016. $18 per year. Given the growth of running and a generally upper-middle-class constituency that has a mesmerizing appeal for advertisers, it was probably inevitable that someone would come along to challenge *Runner's World*, and it was probably just as inevitable that the challenger would be a lean Manhattanite named George A. Hirsch. A 2:38 marathoner who was a founder of both *New York* and *New Times* magazines, Hirsch started laying plans for *The Runner* in 1976, when he was forty-two years old. Following a brief, bitter legal skirmish with *Runner's World* over rights to the title *The Runner*, he brought out his first monthly issue in October 1978. By then he had assembled an able staff and the first of an array of contributing editors that at latest count included three-time Boston Marathon winner Bill Rodgers, Olympic champion Frank Shorter, two-time Boston runner-up Tom Fleming, and miler Marty Liquori, as well as Nina Kuscsik, the 1972 winner of the Boston Marathon's women's division, Gabe Mirkin, co-author of *The Sportsmedicine Book*, Hal Higdon, a defector from the *Runner's World* staff, and Colman McCarthy and Sam Merrill, two of the most graceful, witty and perceptive writers now working the running beat.

From the beginning it was plain that Hirsch and his editor, a cross-country specialist named Marc A. Bloom, didn't plan to assault *Runner's World* head on, but intended, more subtly, to make their challenge where their rival was most vulnerable: in basic journalistic quality. Surrounding themselves with top writers, editors, photographers and layout artists, they put impressive effort into planning not just each issue but the sequence of successive issues. "Ours is the first magazine to come along in this field and publish in a professional way," Hirsch told me. "We've brought together authoritative writers and we put a lot of effort into our choice of subjects. That's critical. If you choose your subjects correctly you prevent repetition. The idea process is paramount with us."

The strategy has borne results. Unlike *Runner's World, The Runner* attempts again and again to offer readers the definitive treatment. It has published full-scale articles on the function of blood and the lungs and on the effects of high-altitude training, as well as solidly written pieces on Shorter's 1979 comeback attempt and John Walker's ill-fated efforts to defend his mile record. With the latter article, through no fault of its own, *The Runner* ran afoul of unlucky timing. Even as the issue in which it appeared was on its way to subscribers, Sebastian Coe unceremoniously broke Walker's record.

Any magazine is blessed if it has a writer or two with grace and style. *The Runner* can count its blessings. Colman McCarthy, who was quoted briefly in Chapter 1, is one of the most artful and lucid literary stylists the running world knows. Sam Merrill, a newcomer to running but an old hand at writing compelling and amusing prose, has a sharp eye for the telling anecdote, and invariably relates it with verve. In an article on the Boston Marathon's unofficial participants, for example, he tells the story of an injured runner who sold his number to a friend who was unable to qualify for the race. As Merrill tells the story, the injured runner phoned his friend one day and began asking searching questions about the progress of his training. The impostor finally asked, "Hey, why the sudden interest?" The other runner replied, "Well, I've got a right to know what shape I'm in, don't I?"

Readers who subscribe to both *Runner's World* and *The Runner* invariably find *The Runner* wittier, more sophisticated and more meticulously written and edited. It is also more inclined to dig for gossip and controversy. It is questionable, however, whether this is a vital ingredient for success. Does an Illinois lawyer trying to break 3:10 really care all that much about a New York City race director's squabbles with a runner who enjoys dressing up in a Superman outfit?

Nonetheless, like its West Coast rival, *The Runner* is gaining readers with every issue. Circulation when it began was a meager 50,000. By late 1979 it was 140,000.

Running Times, 12808 Occoquan Road, Woodbridge, VA
22192. $13.50 per year. Founded in early 1977 by Ed Ayres, a
long-time runner who won the JFK fifty-mile race that year at
the age of thirty-five, *Running Times* covers races more assidu-
ously than any other magazine in the field, devoting page after
page not only to results but also to listings of forthcoming
events. It is unique, too, in having two separate editions, one
for the eastern half of the country and the other for the western. Although its editorial direction occasionally seems less
distinct than that of *Runner's World* or *The Runner*, it is more
inclined to take positions and espouse causes. Not long ago,
for example, Ayres wrote two articles for successive issues in
which he argued the merits of running to and from work instead of driving. The magazine has also criticized commercialism in running and questioned the AAU's and the International Olympic Committee's authoritarian control of the
sport. A readership survey in mid-1979 showed that 77 percent of *Running Times* readers are college graduates, that
most of the remaining 23 percent are full-time students, and
that a full 43 percent hold graduate degrees. Ayres told me his
research suggests that, for whatever reason, his magazine's
readers have significantly higher income and education levels
than the readers of most other running magazines.

Ayres's subscribers are attracted by an editorial point of
view that is both more old-fashioned and more modern than
that of his rivals. On the one hand *Running Times* gazes yearn-
ingly at the good old days of running, before commercialism
and bigness stepped in. On the other, it stresses the importance of contemporary environmental concerns. Ayres says, "I
feel that running is not just a sport but part of a larger life style
that includes a sensitivity to the environment, an awareness
of the importance of being healthy, and an understanding of
the relationship of physical and mental well-being."

Ayres and his staff are proud of the attention they give to
small, uncelebrated races. "We look on the bigness of running
with a somewhat regretful eye," he said. "We're a grass-roots

magazine. We travel around to the small towns and the little races. Ours is an earthier, less glittering approach."

The mixture is plainly working. The press run for the first issue of *Running Times* was a cautious 1,500 copies. At last report paid circulation was 41,000.

Running, Box 350, Salem, OR 97308. $7 for six issues. Published quarterly, *Running* calls itself "the thinking runner's magazine." To judge by the general educational level of American runners, just about any runner these days is likely to be a thinking runner, but why quarrel with such an innocent boast? Based on its year-in, year-out quality, *Running* may be forgiven an exaggeration or two. Edited and published by Jack Welch, who likes to describe himself as a philosopher of running, the magazine is as notable for what it does not contain as for what it does. There are no race results, no personality pieces, no breathlessly euphoric accounts of how some formerly fat man finished his first marathon. Instead, there is a steady diet of solid, unbiased, carefully documented articles on training methods, running physiology, injuries and their prevention, and equipment such as shoes, chronographs and clothing, some of them written by E. C. Frederick, an exercise physiologist and the magazine's founder. Like *Running Times*, *Running* views the present commercialized state of the sport with an uneasy eye. The result is a magazine with an impressive aura of honesty and integrity. Seven years after its founding its circulation has yet to climb above a modest 4,000, but its readers are among the most loyal in the running world.

The Books

A half-dozen years ago practically no books on running were available except the pamphlets and collections of magazine articles that were issued intermittently by World Publications, the publisher of *Runner's World*. Though packed with information, most of them were frustratingly short on style.

Proofread perfunctorily, they were pocked with misspellings and typographical errors. Furthermore, their layout was so forbidding that it required not just enthusiasm but charity to read one of them all the way through. Some other source of information was therefore certain to turn up sooner or later.

It was the growth of interest in running during the closing years of the 1970s that finally awakened book publishers to the opportunities the sport offered. Suddenly running books of every conceivable description (and some that were only barely conceivable) were rushed to the shelves. Anita Bryant wrote one on running and Christianity. So did an Atlanta minister named Earl P. Paulk, Jr. There was a *Joy of Running*, a *Zen of Running*, a *Holistic Running*. There was a *Complete Jogger* and, should the reader remain unsated, a *Beyond Jogging* and even a *Last Word on Running*. There were collections of photographs, collections of cartoons, and works on cross-country running, road racing and marathoning. Nor was the psychology of running neglected. There were, in fact, so many books on various aspects of the subject that you might suppose running wasn't sport at all but psychoanalysis.

A skeptical reader might be forgiven for wondering how much of this outpouring made a genuine contribution to the sum of human knowledge. In pursuit of the answer to that question I kept track for a time of ideas that were repeated from book to book. I soon gave the exercise up as unsportsmanlike, like shooting fish in a barrel.

If, however, there are repetitions and weaknesses in the running literature, there are also books that deserve to endure. They fall into four principal categories: technical works, scientific expositions, medical texts and philosophical studies.

Among the technical books two, both of them antedating the running movement by several years, are preeminent. The first, one of the clearest and soundest works ever written for beginners, is *Jogging*, one of whose authors is William J. Bowerman, the esteemed long-time coach at the University of Oregon. The second, J. Kenneth Doherty's *Modern Track and Field*, contains one of the most comprehensive treatments of distance running ever assembled. It is particularly useful for serious athletes who want to get the most out of their abilities. Two other books that bear repeated consultation are Bob Glover and Jack Shepherd's *Runner's Handbook* and Joan Ullyot's *Women's Running.* For theory and advice about getting yourself ready mentally for the big race, no source is more valuable than Robert M. Nideffer's *The Inner Athlete.*

Many runners are content to run without ever wondering what's going on inside them while they do so. If you're that sort, there's no particular reason to change your ways. If, however, you're curious about the alterations, both temporary and long-term, that hard exercise produces, three books in particular will open your eyes. They are Per-Olaf Åstrand and Kaare Rodahl's *Textbook of Work Physiology,* David L. Costill's *A Scientific Approach to Distance Running* and *The Long Distance Runner,* edited by Paul Milvy. The first, an acknowledged classic, is the most technical; laymen will probably find the latter two more readable. The Milvy book grew out of a landmark 1976 conference that attracted practically all the sport's leading authorities. Costill's book, a much shorter but no less valuable work, is based largely on his own scientific studies at Ball State University, where he directs the Human Performance Laboratory.

Few goals are more important to runners than avoiding injury and, if injured, recovering as quickly as possible. Of the plethora of books on sportsmedicine, three stand out: *Sports Medicine,* edited by Allan J. Ryan and Fred L. Allman, Jr., Gabe Mirkin and Marshall Hoffman's *Sportsmedicine Book,* and Richard Mangi, Peter Jokl and O. William Dayton's *Runner's Medical Guide.* The last book, the most recently published of the three, is conveniently arranged according to parts of the body, so that finding a specific injury is somewhat easier than with the other two. For general discussions of physical fitness and prescriptions for achieving it, Kenneth H. Cooper's *Aerobics* and *The New Aerobics* and Bud Getchell's *Physical Fitness: A Way of Life* are among the most reliable guides. Heart attack victims who want to find their way back to health through exercise will benefit from Terence Kavanagh's *Heart Attack? Counterattack!* A sound nutritional primer is Joseph J. Morella and Richard J. Turchetti's *Nutrition and the Athlete.*

No facet of sport has attracted more attention in recent years than the philosophical aspects of running. Starting with the early writings of Joe Henderson, a host of writers has diligently explored various dimensions of what running ultimately means. The reason for the attention is that for most of us running is not only a physical activity but a reflection of an attitude toward life. Several of the books in this genre remain worthy of close reading. Among them are George Leonard's *The Ultimate Athlete,* for its vividly expressed vision of how sport may be changing; Roger Bannister's *The Four-Minute Mile,* for its lucid demonstration that running is not just struggle but symbol; and George Sheehan's *Dr. Sheehan on Running,* a work remarkable not just for its luminous clarity but for its prescience. Published in the dark ages of running, three years before his more celebrated *Running and Being,* it foreshadowed many of the philosophical themes that were later to become common and thus shaped many later books, including my own *Complete Book of Running.* As an experiment I opened *Dr. Sheehan on Running* at random and came upon this passage:

> After the test comes that marvelous calm that follows completing a marathon or climbing a mountain or running the rapids. ... In that calm, I become the man I would like to be—and perhaps I am.

For me those sentences are as authentic as honest sweat.

A final indispensable philosopher is Johan Huizinga, whose *Homo Ludens: A Study of the Play Element in Culture* may be the most comprehensive book ever written on sport and society. Although Huizinga says little that is specifically about running, his book radiantly illuminates our sport and its meaning.

15 //// Farewell, Pheidippides

A Skeptical Look at Running's Most Ubiquitous Legend

I am running, sweating hard, down a two-lane road that curls through the dusty slopes of southern Greece. I am pressing, not so much because I want to catch the Greek runner bobbing along a couple of hundred yards ahead of me but because I hope, by my diligent effort, to free myself from the dogged American who for the past ten miles has been directing an annoying wheeze at my right shoulder blade. The day is fearfully hot. The organizers of this marathon would, it occurs to me, have benefited from some meditations on Diogenes. With perfectly straight faces they swore that the temperature almost never went above 75 degrees at this time of year, yet here it is in the mid-80s and still climbing. Only the roadside blankets of poppies and Queen Anne's lace and an occasional motionless goat seem at home in this Attic inferno.

Every few miles an official of the Hellenic Amateur Athletic Federation tries to ease our suffering by offering liquid in paper cups. It is a warm orange fluid, and when I try to drink some as I run, it sloshes onto my chest and congeals. Before many miles have passed I begin to feel like an orange lollipop left too long in the sun.

Also in the race are Don Kardong, a member of the 1976 U.S. Olympic marathon team; Chuck Smead, the silver medalist in the 1975 Pan-Am Games marathon, who tuned up by taking a run over Mount Olympus a few days earlier; Dr. Joan Ullyot, an accomplished marathoner and an authority on women's running; and several score other competitors. We have all been lured here by the mesmerizing tug of running's most celebrated legend.

That legend concerns Pheidippides, a foot courier who, after the outnumbered Athenian army's astonishing defeat of 30,000 crack Persian warriors on the Plain of Marathon in 490 B.C., carried a message to Athens, some twenty-five torturous miles to the southwest. Upon his arrival, so the story goes, he announced, "Rejoice! We conquer!" Thereupon, exhausted by the effort of running so far, he died on the spot. Because every modern marathoner is only too familiar with the sense of imminent personal disaster and because the distance Pheidippides is said to have run corresponds so closely with today's official marathon distance of 26.2 miles, he is universally saluted as the patron saint of marathon runners. Our race in Greece, the Spirit of Pheidippides Marathon, was named for him. He turns up in scores of books and magazine articles about running. Jeff Galloway, a former Olympian, has named a brace of sporting goods stores after him and had the name emblazoned across thousands of T-shirts and pairs of shorts. There is scarcely a runner alive who does not revere the name Pheidippides.

Strangely, however, little is known about him. Some scholars think he may have been the same Pheidippides who a few days before the Battle of Marathon ran 150 miles in forty-eight hours to solicit Spartan aid; others say this is a romantic confusion. One modern writer, Xenophon Messinesi, asserts that

Pheidippides made his run "in heavy armor," though on what authority he fails to specify. Other details are similarly sparse. We do not know, for example, how old Pheidippides was, how fast he could run, what part of Attica he came from, or anything else in the way of personal details.

There are some aspects of the story of which we can be reasonably certain, however. We know that the Battle of Marathon, which was a consequence of the first Persian effort to invade Greece, occurred in September, a month when nowadays the average maximum temperature in Athens is 83 degrees. We know, too, that the battle lasted only from breakfast until lunchtime. Finally, we know that an Athenian *hemerodromos*, or professional foot courier, would almost certainly have chosen much the same course that Kardong, Smead and the rest of us followed, because it hugs the relatively level coast instead of needlessly traversing the mountains farther inland.

Beyond that, we can do little but speculate. It is, in fact, hard to resist speculating, because, truth to tell, the Pheidippides story is so patently improbable. Ask yourself: How likely is it, given the fact that thousands of modern marathon runners compete every weekend without mishap, that a trained runner would not just have collapsed but died? Was the mere announcement of victory so urgent that it demanded an effort that cost the messenger his life? Couldn't Pheidippides have run at a less arduous pace and thus lived to run another day?

These questions nagged at me as I ran along the road from Marathon to Athens, as Pheidippides supposedly had done 2,500 years earlier. The Pheidippides legend had, in fact, troubled me ever since I started running more than a dozen years ago. Now, given the opportunity to retrace the steps the hero is supposed to have taken, I hoped to immerse myself in his achievement and thereby become a sort of spiritual brother. If, I reasoned, I could force myself to suffer as he had, and if I could, furthermore, do so in the same rocky setting, I might somehow bridge those twenty-five centuries. I might then penetrate to the elusive truth of the legend or, at the very least, to some approximation of what Pheidippides' run may have been like. Mine was a study in historical probabilities, based on the hunch that the closer I came to the authentic ancient experience, the more I would be able to learn about it.

Three questions were uppermost in my mind:

1) After the Battle of Marathon, was a messenger in fact dispatched to Athens?

2) If such a messenger was dispatched, was he the same person who had earlier run to Sparta?

3) Whoever he was, did he in fact die as a result of the run?

During the weeks before the race I pored over Herodotus, Plutarch and other classical writers. I studied books and articles on Greek military history, training methods, clothing and diet. I interviewed scholars at leading universities. I prodded experienced marathoners to make educated guesses about details of Pheidippides' ordeal. By the time I arrived in Marathon and was issued my number, I felt I should have entered the race under the name Phixx.

The easiest part of Pheidippides' experience to duplicate was the suffering. Even under ideal conditions a marathon is a difficult undertaking; on a hot day it is likely to be grievously demanding. This is why, as we stood in the blazing Greek sunshine near a monument marking the start of the 1896 Olympic marathon, there was little of the bonhomie that usually attends such occasions. There was in fact a clear sense of doom. Nor were our spirits greatly lifted by the antic sight of a Greek runner who had enterprisingly glued two inches of red foam rubber to the soles of his shoes, apparently intending to bound like a rabbit all the way to the marble stadium in Athens.

As an official loaded the starting gun, a Greek with a sense of ceremony handed each of us an olive sprig, to be reverently tossed onto the mound, three miles distant, that marks the mass grave of the Athenians who perished in defense of Marathon. At last the gun sounded and we were on our way, a sweating, polyglot ooze of sentimental athletes.

The early pace was fast, much too fast for the heat. With fatigue beginning to gnaw at me, it seemed increasingly unlikely that the same messenger who had just run 150 miles would be recruited for a second sustained run. Surely the athletics-loving Greeks would have known that such an effort leaves even a well-trained runner fatigued for weeks and sometimes months.

Significantly, the two-messenger theory finds support in the views of the late P. R. Coleman-Norton of Princeton, who refers to the second courier as an "anonymous Athenian runner." If, then, our spirit of romance beckons us to believe that Pheidippides 1 and Pheidippides 2 were the same man, common sense clearly asks us not to. There is, however, no reason thus far to insist that there was no Pheidippides 2 at all. For the moment, let's suppose there was. All that is necessary, to avoid confusion with Pheidippides 1, is to give Pheidippides 2 a distinguishing name. Let us therefore call him Euathlos, a common Athenian name of the period and one that can be translated "Good Athlete."

In one respect Euathlos, if he existed, had an advantage over Kardong and the rest of us. The countryside through which we were running is virtually treeless today; shade is scarcely to be found anywhere. In the fifth century B.C., however, these dry, rocky hills were covered with growth that has long since been chopped down for firewood, or in the case of saplings, nibbled away by goats. As he ran, Euathlos would have enjoyed occasional relief from the relentless September sun. We had none.

In all other respects, however, we modern runners had the advantage.

The road on which we ran, for example, is as smooth and well maintained as any U.S. highway. Euathlos, on the other hand, would have had to negotiate a rough, stony path because, according to Professor Ernst Badian of Harvard's history department, paved roads were all but unknown in 490 B.C. And contrary to a widespread jogger's myth, it is less tiring to run on pavement than on soft surfaces, even grass.

Unlike Euathlos, we wore well-designed running gear. Our clothing was exactly right for the distance and weather. My shirt had such a wide mesh that it was more holes than fabric, the better to allow evaporative cooling. My shorts were featherweight nylon. While Euathlos was almost certainly not burdened with heavy armor ("He would have been a damn silly Greek to run that way," Dean Miller, a professor of history at the University of Rochester, told me), he may well have worn the standard tunic, which would have been impossibly hot compared with present-day running garb. Let us hope he ran naked, like runners pictured on Greek vases of the period.

My shoes were lightweight racing flats no more burdensome than ballet slippers. Euathlos wasn't so lucky. Soldiers of his time wore boots or sandals or else went barefoot. Professor Badian points out that much would have depended on whether he came from Athens or from the countryside, for while footgear was customarily worn in the city, rural folk often went shoeless. W. R. Connor, a Princeton classics professor, thinks it unlikely that Euathlos wore sandals. "I'd hate to run twenty-five miles with a thong between my toes," he said. "I'd rather go barefoot." Of the authorities I consulted, only Professor Helene Foley of the Department of Classics at Stanford thought Euathlos might conceivably have worn boots, "especially if the trail was rough." Halfway to Athens, I felt an ugly blister working its way around the second toe of my right foot. I knew, however, that my predecessor had felt far worse. As I imagined his agony, my pain and his began to merge, almost as if the intervening years had never existed.

Liquid, as I have already mentioned, was offered to us every few miles. No matter how unpalatable, it served to replace the fluids lost as we ran. Euathlos was less fortunate. Few streams or rivers flow through the Attic landscape. Euathlos might occasionally have begged a cup of water at a farmhouse along his route, but the supply would have been undependable at best. The scarcity of water is significant, because few problems that can beset a runner are more dangerous than dehydration.

We modern athletes were all at least passably well trained. Distance running is so common today that athletes know exactly how to prepare for a race. In training, marathoners rarely run fewer than ten miles a day, and they combine long, easy runs with speed work that toughens them for the rigors of racing. In Euathlos' day little was known about such distance training. The longest race in the ancient Olympics was only 4,800 meters, less than three miles. Professor Miller said, "Long-distance running per se just wasn't trained for." As I ran along, I thought of Euathlos, his legs aching, his lungs burning, all because he didn't know the training routines that are rudimentary to present-day runners.

He may well have been hungry, too, and, especially toward the end of his run, weak. Most distance runners today follow the carbohydrate-loading technique, a pre-competition dietary practice that packs muscles with significantly more fuel than they ordinarily contain, and thus postpones exhaustion. Although Euathlos' diet was probably high in carbohydrates such as grains and beans, it is unlikely that he would have eaten particularly well under battlefield conditions. Even if he didn't run nonstop, as modern marathoners do, but alternately ran and walked, he might very easily have suffered from hypoglycemia long before he was anywhere near Athens. (Hypoglycemia, or low blood sugar, can make the ablest and best-trained athlete feel as if he's in one of those nightmarish dreams where mere walking is like wading through quicksand.)

Finally, while we modern marathoners were running purely for the challenge of the race, Euathlos would have had a quite different reason—one that, oddly, is rarely if ever mentioned in published accounts of his run. Consider what had happened that morning. After eight days of uneasy waiting in their encampment, the outnumbered Athenians had finally decided it was time to attack. It was obvious that the battle would be significant, so significant that even Aeschylus, the father of Greek tragedy, was there to record it. Feelings between Greek and Persian ran high. Earlier, the Persian ruler Darius had sent heralds to Athens, demanding submission and symbolic gifts of earth and water. Affronted, the Athenians flung the Persians into a pit, suggesting that they collect their own earth.

At dawn, therefore, the Athenians, 9,000 strong, thundered across the plain and swooped down on the Persians, who, it turned out, had chosen a weak position. By midday, 6,400 of them lay dead. If Herodotus, a shameless flag-waver for the Greek cause, is to be believed, only 192 Athenians lost their lives.

Yet even as they reveled in victory, the Athenians faced a crisis. The Persians, clambering into their ships in retreat, would now head southward and attack Athens itself. This surely is the main reason Euathlos would have been dispatched, not just to carry word of the triumph. "Now he had an urgent message," Professor Connor told me. "It was 'The Persians are coming.'" The dust of battle was still settling as the Athenians packed their gear and began hurrying toward Athens, knowing that the Persians would soon be there. It is thus at least plausible that the Athenian force would have sent a courier ahead to warn the populace. If so, his run would have taken place under quite different conditions from those Kardong, Smead and the rest of us were experiencing. Euathlos would have been running not just for a laurel wreath and a medal, as we were, but for his capital's survival.

Under these circumstances, Euathlos might well have run unwisely, going too quickly and neglecting to stop for water. In hot-weather races, I have often seen runners staggering from heat exhaustion as they try to reach the finish line despite the protests of their bodies. Even Kardong, as experienced and canny a marathon runner as exists today, suffered from its early stages as he approached Athens. "I was on the verge of heat exhaustion," he told me at dinner that night. "I felt dazed and confused."

If Euathlos did in fact die after delivering his message, I think I know what the cause was. In his poem "Pheidippides," Robert Browning attributes it to a heart attack ("Joy in his blood bursting his heart"), but that seems unlikely. Heart attacks, while not unknown in trained runners, are so rare as to be of negligible probability. No, it was almost certainly heat stroke, which can develop when an exhausted athlete pushes on despite physical warnings. "The only thing that can kill a healthy runner, other than cars and buses, is heat stroke," Dr. Ullyot had said just before the marathon. "If you get dizziness

or a headache you're in trouble. Stop running." In imagination, I see Euathlos confused just as Kardong had been and
feeling a headache's first pulsing throbs, yet continuing nonetheless to push down the long road toward Athens and duty. I
see him stumbling into the city and delivering, not his entire
message—"Rejoice! We conquer! The Persians are coming!"
—but only its first part.

But did Euathlos die? I wonder. I was running the other day
with a friend named Stephen Richardson. Speculating on the
legend, Richardson spun out a not entirely fanciful scenario.
What if Euathlos merely collapsed? Furthermore, what if his
collapse was observed by someone who, too impatient to find
out what had really happened, rushed off to report the inci-
dent as the death of one of Marathon's heroes? The story is so
movingly appropriate that any patriotic Athenian would have
wanted to believe it. What would it have mattered if it weren't
precisely true? Are all of our own patriotic legends literally
true? After all, what counts in such legends is metaphorical
truth, the capacity to bring a tear to the eye and make the
heart beat faster.

Here, however, at the shadowy borderline between myth
and reality, a more fundamental question asserts itself. Did
Euathlos (or Pheidippides 1 or 2, or anyone else) really run at
all on that September afternoon twenty-five centuries ago? I
was nearly twenty miles into the race when I found myself irresistibly reflecting on the probabilities. Thus far the course
had been mainly uphill. Suddenly I was at the crest. There, in
the distant sunlight, the Parthenon glowed with a jewel's
white brilliance atop the Acropolis. On the day of the Battle of
Marathon, did an Athenian *hemerodromos* really glimpse that
same Acropolis (on which the Parthenon would not be built
until half a century later)?

Herodotus, the first to describe the battle, says nothing of
such a courier. The story, Professor Badian had pointed out,
doesn't appear until the first century A.D., in Plutarch. Badian
called it "a piece of historical fiction to make a nice ending."
Professor Miller concurred. "It's an agreeable fiction," he said,

"but a very unlikely one. The idea of sending a runner makes a marvelous story, but you'd never send a man if you had horses, and the Athenians almost certainly did have them."

As I ran at last into the historic marble stadium and toward the finish line, I laughed despite my fatigue. Suddenly it seemed ironically appropriate that this race was called the Spirit of Pheidippides Marathon. For spirit, pure spirit, was all the marathoner's hero had probably ever consisted of.

Having finished the race, Chuck Smead, the winner in 2:31, said wearily, "Now I know why Pheidippides died." It's even simpler than that. There is no reason at all to suppose he ever lived.

The Runner's Directory

Equipment, Publications, Organizations and Services Worth Knowing About

Organizations That Encourage Running

American Medical Joggers Association, Box 4704, North Hollywood, CA 91607. $25 a year includes a subscription to the AMJA's provocative newsletter. Membership consists mostly of physicians and heart patients.

National Jogging Association, 2420 K Street, N.W., Washington, DC 20037. $18 a year includes a subscription to the NJA's cheerful and informative newspaper, discounts on running gear, a motivation-bolstering awards program, and other benefits. By special arrangement with the NJA, readers of this book are offered a $3 discount if they include the password "sweatsock."

President's Council on Physical Fitness and Sports, Washington, DC 20201. For a free logbook and procedures for qualifying for a presidential physical fitness award (for boys and girls aged ten to seventeen) or a presidential sports award (for athletes fifteen and over), write the Council.

Road Runners Club of America. The RRC, the nation's leading running organization, has some 250 chapters. To find out about one in your area, send a self-addressed stamped envelope to Sanford Schmidt, 3203 Agnes Boulevard, Alton, IL 62002.

Mail-Order Running Gear

Moss Brown & Co., Inc., 1522 Wisconsin Ave., N.W., Washington, DC 20007. Offers a full line of equipment from major manufacturers. Free illustrated catalogue.

Running Clothes for Women

Gobelle, Box 986, Del Mar, CA 92014; Lady Madonna (for maternity running outfits), 36 East 31st Street, New York, NY 10016; Moving Comfort, Box 2006, Arlington, VA 22202; Pantera, Box 123, New York, NY 10023.

Shoe Repair by Mail

Athlete'Sole, 7911 N.E. 33rd Drive, Suite 150, Portland, OR 97211. A factory-authorized Nike repair center that fixes other brands, too. $14.00 plus $1.50 postage includes new soles, insoles, laces, arch supports if needed.

Filet-of-Sole, 702 East Spring Street, St. Marys, OH 45885. $9.95 plus $1.50 postage for new soles.

Fresh Tracks, 27 West Rayburn Road, Millington, NJ 07946. $12.95 includes choice of soles (zigzag, waffle, etc.), repair of minor tears in uppers, new laces, new insoles if needed.

Ken-Kap, Inc., Box 17674, Tampa, FL 33612. $12.95 plus $1.50 handling includes soles, laces, arch supports and inner soles as necessary.

Mark's Athletic Soles, 4028 S.W. 57th Avenue, Miami, FL 33155. $12.95 plus $1.50 postage includes resoling and repair of stitching and minor tears.

Paul's Sport Shoe Service, 484–486 Main Street, Glen Ellyn,
IL 60137. $14.95, postage paid, for resoling.

Resoling Specialists, Box 12483, Milwaukee, WI 53212.
$12.95, postage paid, for new soles on Adidas, Brooks,
Etonic, New Balance, Nike, Puma and all waffle-bottom
shoes.

Soles and Resoles, 4419 Hollister Avenue, Santa Barbara, CA
93110. $9.75 plus $1.50 postage for new soles.

Do-It-Yourself Resoling

Walker Shoe Service Supply Co., Box 366, Flushing, NY
11367. $9.95 for most styles.

A Way to Make Heels Last Longer

Eternal Sole, Box 3528, Montgomery, AL 36109. $4.95 for two
pairs of long-wearing patches for worn heels.

Computerized Shoe Recommendations

Compute-A-Shoe, Box 99183, San Diego, CA 92109. Fill out a
questionnaire on your running habits and problems and,
for $3, receive a list of three recommended shoes.

A Computerized Medical Evaluation

General Health, 1046 Potomac Street, N.W., Washington, DC
20036. Fill out a 48-page questionnaire and receive a com-
puterized evaluation of your health risks, eating and exercise habits, and mental health. $25. Quantity discounts
available.

A Good Heart-Rate Monitor

Heartwatch, Dart Medical Equipment, Box 18187, Lansing,
MI 48901. $189. A portable, rechargeable pulse monitor.
Several other firms offer instruments that do much the
same thing. For the price, however, this is the best I've seen.

A Way to Measure Your Fat

Fat-O-Meter, Health & Education Services, 2442 Irving Park

Road, Chicago, IL 60618. $9.95. Plastic calipers that are more reliable than bathroom scales for finding out how fat you are.

Shock-Absorbing Heel Cups

Tuli's, 5702 North 19th Avenue, Phoenix, AZ 85015. $9 a pair.

The Best Reflective Gear

Jog-a-Lite, Box 125, Silver Lake, NH 03875. Vests, headbands, wrist or leg bands, sashes, backpacks. Reflective equipment is also available from other sources. This company's line, however, is the best I've found.

A Flashing Light for Night Running

Runner's Beacon, P&M International, Allston, MA 02134. $6.95. A well-made yellow light with an elasticized armband.

Good Rain Gear

The best rain gear I've found are the two-piece suits offered by Adidas, Brooks, Devaney, General Universal Training Supplies, K-Way, Bill Rodgers, Frank Shorter, and Sub 4. All are lightweight and durable, and do a good job of keeping you dry. Some, however, particularly those made of ripstop nylon, are better suited to a light rain than a downpour.

A Reliable Digital Chronograph

Microsel LCD Wrist Chronograph, Microsel, 699 East Brocaw Road, San Jose, CA 95112. $79.95. "Worth its higher price," according to *Running* magazine.

The Best Way to Carry Coins, Keys and Identification

Rippers, Ne-Toe Products, Box 829, Silver Spring, MD 20901. $3.50. A quarter-ounce pocket that fastens to a shoelace. Available in blue, green, yellow and red nylon.

A Cheap Identification Tag

Run-I-Dent, Box 144, Francestown, NH 03043. $2. A stamped metal wrist tag on an elastic band, the Run-I-Dent includes name, telephone and medical insurance plan numbers, blood type, allergies, other medical information.

Two Good Backpacks for Runners

Useful for carrying light cargo while you run. The best come from Runners Diversified, Inc., 400 E. 89th St., New York, NY 10028 ($12.95), and Jog-a-Lite, Box 125, Silver Lake, NH 03875 ($14.95).

An Excellent Home Gymnasium

Total Gym, 7730 Clairemont Mesa Boulevard, San Diego, CA 92111. Flexibility and strength are important to runners. This apparatus will increase both. Two models: $399 and $599.

A Free Fitness Diary

Pocket-sized. From Public Relations Department, Pennsylvania Blue Shield, Camp Hill, PA 17011.

Life Insurance Discounts for the Physically Fit

The Occidental Life Insurance Company of North Carolina (Box 10234, Raleigh, NC 27605) was the pioneer in 1978. Currently a dozen or more companies offer such discounts, so it's worth making some inquiries before buying life insurance.

Running Books by Mail

The Runner Shop, 1 Park Avenue, New York, NY 10016; Runner's Bookservice, Box 161236, Sacramento, CA 95816; World Publications, Inc., Box 366, Mountain View, CA 94042. Free catalogues.

The Best Book on Stretching

Stretching, Stretching, Inc., Box 767, Palmer Lake, CO 80133. $7.95 plus $1.00 postage. Available in bookstores.

Calendars of Forthcoming Running Events

Consult current issues of *The Jogger, The Runner, Runner's World, Running Times* and, for major races by month, *The Complete Runner's Day-by-Day Log and Calendar.*

Running-Related Periodicals

The American Journal of Sports Medicine, 428 East Preston Street, Baltimore, MD 21202. Publication of the American Orthopaedic Society for Sports Medicine. Covers medical aspects of running and other sports. Bimonthly. One year, $30.

American Medical Joggers Association Newsletter, Box 4704, North Hollywood, CA 91607. Scientific aspects of running. Quarterly. One year, $10; free with $25 annual membership.

Athlete's World, 440–442 Whitmore Way, Basildon, Essex, England. All aspects of running, with emphasis on events in Britain. Incorporates *Veteris,* the magazine for masters. Monthly. One year, $35 air; $23 surface.

Athletic Journal, 1719 Howard Street, Evanston, IL 60202. Coaches' analyses of track and field events. One year (ten issues), $6; two years, $11; three years, $15.

British Journal of Sports Medicine, 39 Linkfield Road, Mountsorrel, Loughborough, Leicestershire, England. Exercise physiology, sports injuries, psychology. Quarterly. One year, $15.

California Track News, Box 6103, Fresno, CA 93703. All aspects of California running. One year (ten issues), $7; two years, $12; three years, $16.

Cardio-Gram, La Crosse Exercise Program, Mitchell Hall, University of Wisconsin-La Crosse, La Crosse, WI 54601. Health, fitness and sportsmedicine, with emphasis on rehabilitation of cardiac patients. One year (six issues), $5.

The Coaching Clinic, Prentice-Hall, Inc., Englewood Cliffs, NJ 07632. How-to articles for and by coaches of all sports. Monthly. One year, $24.

Fitness, T. Fleming Associates, Box 4473, Pittsburgh, PA 15205. Physical fitness and nutrition. One year (ten issues), $12.

Foot and Ankle, 428 East Preston Street, Baltimore, MD 21202. A new bimonthly medical journal. (First issue: July 1980.) One year, $35.

Footnotes, 11155 Saffold Way, Reston, VA 22090. Journal of the Road Runners Club of America. Quarterly. Free with membership.

The Harrier, Box 1550, Auburn, AL 36830. Cross-country coverage. Published eight times from September to January, with one spring and one summer issue. One year, $8; two years, $15.

Health Facts, Center for Medical Consumers and Health Care Information, 237 Thompson Street, New York, NY 10012. Bimonthly newsletter, frequently on exercise, published by a nonprofit organization. One year, $6; two years, $11.

The Jogger, 2420 K Street, N.W., Washington, DC 20037. Monthly newspaper of the National Jogging Association. Covers all aspects of running, with emphasis on fitness and fun. Free to members.

Jogging, 13 Golden Square, London W1R 4AG, England. Monthly. £15.25 air, £8.50 surface.

The Journal of Orthopaedic and Sports Physical Therapy, 428 East Preston Street, Baltimore, MD 21202. Publication of the orthopedic and sportsmedicine sections of the American Physical Therapy Association; of interest chiefly to physical therapists, doctors, trainers, coaches. Quarterly. One year, $18.

Marathon Runner, 440–442 Whitmore Way, Basildon, Essex, England. Devoted to races of 26.2 miles and above. Quarterly. One year, $20 air; $15 surface.

Medicine and Science in Sports, 1440 Monroe Street, Madison, WI 53706. Journal of the American College of Sports Medicine. Quarterly. One year, $20.

National Masters Newsletter, 102 West Water Street, Lansford, PA 18232. Monthly. One year, $3.

New York Running News, New York Road Runners Club, Box 1387, GPO, New York, NY 10001. Nine issues yearly. Free with $10 NYRRC membership.

New Zealand Runner, Box 29-043, Auckland 3, New Zealand. A leading running magazine from a leading running nation. Bimonthly. One year, $20 air, $10 surface.

Nor-Cal Running Review, Box 1551, San Mateo, CA 94401. Running in Northern California. One year (eight issues), $8.

The Physician and Sportsmedicine, 4530 West 77th Street, Minneapolis, MN 55435. Medical aspects of sports, including running. Monthly. One year, $26.

The Racer's Edge, Box 321, Lake Orion, MI 48035. Scientific aspects of running. Monthly. One year, $12.

Research Quarterly for Exercise and Sport, 1201 16th Street, N.W., Washington, DC 20036. Scientific aspects of sports, including running. One year, $35.

The Runner, 1 Park Avenue, New York, NY 10016. For a description, see Chapter 14. Monthly. One year, $18.

Runner's World, Box 366, Mountain View, CA 94042. See Chapter 14. Monthly. One year, $13; two years, $24.

Running, Box 350, Salem, OR 97308. See Chapter 14. Quarterly. Six issues, $7.

Running Times, 12808 Occoquan Road, Woodbridge, VA 22192. See Chapter 14. Monthly. One year, $12; two years, $22.

Scholastic Coach, 50 West 44th Street, New York, NY 10036. How-to magazine for coaches and athletic directors. Track articles appear chiefly, though not exclusively, in February, March and April. One year (10 issues), $12; two years, $20; three years, $26. $2 per year less for professional coaches, trainers, athletic directors, etc.

Soviet Sports Review, Box 549, Laguna Beach, CA 92652. Articles translated from the Russian. Quarterly. One year, $12.50; two years, $24.50; three years, $36.

Sports 'n Spokes, 5201 North 19th Avenue, Suite 108, Phoenix, AZ 85015. Devoted to wheelchair sports, including track and field and road racing. Bimonthly. One year, $5.50.

Track and Field News, Box 296, Los Altos, CA 94022. World-
wide coverage of men's and women's track and field.
Monthly. One year, $13.50.

Track and Field Quarterly Review, 1705 Evanston Avenue,
Kalamazoo, MI 49008. Journal of the U.S. Track Coaches
Association. One year, $12.

TrackMaster, 900 South Washington Street, Suite G-11, Falls
Church, VA 22046. On masters' running, chiefly in the East.
One year, $12.

Track Newsletter, Box 296, Los Altos, CA 94022. Summaries of
important track and field meets the world over. One year
(18 issues), $20.

Track Technique, Box 296, Los Altos, CA 94022. Technical developments in track and field. Quarterly. One year, $8.

More Reading About Running

A Selected Bibliography

Abbreviations: *AJE = American Journal of Epidemiology. JAMA = Journal of the American Medical Association. MSS = Medicine and Science in Sports. NEJM = New England Journal of Medicine. NYT = New York Times. PFRD = Physical Fitness Research Digest. P&SM = The Physician and Sportsmedicine. RW = Runner's World. RT = Running Times. TJ = The Jogger. TR = The Runner.*

ADAMS, GENE M. and DEVRIES, HERBERT A. "Physiological Effects of an Exercise Training Regimen Upon Women Aged 52 to 79." *Journal of Gerontology*, January 1973.

ALEXANDER, MORRIS. *The Comrades Marathon Story*. Capetown: Juta, 1976.

ALTSHUL, VICTOR A. "The Ego-Integrative (and Disintegrative)

Effects of Long-Distance Running." *Current Concepts in Psychiatry*, July–August, 1978.

AMDUR, NEIL. "Footing the Bill." *TR*, June 1979.

———. "Jumbo Elliott: Ingenious Giant of U.S. Track." *NYT*, April 23, 1979.

———. "What Makes the Seventies Run?" *TR*, October 1978.

American College of Sports Medicine. "Position Statement on the Recommended Quantity and Quality of Exercise for Developing and Maintaining Fitness in Healthy Adults." *MSS*, Vol. 10, No. 3, 1978.

ANDERSEN, ROBERT. "Running: A Road to Mental Health." *RW*, July 1979.

ANDERSON, NANCY. "Why Women Don't Race." *Footnotes*, Summer 1979.

ANDERSON, ROBERT A. *Stretching*, rev. ed. Bolinas, Calif.: Shelter Publications, 1980. A comprehensive treatment of the subject.

ANDREWS, VALERIE. "Dreams and the Runconscious." *TR*, October 1978.

———. *The Psychic Power of Running.* New York: Rawson, 1978.

ÅSTRAND, PER-OLAF and RODAHL, KAARE. *Textbook of Work Physiology.* New York: McGraw-Hill, 1977.

AYRES, ALEX. "Craig Virgin." *RT*, August 1979.

———. "Who Said Running Is a Religion?" *RT*, December 1978.

AYRES, ED. "The Death of a Runner." *RT*, December 1978. On the collapse while running of Congressman Goodloe Byron.

———. "The Myth of Indestructibility." *RT*, January 1979.

———. "Overthrowing the Junk-Food Tyranny." *RT*, April 1979.

———. "Pain." *RT*, October 1978.

BANNISTER, ROGER. *The Four-Minute Mile.* New York: Dodd, Mead, 1955.

———. "Four Minutes That Were an Eternity." *RW*, June 1979.

BARNES, LAN. "Blood Boosting: Success and Controversy." *P&SM*, July 1978.

BARNES, TONY. "What It Takes to Make a Champion." *Jogging,* July 1979.

BARRY, ALAN J., et al. "The Effects of Physical Conditioning on Older Individuals." *Journal of Gerontology,* April 1966.

BASSLER, THOMAS J. "Megavitamins and Megamiles: The Folklore of Marathoning." *Medicine and Sport,* Volume 12.

BATES, BARRY T., JAMES, STANLEY L. and OSTERNIG, LOUIS R. "Foot Function During the Support Phase of Running." *Running,* Fall 1978.

BATTEN, JACK. *The Complete Jogger.* New York: Harcourt Brace Jovanovich, 1977.

BELAKOVSKY, O. M. "Don't Be Afraid of Heavy Loads." *Soviet Sports Review,* July 1979.

BENYO, RICHARD. "The Race Went to the Smartest." *RW,* November 1978.

BERG, KRIS. "How to Maximize Running Efficiency." *RW,* April 1979.

BERGMAN, MYRON A. "Calluses." *TJ,* April 1979.

———. "Morton's Foot, Morton's Toe, Morton's Neuroma." *TJ,* November 1978.

———. "Stress Fractures." *TJ,* December 1978–January 1979.

BERLAND, THEODORE. "Pledge Allegiance to Your Diet." *New York Post,* July 5, 1979.

BIERMAN, JUNE and TOOHEY, BARBARA. *The Diabetic's Sports and Exercise Book.* New York: Harcourt Brace Jovanovich, 1978.

BILLINGTON, LYN. "Let Women Run on Equal Terms with the Men." *Jogging,* August 1979.

BISHOP, BOB. "How Walt Stack Created the D.S.E. [Dolphin South End running club]." *Footnotes,* Spring 1979.

BLACK, JONATHAN. "The Brain According to Mandell." *TR,* April 1979.

———. "The Private Obsession of Ted Corbitt." *TR,* December 1978.

BLOOM, MARC A. *Cross Country Running.* Mountain View, Calif.: World Publications, 1978.

BONEN, AREND and BELCASTRO, ANGELO N. "Comparison of Self-

Selected Recovery Methods on Lactic Acid Removal Rates." *MSS*, Vol. 8, No. 3, 1976.

BORTOLOTTI, PETE. "Diary of an Athletic Shoe Salesman." *Running Review*, September 1978.

BOURNE, RICHARD. "Hypnosis: Key to Relaxed Running." *RW*, August 1978.

BOWERMAN, WILLIAM J. "Fartlek Workouts Improve Speed and Style Through Running Games." *RW*, January 1979.

———. "Marathon Training." *RW*, October 1978.

———. "Modifying the Natural Running Style." *RW*, November 1978.

——— and HARRIS, W. E. *Jogging*. New York: Grosset & Dunlap, 1967.

BOYER, JOHN M. "Effects of Chronic Exercise on Cardiovascular Function." *PFRD*, July 1972.

BRADLEY, JEFF. "Running . . . Naturally." *Running Review*, September 1978.

BRAND, RICHARD J., PAFFENBARGER, RALPH S., JR., SCHOLTZ, ROBERT I. and KAMPERT, JAMES B. "Work Activity and Fatal Heart Attacks Studied by Multiple Logistic Risk Analysis." Paper presented to the American Heart Association, Miami Beach, Fla., November 15–18, 1976.

BRANSFORD, DONALD R. and HOWLEY, EDWARD T. "Oxygen Cost of Running in Trained and Untrained Men and Women." *MSS*, Vol. 9, No. 1, 1977.

BRASHER, CHRISTOPHER. "[Sebastian] Coe's Mileage Ingredient." *The Observer* (London), July 22, 1979.

BRODY, DAVID and FRIEDMAN, MEYER. "Is Jogging Really Good for You?" *U.S. News and World Report*, April 19, 1979. A debate.

BRODY, JANE E. "Exercising to Turn Back the Years." *NYT*, June 6, 1979.

———. "It's OK (and Cheap) to Eat Starches." *NYT*, April 25, 1979.

———. "Latest Data Suggest Exercise Helps Curb Heart Attacks." *NYT*, March 27, 1979.

———. "Study of 17,000 Men Indicates Vigorous Sports Protect Heart." *NYT*, November 29, 1977.

BROOKS, MARVIN and YOLLES, MARILYN. "Running on Empty." *TR*, June 1979.

BROWER, JONATHAN J. "Making Miki a Marathoner." *RW*, February 1977. On Miki Gorman.

BROWN, BILL. "London to Brighton." *Road Runners Club Newsletter* (United Kingdom), January 1979.

BROWN, JACQUELYN and JONES, DIANA. "[Joan] Benoit: Royalty in a Baseball Cap." *TR*, July 1979.

BROWN, JAMES C. *The Therapeutic Mile.* Irmo, South Carolina: Human Growth and Development Books, 1979.

BROWN, ROBERT S., RAMIREZ, DONALD E. and TAUB, JOHN M. "The Prescription of Exercise for Depression." *P&SM*, December 1978.

BRUCK, CONNIE. "Caution: Children at Play." *TR*, July 1979.

BRYANT, ANITA and GREEN, BOB. *Running the Good Race.* Old Tappan, N.J.: Revell, 1976.

BRYNTESON, PAUL and SINNING, WAYNE E. "The Effects of Training Frequencies on the Retention of Cardiovascular Fitness." *MSS*, Vol. 5, No. 1, 1973.

BURFOOT, AMBY. "Downhill Racer." *RW*, August 1979.

———. "The Joys of Vegetarian Carbohydrate-Loading." *RW*, January 1979.

———. "The Race to Decide the King of the Road." *RW*, November 1978. On the Falmouth Road Race.

———. "Ten Steps to Running Under Three Hours." *RW*, February 1979.

———. "The Triple Crown of Marathoning." *RW*, December 1978.

BURGER, ROBERT E. *The Jogger's Catalogue: The Source Book for Runners.* New York: M. Evans, 1978.

Business Week, editors of. "'Mapping' Feet That Feel Ill." June 18, 1979.

BUTT, DORCAS S. *Psychology of Sport.* New York: Van Nostrand Reinhold, 1976.

CAMPBELL, GAIL. *Marathon: The World of Long-Distance Athletes.* New York: Sterling, 1977.

———. "The Women of Marathoning." *RW*, September 1977.

CANTWELL, JOHN D. "Running." *JAMA*, September 22, 1978.

CARR, JIM. "The Challenge of Pikes Peak." *The Marathoner*, Fall 1978.

CASEY, SUSAN. "No One Her Age Comes Close to Matching Mavis," *RW*, February 1979. On marathoner Lindgren.

CAVANAGH, PETER and WILLIAMS, KEITH R. "Should You Change Your Stride Length?" *RW*, July 1979.

CHAPLIN, MEREDITH. "Exercise and Pregnancy." *New York Post*, April 26, 1979.

CHRETIEN, JANE HENKEL and PAFFENBARGER, RALPH S., JR. "Occupational Preselection." Letters to *NEJM*, July 9, 1970.

CLAPP, STEVE. "The Nutrition Connection." *Footnotes*, Winter 1978.

CLARKE, CAROLYN. "Psyching to Lose." *RW*, March 1978.

CLARKE, H. HARRISON, ed. "Athletes: Their Academic Achievement and Personal-Social Status." *PFRD*, July 1975.

———. "Characteristics of Athletes." *PFRD*, April 1973.

———. "Circulatory-Respiratory Endurance." *PFRD*, July 1973.

———. "Exercise and the Abdominal Muscles." *PFRD*, July 1976.

———. "Exercise and Aging." *PFRD*, April 1977.

———. "Exercise and Blood Cholesterol." *PFRD*, July 1972.

———. "Exercise and Fat Reduction." *PFRD*, April 1975.

———. "Exercise and the Knee Joint." *PFRD*, January 1976.

———. "Jogging." *PFRD*, January 1977.

———. "Joint and Body Range of Movement." *PFRD*, October 1975.

———. "Physical Activity and Coronary Heart Disease." *PFRD*, April 1972.

———. "Physical Activity During Menstruation and Pregnancy." *PFRD*, July 1978.

———. "Physical Fitness Practices and Programs for Elementary and Secondary Schools." *PFRD*, October 1976.

———. "Rope Skipping, Dancing, Walking and Golf-Pack Carrying." *PFRD*, October 1977.

———. Summary of physiological effects of exercise (untitled). *PFRD*, October 1972.

———. "The Totality of Man." *PFRD*, October 1971.

————. "Update: Physical Activity and Coronary Heart Disease." *PFRD*, April 1979.

COCKRILL, MARK. "Heat Adaptation." *RW*, May 1979.

COHEN, KENNETH R. "Seeing Your Way Clear to Good Eye Protection." *RW*, March 1979.

COLKER, DAVID. *Running Away from Home*. New York: Harcourt Brace Jovanovich, 1979.

CONCANNON, JOE. "Second Best, But Still in the Running." *Boston Globe*, April 13, 1979. On distance runner Randy Thomas.

CONNIFF, JAMES C. G. "All About Body Fat." *TR*, October 1978.

————. "Heat: The Runner's Worst Enemy." *TR*, June 1979.

————. "The Many Mysteries of Breath." *TR*, February 1979.

CONRAD, C. CARSON. "When You're Young at Heart." *Aging*, April 1976.

COOPER, KENNETH H. *Aerobics*. New York: Bantam, 1968.

————. *The Aerobics Way*. New York: M. Evans, 1977.

————. *The New Aerobics*. New York: Bantam, 1970.

COOPER, MILDRED and COOPER, KENNETH H. *Aerobics for Women*. New York: Bantam, 1973.

CORBITT, TED. "Ultramarathon Scene." *New York Running News*, Fall 1978.

————. "Warm Up, Warm Down." *TR*, March 1979.

COSTILL, DAVID L. *A Scientific Approach to Distance Running*. Los Altos, Calif.: Track & Field News, 1979.

————, et al. "Training Adaptations in Skeletal Muscle of Juvenile Diabetics." Unpublished paper; undated.

CREFF, ALBERT and WERNICK, ROBERT. *Dr. Creff's 1–2–3 Sports Diet*. New York: Coward, McCann & Geoghegan, 1979.

DALE, EDWIN, et al. "Physical Fitness Profiles and Reproductive Physiology of the Female Distance Runner." *P&SM*, January 1979.

D'ALTON, MARTINA. *The Runner's Guide to the U.S.A.* New York: Summit, 1978.

DARMAN, JEFF. "Breakfast of Champions?" *Footnotes*, Winter 1978. On beer as an athlete's drink.

DELLINGER, BILL. "Peaking for Competition." *TR*, April 1979.

DE VRIES, HERBERT A. "Physiological Effects of an Exercise

Training Program Upon Men Aged 52–88." *Journal of Gerontology*, October 1970.

DILFER, CAROL. *Your Baby, Your Body*. New York: Crown, 1977.

DODD, ED. "The Twenty-Four-Hour Ordeal." *The Marathoner*, Fall 1978.

DOHERTY, J. KENNETH. *Modern Track and Field*. Englewood Cliffs, N.J.: Prentice-Hall, 1963.

DRAKE, LLOYD. "Coronary Thrombosis and the Runner." *New Zealand Runner*, March–April 1979.

———. "High Altitude Training." *New Zealand Runner*, August–September 1978.

——— and WHEELER, JOHN R. "Medical Forum." *New Zealand Runner*, March–April 1979.

DRESSENDORFER, RUDOLPH H. "Endurance Training of Recreationally Active Men." *P&SM*, November 1978.

——— and GAHAGEN, HARRY. "Serum Lipid Levels in Male Runners." *P&SM*, January 1979.

DRINKWATER, B. L. and HORVATH, S. M. "Heat Tolerance and Aging." *MSS*, Vol. II, No. 1, 1979.

DULLEA, GEORGIA. "Health Survey Finds Poor Habits Prevail." *NYT*, April 26, 1978.

DYCHTWALD, KEN. "Bodymind Stretching for Runners." *TJ*, December 1978–January 1979.

EISCHENS, ROGER, GREIST, JOHN H. and MC INVAILLE, TOM. *Run to Reality*. Madison, Wis.: Madison Running Press, 1977.

EISENMAN, PATRICIA A. and GOLDING, LAWRENCE A. "Comparison of Effects of Training on Vo₂max in Girls and Young Women." *MSS*, Vol. 7, No. 2, 1975.

ELLIOTT, LIZ. "Grete Waitz." *TJ*, April 1979. An interview with the women's marathon record holder.

ELLISON, DAN. "The Cold Facts on Winter Running." *RW*, December 1978.

———. "Running After 40." *RW*, March 1979.

ERICKSON, DONALD J. "Exercise for the Older Adult." *P&SM*, October 1978.

EVANS, BILL. "Sugar: Another Viewpoint." *Ball State University Adult Fitness Newsletter*, March 1978.

Family Practice, editors of. "Exercise-Induced Asthma Is

Found to Trip the Unsuspecting on Jogging Trail." November–December 1978.

FARQUHAR, JOHN W. *The American Way of Life Need Not Be Hazardous to Your Health.* Stanford, California: Stanford Alumni Association, 1978.

FELTS, PHILIP W. and MARSHALL, WILLIAM F. "What's New in Exercise." *Diabetes Forecast,* March–April 1979.

FERAN, TOM. "A Dangerous Mania." *Greenwich* (Connecticut) *Time,* February 8, 1979.

FIXX, JAMES F. "Off and Running: A Viewer's Guide to the [New York City] Marathon." *New York,* October 24, 1977.

FLEMING, TOM. "Your Days Are Numbered." *TR,* July 1979. On racing frequency.

FLOOD, THOMAS. "Who's Running?" *Diabetes Forecast,* March–April 1979.

FOSTER, C., COSTILL, DAVID L. and FINK, W. J. "Effects of Preexercise Feedings on Endurance Performance." *MSS,* Vol. 2, No. 1, 1979.

FOX, EDWARD L., et al. "Intensity and Distance of Interval Training Programs and Changes in Aerobic Power." *MSS,* Vol. 5, No. 1, 1973.

FRANKLIN, BARRY A., FORGAC, M. TABERNIK and HELLERSTEIN, HERMAN K. "Accuracy of Predicted Marathon Time: Relationship of Training Mileage to Performance." *Research Quarterly,* Vol. 49, No. 4, 1978.

————, LUSSIER, LOUIS and BUSKIRK, ELSWORTH R. "Injury Rates in Women Joggers." *P&SM,* March 1979.

FREDERICK, E. C. "Running Away from Aging." *Running,* Winter 1979.

————. "Running in the Cold." *Running,* Fall 1978.

FRIDLEY, CAROL. "Equal but Different." *Running Review,* September 1978. On running shoes for women.

FU, FRANK H. "The Effects of Physical Training on the Lung Growth of Infant Rats." *MSS,* Vol. 8, No. 4, 1976.

GATTI, CHARLES. "Maintaining Endurance." *RW,* December 1978. On staying fit while injured.

GERWIG, KATE. "The Fastest Boy in the World." *RT,* January 1979.

GETCHELL, LEROY H. "Individualizing Physical Fitness Training." *Journal of Physical Education*, January–February 1978.

———. *Physical Fitness: A Way of Life.* New York: Wiley, 1979.

GILLUM, RICHARD F. and PAFFENBARGER, RALPH S., JR. "Sociocultural Mobility as a Precursor of Coronary Heart Disease and Hypertension." *AJE*, Vol. 108, No. 4, 1978.

GISOLFI, CARL V. and COHEN, JUDITH S. "Relationships Among Training, Heat Acclimation, and Heat Tolerance in Men and Women: The Controversy Revisited." *MSS*, Vol. 2, No. 1, 1979.

GLOVER, BOB. "Novice Marathoning." *New York Running News*, Fall 1978.

———. "Tips for Novice Racers." *TJ*, December 1978–January 1979.

———. "Women and Runnerhood." *TJ*, April 1979.

——— and SHEPHERD, JACK. *The Runner's Handbook.* New York: Penguin, 1978.

GODBEY, GEOFFREY. "The Theory of the Leisure Mass." *Public Opinion*, August–September 1979.

GOLDBERG, LESLIE. "Grete Waitz: Northern Lightning." *TR*, April 1979.

———. "Walt Stack: A Very Young Old Man." *TR*, February 1979.

GOULART, FRANCES SHERIDAN. *Eating to Win.* Briarcliff Manor, N.Y.: Stein & Day, 1978.

GRANT, MARK N. "Park Barner: The Human Treadmill." *TR*, October 1978.

GREIST, JOHN H., et al. "Running Out of Depression." *P&SM*, December 1978.

GRIFFIN, JON. "Overdistance—A Way Around the Wall." *Running*, Fall 1978.

Grit, editors of. "Congregation Jogs After It Prays." June 17, 1979.

HANNER, RICHARD. "Doing It Their Way." *RW*, July 1979.

HANSEN, JACQUELINE. "Fighting for Recognition." *Footnotes*, Spring 1979. On competition for women.

HARPER, PAULA. "26 Miles to the Finish Line." *Diabetes Forecast*, March–April 1979.

HARRIS, LEONARD. "Chris Brooks, Supercoach." *TR*, March 1979.

Harris, Louis, and Associates, Inc. "The Perrier Study: Fitness in America." New York: Great Waters of France, 1979.

HAUDA, WILLIAM E. "Traffic Accidents." *Footnotes*, Summer 1979.

HEIDENREICH, STEVE and DORR, DAVID. *Running Back.* New York: Hawthorn, 1979. The true story of an athlete's return to running after an automobile accident.

HEINICKE, MARK. "A Guide to Running Camps for People of All Ages and Abilities." *RT*, May 1979.

HELLER, ROBERT. "The Man in the Pin-Stripe Tracksuit." *Jogging*, May 1979.

HENDERSON, JOE. "Elements of Style." *RW*, September 1977.

———. "Running Commentary." *RW*, September 1978.

——— and BURFOOT, AMBY. "In Quest of the Magic Mile." *RW*, June 1979.

HENNING, JOEL. *Holistic Running.* New York: Atheneum, 1978.

———. "The Simple Truth About Blisters." *RW*, September 1978.

HERMAN, HANK. ". . . But Will They Still Be Running in 1989?" *Family Health*, April 1979.

HERXHEIMER, H., RIFAS, DONALD C., BASSLER, THOMAS J., SCAFF, JACK H., JR., ROBINSON, DEREK, CANTON, IRVING D. and PAFFENBARGER, RALPH S., JR. "Exercise, Running and the Heart." Letters to *NEJM*, June 12, 1975.

HIGDON, HAL. *Beginner's Running Guide.* Mountain View, Calif.: World Publications, 1978.

———. "Getting to the Foot of the Problem." *RW*, April 1978.

HILL, M. DEAN. "Dealing with the Growing Pains." *RW*, September 1977.

HLAVAK, HARRY F. *The Foot Book.* Mountain View, Calif.: World Publications, 1977.

HOFFMAN, TERRENCE, STAUFFER, ROBERT W. and JACKSON, ANDREW S. "Sex Difference in Strength." *American Journal of Sports Medicine*, July–August 1979.

HOLDT, DAVID M. "In Pursuit of the Perfect Shoe." *TR*, October 1978.

HUGHSON, RICHARD L. and SUTTON, JOHN R. "Heat Stroke in a

'Run for Fun.'" *British Medical Journal*, October 21, 1978.

HUIZINGA, JOHAN. *Homo Ludens: A Study of the Play Element in Culture*, translated by R. F. C. Hill. London: Routledge and Kegan Paul, 1949.

IVY, J. L., et al. "Influence of Caffeine and Carbohydrate Feedings on Endurance Performance." *MSS*, Vol. 2, No. 1, 1979.

JACKSON, J. ARTHUR, GASS, GREGORY C. and CAMP, ELIZABETH M. "The Effects of Posthypnotic Suggestion on Maximum Endurance Performance and Related Metabolic Variables." Unpublished article. Undated.

JEANSONNE, JOHN. "Rights of Passage." *TR*, December 1978.

JELLEY, ARCH. "Planning a Schedule." *New Zealand Runner*, August–September 1978.

JEROME, JOHN. "The Year of the Foot." *TR*, March 1979.

The Jogger, editors of. "The ABC's of Geriatric Jogging." April 1979.

Jogging, editors of. "The Amazing Touch of Acupressure." May 1979.

———. "How You Yourself Can Prepare for the Marathon." April 1979.

———. "If You Feel Any Discomfort at All, Stop and Walk." May 1979. On running while pregnant.

———. "Running a Family." May 1979. How running mothers cope.

———. "A Second Wind for the Invincible Man." May 1979. On marathoner Ian Thompson.

———. "Taking Out the Agony by Putting on the Style." June 1979.

JONES, RICHARD. "Whither Sportsmedicine?" *Footnotes*, Spring 1979.

JUKES, THOMAS. "The Simple Truth About Sugar." *RW*, December 1978.

KAISER, DENNIS L. "Choosing Your Optimum Pace." *Running*, Spring 1979.

KARLGAARD, RICHARD. *The Last Word on Running*. Thornwood, N.Y.: Caroline House, 1978.

KEENAN, TOM. "Heart Attack, Sudden Death and Running." *Sugarloaf Sun*, May 12, 1979.

KELLEY, JOHN. "The Guide to Running Cross-Country in America." *RW*, September 1978.

KEVLES, BARBARA. "Running Clothes—Designed for Women by Women." *Running Review*, February 1979.

———. "Selling out the Big Run." *Running Review*, November–December 1978.

———. "Women Marathon Runners: The New Breed Sportswomen." *Running Review*, December 1978–January 1979.

KOPP, DALE. "Sports Medicine Center Aids Athletes at Fast Rate." *Running Review*, March 1979. Interview with podiatrist Gary Gordon.

KAPLAN, JANICE. *Women and Sports*. New York: Viking, 1979.

KAVANAGH, TERENCE. *Heart Attack? Counterattack!* Toronto: Van Nostrand Reinhold, 1976.

KNUTTGEN, H. G., et al. "Physical Conditioning Through Interval Training with Young Adult Males." *MSS*, Vol. 5, No. 4, 1973.

KONISHI, FRANK. *Exercise Equivalents of Foods: A Practical Guide for the Overweight*. Carbondale, Ill.: Southern Illinois University Press, 1975.

KOSTRUBALA, THADDEUS. *The Joy of Running*. Philadelphia and New York: Lippincott, 1976.

KUSCSIK, NINA. "A Coach of One's Own." *TR*, February 1979.

KYLE, CHESTER R. "Cutting Through the Wall of Air." *RW*, May 1979.

LADOU, JOSEPH. "Circadian Rhythms and Athletic Performance." *P&SM*, July 1979.

LAPP, LINDA. "Let Your Mind Run Free: The Jogger and Mental Health." *TJ*, December 1978–January 1979.

LARNED, DEBORAH. "The Seven Percent Solution." *The Runner*, May 1979. On blood and its functions.

LATIMER, DOUG. "Grete Waitz: Marathon Woman." *Women's Sports*, January 1979.

LEE, H. B. "Hypothermia—When It's Too Cold!" *Road Runners Club Newsletter* (United Kingdom), January 1979.

LEONARD, GEORGE. *The Ultimate Athlete*. New York: Avon, 1977.

LEVY, ROBERT I. "Heart Attack." *The Sciences*, May–June 1979.

LEWIS, RICHARD. "A Grain of Salt." *TR*, March 1979.

————. "Myths About Meat." *TR*, December 1978.

————. "Soup to Nuts." *TR*, May 1979.

————. "Sugar Simple and Complex." *TR*, February 1979.

LEWIS, THOMAS. *Diseases of the Heart*. London: Macmillan, 1946.

LILLIEFORS, JIM. "Fasting." *RW*, September 1977.

————. "Running to Break 2:20." *RW*, February 1977.

LIQUORI, MARTY. "Your Best Workouts." *TR*, August 1979.

———— and MYSLENSKI, SKIP. *On the Run*. New York: Morrow, 1979.

LYDIARD, ARTHUR. "Training and Racing." *RW*, December 1978.

————, with GILMOUR, GARTH. "Tactics on the Track." *RW*, August 1978.

MCCARTHY, COLMAN. "Runners Asked for the Backlash." *Minneapolis Tribune*, October 28, 1978.

MCCUTCHEON, LYNN E. "Birth Order and Distance Running." *Running Review*, September 1979.

MCGREGOR, ROB ROY. "Get Off on the Right Foot!" *Diabetes Forecast*, March–April 1979.

MANGI, RICHARD, JOKL, PETER and DAYTON, WILLIAM O. *The Runner's Medical Guide*. New York: Summit, 1979.

MARON, DONALD. "Prevention of Overuse Injuries in the Distance Runner." *Running*, Winter 1979.

MARSHALL, NICK. "A Woman on the Way to Running's Outer Limits." *RW*, January 1979. On ultramarathoner Sherry Horner.

MARTIN, BRUCE J., et al. "Effect of Warm-up on Metabolic Responses to Strenuous Exercise." *MSS*, Vol. 7, No. 2, 1975.

MERRILL, SAM. "John Walker's Fight to Stay on Top." *TR*, August 1979.

MILVY, PAUL, ed. *The Long Distance Runner*. New York: Urizen, 1978.

MIRKIN, GABE. "Coping with Cold Weather." *TR*, February 1979.

————. "A Deceptive Injury." *TR*, December 1978. On Achilles tendinitis.

————. "Endurance." *TJ*, April 1979.

————. "Exercise and Menstruation." *TJ*, November 1978.

———. "Quit Your Belly Aching." *TR*, May 1979.

———. "Stop Popping Those Vitamin Pills!" *Footnotes*, Winter 1978.

——— and HOFFMAN, MARSHALL. *The Sportsmedicine Book*. Boston: Little, Brown, 1978.

MOLLEN, ART. *Run for Your Life*. Garden City, N.Y.: Doubleday, 1978.

MORELLA, JOSEPH J. and TURCHETTI, RICHARD J. *Nutrition and the Athlete*. New York: Mason/Charter, 1976.

MORGAN, WILLIAM P. "Negative Addiction in Runners." *P&SM*, February 1979.

———. "Psychological Factors Influencing Perceived Exertion." *MSS*, Vol. 5, No. 2, 1973.

———. "Running Into Addiction." *TR*, March 1979.

MORRIS, J. N., HEADY, J. A. and RAFFLE, P. A. B. "Coronary Heart Disease and Physical Activity of Work." *The Lancet* 2, 1953.

———. "Physique of London Busmen: The Epidemiology of Uniforms." *The Lancet* 2, 1956.

MOSS, MICHAEL. "Trucking Along at 71." *RT*, April 1979. On marathoner Mavis Lindgren.

MURPHY, DIANA. "Women's Running." *RW*, January 1979.

MURRAY, TOM. "The Top 10 Milers of All Time." *RW*, June 1979.

MYSLENSKI, SKIP. "Marty Liquori." *RW*, March 1979.

NAPOLI, MARYANN. "Exercise." *Health Facts*, May–June 1979.

NEUHOFF, CHRIS. "The Magic of 3–5 Minute Repeat Runs." *Running*, Fall 1978.

———. "Specificity of Training—The Secret of Olympians." *Running*, Summer–Fall, 1979.

New Zealand Runner, editors of. "Fun Run Fever Hits N.Z.!" June–July 1978.

NEWTON, ARTHUR. "The Man Who Ran Non-Stop for Twenty-Four Hours." *Jogging*, June 1979.

NIDEFFER, ROBERT M. *The Inner Athlete: Mind Plus Muscle for Winning*. New York: Crowell, 1976.

NIEDERMANN, TIMOTHY. "Who Is Grete Waitz?" *New York Running News*, January 1979.

NORFOLK, DONALD. "Six Slim-Guides for Those Who Hate Dieting." *Jogging*, May 1979.

OLNEY, ROSS R. *The Young Runner*. New York: Lothrop, Lee & Shepard, 1978.

OLSEN, ERIC. "Altitude Highs and Lows." *TR*, July 1979.

———. "Frank Shorter's Comeback: Still a Question." *TR*, August 1979.

———. "Henry Rono: Around the World Records in 80 Days." *TR*, April 1979.

———. "34 Below in International Falls." *TR*, April 1979.

———. "A View from the Top." *TR*, December 1978. On the Pikes Peak Marathon.

OSLER, TOM. *On the Conditioning of Distance Runners*. Los Altos, Calif.: Tafnews Press, 1977.

———. *The Serious Runner's Handbook*. Mountain View, Calif.: World Publications, 1978.

OSMUN, MARK. *The Honolulu Marathon*. Philadelphia and New York: Lippincott, 1979.

PAFFENBARGER, RALPH S., JR., et al. "Characteristics of Longshoremen Related to Fatal Coronary Heart Disease and Stroke." *American Journal of Public Health*, July 1971.

———. "Chronic Disease in Former College Students: Implications for College Health Programs." *Journal of the American College Health Association*, October 1967.

———. "Countercurrents of Physical Activity and Heart Attack Trends." In *Proceedings of the Conference on the Decline in Coronary Heart Disease Mortality*. Washington, D.C.: National Institutes of Health, May 1979.

———, et al. "Early Precursors of Fatal Coronary Heart Disease." *AJE*, Vol. 83, No. 2, 1966.

———, et al. "Energy Expenditure, Cigarette Smoking, and Blood Pressure Level as Related to Death from Specific Diseases." *AJE*, Volume 108, No. 1, 1978.

———. "Factors Predisposing to Fatal Stroke in Longshoremen." *Preventive Medicine* 1, 1972.

———. "Habitual Physical Activity and Heart Attack Risk." Report presented at the Conference on Stress, Strain, Heart Disease and the Law, Boston, January 1978.

————, et al. "Methods of Study and Observations on Mortality from Coronary Heart Disease." *American Journal of Public Health*, June 1966.

————. "Physical Activity and Fatal Heart Attack: Protection or Selection?" In *Exercise in Cardiovascular Health and Disease*. New York: Yorke Medical Books, 1977.

————. "Questionnaire's Disease." *Harvard Magazine*, July–August 1978.

————, et al. "Work-Energy Level, Personal Characteristics, and Fatal Heart Attack: A Birth-Cohort Effect." *AJE*, Vol. 105, No. 3, 1977.

————, et al. "Work Activity of Longshoremen as Related to Death from Coronary Heart Disease and Stroke." *NEJM*, May 14, 1970.

———— and ASNES, DANIEL P. "Precursors of Suicide in Early and Middle Life." *American Journal of Public Health*, July 1966.

———— and HALE, WAYNE E. "Work Activity and Coronary Heart Mortality." *NEJM*, March 13, 1975.

————, KING, STANLEY J., and WING, ALVIN L. "Characteristics in Youth that Predispose to Suicide and Accidental Death in Later Life." *American Journal of Public Health*, June 1969.

————, THORNE, MELVYN C. and WING, ALVIN L. "Characteristics in Youth Predisposing to Hypertension in Later Years." *AJE*, Vol. 88, No. 1, 1968.

———— and WILLIAMS, JAMES L. "Chronic Disease in Former College Students: Early Precursors of Fatal Stroke." *American Journal of Public Health*, August 1967.

———— and WING, ALVIN L. "Characteristics in Youth Predisposing to Fatal Stroke in Later Years." *The Lancet*, April 8, 1967.

———— and WING, ALVIN L. "Early Precursors of Adult-Onset Diabetes Mellitus." *AJE*, Vol. 97, No. 5, 1973.

———— and WING, ALVIN L. "Early Precursors of Nonfatal Stroke." *AJE*; Volume 94, No. 6, 1971.

———— and WING, ALVIN L. "The Effects of Single and Multiple Characteristics on Risk of Fatal Coronary Heart Disease." *AJE*, Vol. 90, No. 6, 1969.

————, WING, ALVIN L. and HYDE, ROBERT T. "Characteristics in

Youth Indicative of Adult-Onset Hodgkin's Disease." *Journal of the National Cancer Institute,* May 1977.

————, WING, ALVIN L. and HYDE, ROBERT T. "Characteristics in Youth Predictive of Adult-Onset Malignant Lymphomas, Melanomas, and Leukemias." *Journal of the National Cancer Institute,* January 1978.

————, WING, ALVIN L. and HYDE, ROBERT T. "Early Precursors of Peptic Ulcer." *AJE,* Vol. 100, No. 4, 1974.

————, WING, ALVIN L. and HYDE, ROBERT T. "Physical Activity as an Index of Heart Attack Risk in College Alumni." *AJE,* 108, 1978.

PAGLIANO, JOHN. "Preventive Podiatry." *RW,* May 1979.

————. "The Use of Ice in Athletic Injuries." *Running,* Fall 1978.

PALMER, BILL. "Wounded Marathoner Completes Race." *TJ,* December–January 1979.

PARROTT, GEORGE L., MANSOOR, JIM and UNDERWOOD, ABE. "Ultramarathoners: Correlates of Success and Characteristics of Participants." *Running,* Summer–Fall, 1979.

PATE, RUSSELL R., MAGUIRE, MOLLY and VAN WYK, JON. "Dietary Iron Supplementation in Women Athletes." *P&SM,* September 1979.

PAULK, EARL P., JR. *Divine Runner.* Atlanta: Cross Roads Publications, 1978.

PEDERSEN, PREBEN K. and JORGENSEN, KURT. "Maximal Oxygen Uptake in Young Women with Training, Inactivity, and Retraining." *MSS,* Volume 10, No. 4, 1978.

PERLMAN, PHILLIP R. "Shoes and Feet." *RW,* April 1979.

Physical Fitness Research Digest, editors of. "National Adult Physical Fitness Survey." Washington, D.C.: President's Council on Physical Fitness and Sports, April 1974.

The Physician and Sportsmedicine, editors of. "Strenuous Sports Better for Heart, MD Reports." January 1978.

————. "Women Marathoners Describe Bra Needs." December 1977.

PINKERTON, ELAINE. "Women's Running." *RW,* April 1979.

POLLOCK, MICHAEL L., et al. "Effects of Frequency and Duration of Training on Attrition and Incidence of Injury." *MSS*, Vol. 9, No. 1, 1977.

———. "How Much Exercise Is Enough?" *P&SM*, June 1978.

———, MILLER, HENRY S., JR. and RIBISL, PAUL M. "Effects of Fitness on Aging." *P&SM*, August 1978.

———, MILLER, HENRY S., JR. and WILMORE, JACK. "A Profile of a Champion Distance Runner: Age 60." *MSS*, Vol. 6, No. 2, 1974.

POWERS, PETER L. "The Sweet and Long of It: Running with Diabetes." *Running*, Spring 1979.

President's Council on Physical Fitness and Sports Newsletter, editors of. "Is Fitness, Sports Boom Being Oversold?" August 1977.

———. "National Poll Lists Barriers to Maintenance of Health." March 1979.

———. "Study Shows 39% of Boys Overweight." August 1977.

———. "Survey Finds 90% of Teachers Not in Good Shape." December 1978.

PRITIKIN, NATHAN. *The Pritikin Program for Diet & Exercise*. New York: Grosset & Dunlap, 1979.

QUINN, SUSAN. "The Miracle Workers." *Boston*, June 1978. On doctors who treat athletes.

RAGSDALE, MIKE and POWERS, SCOTTY. "Effects of Stride Length on Distance Running Performance." *Running*, Winter 1979.

RAND, JIM and WALKER, TONY. *This Is Orienteering*. London: Pelham, 1976.

RENNIE, DOUG. "The Son of 'Less Is More.'" *Running*, Spring 1979.

RENSBERGER, BOYCE. "Research Yields Surprises About Early Human Diets." *NYT*, May 15, 1979.

RESTON, JAMES. "In Praise of Fishing." *NYT*, September 19, 1979.

RHODES, MARTHA E. "The 'Natural' Food Myth." *The Sciences*, May–June 1979.

Road Runners Club Newsletter (United Kingdom), editors of. "The Big Business Boom." August 1979.

RODGERS, BILL, WITH JOE CONCANNON. *One for the Road.* New York: Simon & Schuster, 1980.

———. "Road Racing Strategy." *TR*, May 1979.

ROSKELLY, NICK. "The Long Road on Very Short Legs." *RW*, October 1978. A three-year-old runner's story.

ROTH, PETER. *Running U.S.A.: The Complete Guide to Running in 125 American Cities.* New York: Aardvark, 1979.

The Runner, editors of. "Largest Races of '78." June 1979.

Runner's World, editors of. *The Complete Woman Runner.* Mountain View, Calif.: World Publications, 1978.

———. "Running Carefully Through Civilization." March 1979.

———. "Running Through Nature Unscathed." February 1979.

———. "Training Tips from the World's Best." April 1979.

Running, editors of. "Chronographs for Runners." Winter 1979.

Running Review, editors of. "Construction of a Running Shoe." September 1978.

Running Times, editors of. "Form Versus Conditioning." May 1979.

———. "How to Select a Pair of Running Shoes." October 1978.

———. "Optimal Builds of Elite Female Distance Runners." September 1979.

———. "Six Miles a Day Keeps the Doctor Away." December 1978.

RYAN, ALLAN J., et al. "Exercise and the Cardiovascular System." *P&SM*, September 1979.

——— and ALLMAN, FRED L. *Sports Medicine.* New York: Academic Press, 1974.

RYUN, JIM. "Reflecting on the First Schoolboy Sub-4." *RW*, June 1979.

SANDER, NORBERT. "Comparing Men and Women." *New York Running News*, August 1979.

———. "Endurance vs. Fatigue." *New York Running News*, Fall 1978.

————. "Light at the End of the Run." *RW*, May 1979. On losing weight.

SANGER, DAVID E. "'Superman' as the Marathon Man." *NYT*, May 6, 1979.

SCHEERER, PENELOPE and SCHWANBECK, JOHN. *The Traveling Runner's Guide.* New York: Dutton, 1979.

SCHMECK, HAROLD M. "Researchers Find Surprises in Process of Aging." *NYT*, June 19, 1979.

SCHNEIDER, HOWARD. "Steve Ovett." *RW*, August 1979.

SCHNEIDER, MYLES J. "What to Do Until the Podiatrist Arrives." *Footnotes*, Winter 1978.

SCHUSTER, RICHARD O. "Fun Running and Its Potential Hazards." *Running Review*, November–December 1978.

————. "Interpretation of Wear on Running Shoes." *Running Review*, March 1979.

————. "More About Shin Splints." *Running Review*, October 1978.

————. "Orthotic Foot Devices for Runners." *Running Review*, February 1979.

————. "Running Footgear." *Running News*, September 1978.

SCRANTON, PIERCE E. and STANITSKI, CARL L. "A Simple Look at Major Running Overuse Injuries." *RW*, October 1978.

SEVENE, BOB. "Beginning Running." *RW*, June 1979.

SHANEBROOK, J. RICHARD and JASZCZAK, RICHARD D. "Aerodynamic Drag Analysis of Runners." *MSS*, Vol. 8, No. 1, 1976.

SHANGOLD, MONA M. "How Running Affects Pregnancy." *TR*, March 1979.

SHAPIRO, JIM. "On the Road from London to Brighton." *RW*, March 1979.

————. *On the Road: The Marathon.* New York: Crown, 1978.

————. "Space Travel on Foot: The Ultimate Challenge of the Ultramarathon." *Harvard Magazine*, September–October 1978.

SHEEHAN, GEORGE A. *Running and Being.* New York: Simon & Schuster, 1978.

————. *Dr. Sheehan on Running.* Mountain View, Calif.: World Publications, 1975.

———. "When the Stress of Modern Living Becomes Too Much, Run." *RW*, November 1978.

SHEPHARD, ROY J. *The Fit Athlete.* New York: Oxford 1978.

SHEPHERD, JACK. "Master [Fritz] Mueller." *TR*, October 1978.

SHORTER, FRANK. "Building for Speed." *TR*, October 1978.

———. "A Different Stress." *TR*, December 1978.

SHUMAN, CHARLES. "Reviewing the Shoe Reviews." *Footnotes*, Winter 1978.

SIEGEL, ARTHUR J. "Jogamute: New Word, New Life-Style." *TJ*, October 1978.

SLOVIK, PAUL. "Predicting Marathon Times." *The Marathoner*, Fall 1978.

SMEAD, CHUCK. "There's Speed in Them Thar Hills." *RW*, November 1978.

———. "The Ups and Downs of Mountain Racing." *Running*, Winter 1979.

SMITH, LINDA. "What Runners Eat." *Footnotes*, Spring 1979.

SMITZ, GREG. "Weight Training for a Runner." *RT*, January 1979.

SMYTHE, PAT. "The Western States 100." *The Marathoner*, Fall, 1978.

SPINO, MIKE. *Beyond Jogging.* Millbrae, Calif.: Celestial Arts, 1976.

STAMFORD, BRYANT A. "Effects of Chronic Institutionalization on the Physical Working Capacity and Trainability of Geriatric Men." *Journal of Gerontology*, October 1972.

STEADWARD, ROBERT D. and SINGH, MOHAN. "The Effects of Smoking Marihuana on Physical Performance." *MSS*, Vol. 7, No. 4, 1975.

STEFFNY, MANFRED. "Marathoning." *The Marathoner*, Fall 1978.

STEWART, DOUG. "So You Want to Run Faster!" *Sugarloaf Sun*, May 12, 1979.

SUBOTNICK, STEVEN I. "The Foot Doctor." *RW*, August 1978.

———. *The Running Foot Doctor.* Mountain View, Calif.: World Publications, 1977.

———. "Running and Injuries." *TJ*, April 1979.

———. "Shoes and Feet." *RW*, February 1979.

SUOMINEN, HARRI, et al. "Effect of Eight Weeks' Physical Train-

ing on Muscle and Connective Tissue of the M. Vastees Li-
teralis in 69-Year-Old Men and Women." *Journal of Gerontology*, January 1977.

SUSSMAN, VIC. "Outrunning the Meat-Eaters." *RT*, June 1979.

TAUNTON, J. E. "Achilles Tendonitis [sic]." *Running*, Winter
1979.

TEMPLE, CLIFF. "The Girl Who Knocked the Marathon for Six."
Jogging, August 1979. On women's marathon record-holder
Grete Waitz.

———. "A Religious Experience? My Foot!" *Jogging*, April
1979.

———. "Roger Bannister: The First to Break 'Four.'" *RW*,
June 1979.

TEXAS, JAMES. "Take the Money and Run." *TR*, January 1979.

THORNE, MELVYN C., WING, ALVIN L. and PAFFENBARGER, RALPH S.,
JR. "Early Precursors of Nonfatal Coronary Heart Disease."
AJE, Vol. 87, No. 3, 1968.

TRACEY, MICHAEL V. "Human Nutrition." In Ronald Duncan
and Miranda Weston-Smith, eds., *The Encyclopedia of
Human Ignorance*. New York: Pocket Books, 1978.

TULLOH, BRUCE. "Meet the People Who Live in the Thin Air."
Jogging, July 1979. On Mexico's Tarahumara Indians.

———. "What the Kenyans Can Teach Us About Running."
Jogging, May 1979.

TYMM, MIKE. "The Trauma of Turning Forty." *RW*, September
1977.

UHER, MARTIN. "The Mechanics of Running Up and Down
Hills." *RT*, August 1979.

ULLYOT, JOAN. *Women's Running*. Mountain View, Calif.:
World Publications, 1976.

VALMASSY, RON. "Injuries: Who Gets Hurt?" *RT*, March 1979.

VAN AAKEN, ERNST. "Workouts for New Runners." *RW*, January
1979.

VAN DOORN, JOHN. "An Intimidating New Class: The Physical
Elite." *New York*, May 29, 1978.

VAN GELDER, LAWRENCE. "Girls in Athletics Provide New Focus
for Doctors." *NYT*, August 10, 1979.

VARE, ROBERT. "I Run to Eat." *Food & Wine*, June 1979.

VEBLEN, THORSTEIN. *The Theory of the Leisure Class.* Boston: Houghton Mifflin, 1973.

WALLAN, PETER. "The Dinger Method: Breakthrough Training for Non-Elite Runners." *Running,* Summer–Fall 1979.

WARDE, ROBERT. "Coming on Strong After 50." *RW,* November 1977. On marathoner Alex Ratelle.

WEIMER, MARGE. "Women's Running." *RW,* February 1979.

WELLS, CHRISTINE L. "Sexual [sic] Differences in Heat Stress Response." *P&SM,* September 1977.

WHEELER, JOHN R. "The Immediate Treatment of Soft Tissue Injuries in Distance Runners." *New Zealand Runner,* October–December 1978.

———. "The Prevention of Running Injuries." *New Zealand Runner,* January–February 1979.

WHITAKER, JULIAN. "How Much Protein Do Runners Need?" *RW,* February 1979.

WHITNEY, RUTH SAUER. "What Your Children Can Lose by Running." *RW,* February 1979. On weight loss.

WILBOURN, KAREN. "The Lung Distance Runners." *RW,* August 1978.

WILLIAMS, KATIE. "Getting Thin." *RT,* July 1979.

WILMORE, JACK H. and BROWN, C. HARMON. "Physiological Profiles of Women Distance Runners." *MSS,* Vol. 6, No. 3, 1974.

———, MILLER, HENRY L. and POLLOCK, MICHAEL L. "Body Composition and Physiological Characteristics of Active Endurance Athletes in Their Eighth Decade of Life." *MSS,* Vol. 6, No. 1, 1975.

WIRTH, VICTORIA, EMMONS, PATTY and LARSON, DANIEL. "Running Through Pregnancy." *RW,* November and December 1978 (two parts).

WOOD, PETER D. "Running Away from Heart Disease." *RW,* June 1979.

WOOD, STEPHEN. "Summer Is the Time to Get Out and Get Going." *Jogging,* July 1979.

YATES, ROSS. "The Hidden Rot of Commercialism." *Running Review,* December 1978.

YOLLES, MARILYN. "Lose Weight, Run Faster." *TR,* March 1979.

YOUNG, R. JOHN and ISMAIL, A. H. "Personality Differences of Adult Men Before and After a Physical Fitness Program." *Research Quarterly*, October 1976.

ZIEGEL, VIC and GROSSBERGER, LEWIS. *The Non-Runner's Book.* New York: Collier, 1978.

Index

236 ◢◢◢

Schumacher, Fred, 46, 47, 58
Schuster, Richard O., 124, 147
Scientific Approach to Distance Running, A
  (Costill), 186
Select Committee on Nutrition and Human
  Needs (U.S. Senate), 132, 140
Shapiro, Jim, 158–59
Sheehan, George, 9, 41–42, 139, 147, 179, 187
Shepherd, Jack, 186
Shierman, Gail, 46
shoes, 74, 121, 123–25
Short, Mike, 174
Shorter, Frank, 4, 181, 182
Sidney, Kenneth, H., 36
Siegel, Arthur J., 58
Sime, Wesley E., 36
Singh, Mohan, 76
Smead, Chuck, 84, 190, 196, 198
Smith, Bill, 173
Solomon, Earl G., 37
Spackman, Bob, 56–57
Spade, Lee, 45
Spirit of Pheidippides Marathon, 190, 198
Sport Psychology Laboratory (University of
  Wisconsin), 40
Sports Medicine (eds. Ryan and Allman), 186
Sportsmedicine Book, The (Mirkin and Hoff-
  man), 113, 138, 186
Sports Medicine Resource, Inc., 150
Stamford, Bryant A., 106
Stauffer, Robert W., 90
Steadward, Robert D., 76
Steinmetz, Christine, 123, 148–49, 158
Stowe, Jerry, 170
Stress Physiology Laboratory (University of
  Iowa), 96
stretching, 73–74
stride length, 78
stroke, prediction of, 23
Subotnick, Steven I., 128, 147, 179
Sundown Salute Marathon, 111
Suominen, Harri, 106

Telford, Max, 159, 171
Textbook of Work Physiology (Åstrand and Rodahl), 186
Turkey Trot (25-kilometer) race, 140
Tharp, Gerald D., 36–37
Theory of the Leisure Class (Veblen), 5
Therapeutic Mile, The (Brown), 38
Third International Amsterdam Marathon, 60
Thomas, Randy, 62, 133
training, 65–80; biorhythms, 77; blood doping,
  79; breathing rhythm, 75; coffee, 75–76; hot-
  weather racing, 78; how far to run at first,
  66–71; intensity, 72; jet lag and, 77; marijuana smoking and, 39, 76; in mountains,
  78–79; overtraining, 72–73; puddles and,
  79–80; recovering from fatigue, 74; shoes for

training, 74; starting, 66; stretching, 73–74;
  stride length, 78; warmups, 73; wind, 74–75
Trevelyan, George M., 11
Tulloh, Bruce, 159
Turchetti, Richard J., 135, 187

Ullyot, Joan, 97, 186, 190, 196–97
Ultimate Athlete, The (Leonard), 187
ultramarathoning, 155–61; popularity of, 159
Underwood, Abe, 160
University of Wisconsin, 36
U.S. Administration on Aging, 104–5
U.S. Public Health Service, 17

Veblen, Thorstein, 5
Virgin, Craig, 62, 147
Virginia (10 miles) race, 84
Vitamin C, 136, 138
vitamins and minerals, 136, 137–38
Volkmer, Donald D., 52

Wagner, John O., 167, 168–69
Waitz, Grete, 88–90, 97
Walker, John, 79, 171, 182
Wall Street Journal, 178
warmup suits, 121–22
warmup, uses of, 73
Washington Post, 9
Weber, Sarah R., 57
Welch, Jack, 184
Wells, Jeff, 62, 147
Western States 100-Mile Endurance Run, 15,
  22, 159
White, Max, 158
White, Paul Dudley, 19
Williams, Susan, 150–51
Wilmore, Jack H., 92
Wilson, Philip K., 49
wind resistance, overcoming, 74–75
Wisconsin Mayfair Marathon, 102
women runners, 85–97; advantages of, 91–92;
  cardiovascular system, 90–91; cosmetic ben-
  efits, 93; gear, 122–23; injuries, 91, 92; men-
  strual cycle, 88, 94–95; reproductive system,
  94–96; training of, 96–97
Women and Sports (Kaplan), 94
Women's Running (Ullyot), 97, 186
Wood, Barbara L., 47
Wood, Peter D., 28, 31–32, 91, 179

Yankelovich, Skelly and White, 11
Yonkers Marathon, 108–9
Young, R. John, 106
Young Men's Christian Association (YMCA),
  46, 50, 53, 66, 108, 167
youth, running and, 110–18; principles (President's Council on Physical Fitness and
  Sports), 117–18; psychological dimensions
  of, 115–16

About the Author

JAMES F. FIXX has written four other books, including the record-breaking best-seller *The Complete Book of Running*, which the Road Runners Club of America voted 1977's most distinguished work on the sport. Fixx, who runs ten or more miles a day and has competed in eight Boston Marathons, is a former editor for *Saturday Review, McCall's* and *Life*. He is a consultant to the President's Council on Physical Fitness and Sports, a regular contributor to national magazines, a frequent television and radio guest, and author of the annual *Complete Runner's Day-by-Day Log and Calendar*. He is married, has four children and lives in Riverside, Connecticut.